Breaking Through

Breaking Through

The Making of Minority Executives in
Corporate America

David A. Thomas • John J. Gabarro

HARVARD BUSINESS SCHOOL PRESS
BOSTON, MASSACHUSETTS

Printed in the United States of America
03   5 4

Thomas, David A., 1956–
    Breaking through : the making of minority executives in corporate
America / David. A. Thomas, John J. Gabarro.
        p.   cm.
    Includes bibliographical references and index.
    ISBN 0-87584-866-4 (alk. paper)
    1. Minority executives—United States.   2. Executives—United
States.   3. Discrimination in employment—Unites States.
    4. Diversity in the workplace—Unites States.   I. Gabarro, John J.
    II. Title.
    HD38.25.U6T47   1999
    331.13'3'0973—dc21   98-55291
                                                                        CIP

*The paper used in this publication meets the requirements of the American National
Standard for Permanence of Paper for Printed Library Materials Z39.49-1984.*

TO DR. LEROY WELLS, JR., MENTOR, FRIEND, AND INSPIRATION.

Dr. Leroy Wells, Jr., died just as David was in the midst of writing the first draft. Leroy was David's closest friend and first professional mentor. His death was a shocking, almost paralyzing event. With prayers and a deepening faith, Leroy was ultimately the source of inspiration that led this project to completion. His direct and indirect contributions to this book are immeasurable. We hope the final product would please him.

Contents

◢ Acknowledgments

THIS PROJECT WAS MORE than six years in the making. It is the product of two careers and multiple streams of research merging around one phenomenon, minority executive development, that is of deep intellectual and personal interest to us both. The possibility that we could actually undertake such a project first dawned on us during a seven-hour dinner conversation in which we spun the common threads of our research and began to forge the deeply personal bond of our relationship.

Our first year of attempting to gain access to companies made us keenly aware of why no other studies such as ours exist. It was difficult to identify any companies with more than one or two executives of color in 1992. Even more challenging was the task of gaining access to companies willing to open themselves up to examination. Race was then, and continues to be, a sensitive topic, consciously and unconsciously associated with intractable problems and litigious quagmires. Most corporate attorneys advise their clients to steer clear of openly discussing issues of race, even in the service of learning. And many individuals feel vulnerable speaking about such controversial topics or drawing attention to themselves in ways that might diminish their personal achievements and perspectives by highlighting their race.

Understanding this reality, we are deeply indebted to the three companies and fifty-four executives and managers who agreed to participate in our study. Our commitment to guaranteeing their anonymity prevents us from acknowledging them by name. We hope that they gain some measure of satisfaction in the contribution they have made to the development of management theory and practice and to helping individuals better navigate the corporate mainstream.

A project of this length and magnitude does not happen without the support of many people. Only two names grace the cover of this book, but several people took pride and felt ownership in it, ensuring that the project reached its potential. In the first three years of our field research, Debra Woog was the research associate who organized our data collection efforts and conducted many of the subordinate, peer, and supervisor interviews. Debra brought energy and enthusiasm to our team at critical points when the task of collecting more data was overwhelming. We are deeply indebted to her.

We cannot say enough about the vital role that Emily Heaphy played in the final eighteen months of this project. Although she joined us late, her contribution is evident throughout the final product. Her title, research associate, understates the magnitude of her place in the life of this project. Others who provided us research support at various points include Modupe Akinole, Lisa Chadderdon, Jaan Elias, Deborah Evans, John Hammond, and Elise Phillips. Each has our gratitude and appreciation.

Throughout all but the last year of this project, Tracey Foxworth kept track of schedules, research memos, and communications generated over the life of this project—providing excellent administrative support.

Janice Simmons prepared this manuscript for us with an inspiring and impressive level of care and responsiveness. She met unbelievably tight revision deadlines. Without complaint, she typed and retyped each chapter more times than we care to remember. Janice often alerted us to inconsistencies and fixed our mistakes before we even recognized them. We are also indebted to Janice's colleagues in the Harvard Business School's Word Processing Department. Aimee Hamel, Ann O'Connell, and Joan O'Connor transcribed our interviews and worked on early drafts of the manuscript.

Academics write books, but it is often editors who make them readable. In the early stages of writing this book, Barbara Feinberg was our developmental editor. She deserves credit for helping us develop a structure for presenting our findings. To aid in editing the final draft of this book, we were fortunate to enlist the services of Barbara Rifkind. She brought calm under pressure and great awareness of the readers' needs and the authors' intentions in digesting a study such as ours. Her keen editing and perceptive suggestions greatly improved the flow and presentation of the ideas herein.

Editorial assistance was also provided by David's nine-year-old daughter, Sommer Thomas, who each day demanded that her father report his progress and show her the completed pages. She also corrected poor handwriting and his bad habit of scratching out instead of erasing mistakes.

Nikki Sabin, our editor at the Harvard Business School Press, saw the worth of this project long before it took clear or final form. Helen Reese helped broker the match by convincing us that Nikki really "understood this book." To both of them, we say thank you.

Just as the development of minority executives must be understood as a process embedded in an institutional context, so too must this work. We were fortunate throughout the last six years to have the support of the Harvard Business School, especially the financial sponsorship of the Division of Research. Jay Lorsch, Richard Tedlow, and Teresa Amabile each served as our director of research during a period of the study. Their advice and support was critical to keeping us on track. John McArthur was dean of the school when we began this project. He encouraged David to pursue it even when many thought the project was not prudent or possible. In this way, he provided the kind of leadership that helps an individual achieve new heights in their own development.

We have been most fortunate over the course of this project to be part of a wonderful group of colleagues, the Organizational Behavior Unit, at the Harvard Business School. Without exception, our colleagues have supported us and communicated a belief in the value of our work. They have been forthright with both their criticism and praise. Mike Beer, Jeff Bradach, Linda Hill, Herminia Ibarra, John Kotter, Paul Lawrence, Jay Lorsch, Nitin Nohria, and Carl Sloane each read the entire length of the manuscript, some more than once, to give us useful feedback.

Helpful feedback was also forthcoming from individuals outside the unit. Jim Baron, Stacey Blake, Jim Cash, Dwight Crane, and David Porter provided comments that refined our thinking and led this book to have broader appeal than would have been the case otherwise. A number of other colleagues provided criticism, suggestions, and other comments on various parts of this project. We would especially like to thank Clay Alderfer, Robin Ely, Kathy Kram, Barbara Lawrence, and Tim Hall.

Our families have been with us throughout the ups and downs of this project. In particular, Willetta has suffered David's waking at 6:00 A.M. and coming to bed at 2:00 A.M. after full days of writing. Neither she nor Jack's wife, Marilyn, begrudged us the time or the passion we gave to this project. Our children, too, made the sacrifice of time in support of this work. Perhaps the only consolation is that what we have learned may contribute to their generation's inheritance of a world better able to remove the barriers to equal opportunity.

Introduction

"The problem of the twentieth century will be the color line."

W.E.B. DUBOIS (1903)

A REFLECTIVE LOOK AT the social history of the United States almost a full century after W. E. B. DuBois spoke these words would give hearty support to his prediction. Census data and opinion polls continue to document that race is a salient predictor of difference in experience, political affiliation, lifestyle preferences, health status, and economic well-being. Americans continue to live and worship largely separate from one another.[1]

This separateness exists even though the country has, for the last half century, been striving to live out its creed that all people are created equal. This movement has been largely associated with change efforts in the political and social arenas of civic life. In the last quarter century, however, the emphasis has shifted to

1

the economic sphere. Particularly prominent is the issue of equal opportunity in employment.

Increasingly, the focus on economic participation has moved to what many feel is the ultimate source of power and success in corporate America—executive jobs. Commentators in this arena have noted that until Franklin Raines was selected CEO of Fannie Mae in 1998, no African American, Asian American, or native-born Hispanic had ever been CEO of a *Fortune* 500 corporation. The symbolism of this fact is not that corporate America is unwilling to hand a million-dollar paycheck to a person of color. We know that it is willing because some athletes, entertainers, artists, writers, and even a few people of color in business command huge sums, more than many CEOs of *Fortune* 500 companies. Instead the critical question is why well-trained, highly committed people of color cannot make it into the executive ranks of U.S. corporations.

There is some reason to be optimistic if one reads the business press. There are now a small number of minorities who have made it to very senior executive jobs. Often, there is a surprising amount of fascination with these individuals, some of whom become the object of considerable media attention.

Kenneth Chenault, president and chief operating officer of American Express, Barry Rand, former executive vice president of Xerox, Tom Jones, co-chairman and CEO of Citigroup's Asset Management Group, Solomon Trujillo, president and CEO of USWest, Ann Fudge, president of Maxwell House, and Rajat Gupta, president and CEO of McKinsey & Company, are all persons of color—African American, Hispanic American, or Asian American—who rose to the executive level of major U.S. firms. Their renown extends well beyond their organizations and industries, much further than most of their white counterparts or predecessors. The fascination with these individuals is in part related to their embodiment of the tensions and potential resolutions of the combined issues of race, power, and the opportunity to lead in corporate America. Like it or not, the probabilities that these individuals would hold these positions is small. According to recent statistics, the chances of a person of color holding an executive position in a *Fortune* 500 corporation are about 33 to 1 compared to those for whites.[2] Take away those minorities who are executives in pure staff roles such as human resources, public relations, and general counsel's office, and the odds fall even more dramatically.[3] How did these executives beat the odds?

The aim of this book is to articulate the processes of development and advancement that produce minority executives. It represents a six-year endeavor to examine both the individual and organizational factors that influence minority advancement. We believe that our findings and the lessons they render are relevant to three audiences: academics interested in careers, race relations in organizations, and the sociology of occupations; general managers, HR executives, and others concerned with the development and advancement of minorities in management; and finally, minority managers and professionals who aspire to executive responsibility in corporate America.

In conducting this study, we have made several critical choices. The first was to make this research comparative; we have studied both minorities and whites, both executives and non-executives (i.e., managers whose careers have plateaued at the middle management level). The second choice we made was to focus on this phenomenon intensively in three companies. We selected these companies because they were clearly leaders in their ability to develop people of color from the entry-level management to the executive level. We also chose them because they operated in very different industries and contexts, and all three were leaders in market share and reputation.

◢ RACE AND EXECUTIVE DEVELOPMENT

Hundreds of books and thousands of research articles have appeared in the last two decades on executive development and leadership. Yet virtually all of this literature is silent on the issue of race.[4] The only possible exonerating defense for this omission is that there were so few minority senior managers and executives in the companies where much of this research was undertaken. In the absence of research on the effects of race on executive development, we do not know if systematic differences exist between the career paths taken by whites and minorities to reach the executive suite, or in the way they experience that climb.

We are not the first researchers to examine issues of race and opportunity. There is a long tradition of race relations research in the social science disciplines of sociology, psychology, and economics.

Unfortunately, little of it has focused on executive leadership in corporations or on developing theory that might be useful to minorities who find themselves trying to succeed in large corporations. Within the careers literature in the organizational sciences there is a small but growing body of empirical studies that has begun to address the links among race, professional development, and opportunity in organizations. This work has been especially useful in shedding light on factors that impede minority advancement in organizations. These career studies generally start with the observation that there is a paucity of African Americans, Asian Americans, and Hispanics in the executive suites of large U.S. corporations. With this lens the studies examine the experiences and opportunity structures that limit minority advancement.[5] As a body of work, it has yielded a sharper and deeper understanding of the barriers to advancement but not of the experiences and opportunity structures that lead to advancement. Even in large survey studies of racial dynamics in organizations, the nonwhite respondent samples are dominated by those who have *not* reached the executive suite.[6] Similarly, studies focused on understanding processes such as mentoring and social support have tended to focus on minorities in subordinate positions, such as young protégés and lower-level managers.[7] The net result is that we know little of the experiences of minorities who *do* break through the glass ceiling for race.

One way of conceptualizing much of this body of work is as attempts to understand the phenomenon of the glass ceiling by examining the experiences of those beneath it. To a large extent, it reflects an empirical reality. This approach makes sense in light of the fact that the odds are high that people of color will disproportionately end up beneath that ceiling even when one controls for those human capital assets that should affect opportunity, such as education, training, and social class. What these studies provide is a clear picture of the challenges facing people of color as they attempt to rise up the corporate ladder. In the next chapter, we discuss these challenges.

The exceptions are benchmark studies of corporations that have done relatively well at creating a diverse workforce.[8] These studies have been especially useful in identifying programmatic efforts in companies that produce a diverse and well-managed workforce. But the actual career experiences of individuals moving through the corporations are not addressed. Even the criteria for choosing these remarkable companies can sometimes be problematic. Typically, best practice companies are chosen on the basis of their overall percentage of managers of color, with almost no attention to what these individuals actually do, what levels they attain, or what resources they control. Such studies illuminate critical factors that effect corporate diversity, but do not speak directly to the processes that give rise to the development and advancement of minority executives. As a result, we know little of the experiences—either individual or organizational—that correspond with the cracking, and ultimately the breaking, of the glass ceiling for racial minorities.

◢ WHY FOCUS ON WINNERS?

Perhaps not everyone would agree that the dearth of studies on the experiences of minority executives is a serious deficiency in the existing body of knowledge on race and management development. Indeed, soon after this project was launched, a colleague asked: "Why are you studying *winners*? Isn't there more to be gained by looking at those who are not succeeding—those who don't make it to the management level, let alone executive level?" Another asked, "Is the glass 99 percent empty or 1 percent full; why are you studying the 1 percent?" Both questions imply that studying an elite class of minority executives and their development might gloss over the very real, and sometimes insurmountable, obstacles that a majority of nonwhites face in their quest for advancement in corporate America. Our belief, then and now, is that lessons drawn from success frequently suggest how to identify sources of leverage that can help surmount the obstacles to advancement. In a manner of speaking, we believe that the minority executives we have studied are similar to the handful of frontier pioneers who forged a trail over rough and uncharted territory to settle a new land, clearing a path for the many who followed.

Nevertheless, caution is appropriate. In this era of winner-takes-all superstardom, it would be a mistake to permit this sort of research to spawn new myths—as some magazine articles have done—about a new breed of heroic, nonwhite Horatio Algers. Given the reality, this would do no one a favor. One need only read recent accounts of minorities' experiences of racism and discrimination in corporate America to see that institutional barriers to their advancement persist.[9] There remain companies in which no amount of individual effort, preparation, or performance is likely to propel a person of color into an executive position with the power to shape key business decisions.

We are not suggesting that other ways of studying the problem of minority advancement are not useful. Rather, we believe that a careful, comparative examination of individuals who break through the glass ceiling and of their contexts and careers will help to illuminate some of the issues (and potential sources of leverage) that are salient to eliminating or overcoming barriers. In this regard, our intention is to complement existing research that focuses on identifying the specific barriers themselves.

A STUDY OF MINORITY EXECUTIVE DEVELOPMENT AND ADVANCEMENT

The focus of our book is on the lessons that can be learned from the career experiences of successful minority executives. The primary data for the book are twenty case studies of minority executives at three major U.S. companies whose identities we have disguised. The minority executives included African Americans, Asian Americans, and Hispanic Americans. For comparison purposes, we also conducted equally in-depth studies of thirty-four other white and minority executives and non-executives from the same three companies.

The three companies were selected for a number of reasons. First, as stated before, all three are leaders in their particular industries in efforts to improve racial diversity in their management ranks. Second, they represent disparate industries with different levels of technological intensity required in their core operations. Third, our preliminary assessments indicated that the cultures and employment practices of the three companies were quite different from each other. These differences in their approaches to diversity enabled us to analyze more clearly the influence of corporate context on minority advancement. The three companies, their products, and their organizations are described in detail in Chapter 2. Herein we will refer to these companies by their pseudonyms: Acme Industries, Advanced Technology, and Gant Electronics.

Definitions and Criteria

Who is an executive? We have used a rather stringent definition of executive. Our interest was in understanding the development and advancement of minority executives who either had general management responsibility or had major responsibility for a core business function, such as finance, manufacturing, or engineering. This meant that some persons of color in each firm whose title and compensation category qualified them as an executive were not eligible for our study. Other studies of minority executives, such as those by Sharon Collins and John Work, suggest that most minority executives today tend to hold high-level staff positions outside core business areas, largely in corporate staffs such as human resources, community and government relations, and legal. Such jobs, while important in their own right, seldom lead to the CEO position or other senior operating roles and do not carry authority for setting strategic direction or profit and loss responsibility.[10]

Each of the three companies in the study had its own definition of the level at which executive status was conferred. For purposes of ensuring comparability across companies, we defined an executive as someone who was a corporate officer or a direct report of a corporate officer with responsibility for an integrated business unit (e.g., division president or vice president/general manager) or leadership of a corporate function (e.g., corporate controller or vice president for purchasing). In all cases, this definition was more restrictive than the definitions used by the companies. The types of jobs occupied by our study participants are among the most coveted by managers of any race and, so far, the most elusive for minorities.

In order to understand fully the experience of minority executive development and advancement, we needed to include both white executives and non-executive plateaued minority managers in the study. We studied comparable white executives in order to identify both what was common and what was unique to the experiences and career patterns of minority executives. Our interest in studying plateaued minority managers was to understand what experiences they had in common with minority executives and, equally important, how differing career experiences, assignment patterns, and developmental opportunities might have accounted for the plateauing of one group and the advancement of the other.

We chose plateaued minority middle managers as the comparison group because they were individuals who had achieved a fairly significant level of managerial responsibility (upper-middle management), but were seen by their companies as being unlikely to make it to the executive level as we defined it. This ensured that the comparison group of plateaued managers consisted of people who had demonstrated their ability to contribute to the corporation and had been successful enough to reach upper-middle management. We thus avoided the risk of comparing minority executives to minorities whose careers included little advancement beyond individual contributor or first-level management. Five criteria were employed in the selection of the non-executive, plateaued managers:

1. They were currently in a managerial role that involved supervision of other managers;

2. they were in a core business function and not a support staff department;

3. their tenure at their current level of upper-middle management was longer than the average for that level;

4. they were not currently designated by their organization as having the potential to move to the executive level; and

5. they were deemed an effective performer in their current job.

The individuals who met these criteria were all upper-middle managers whose responsibilities typically involved heading a functional department within a business unit. Common titles were plant manager, director of marketing, and branch manager. Plateaued managers in the study most often reported to an executive such as a division vice president/general manager or head of a corporate function.

Selecting the Participants

After gaining approval to conduct our research in each site, we asked our company liaisons to provide us with a list of African Americans, Asian Americans, and Hispanic Americans who met our executive criteria. We then selected a subset of these individuals and invited them to participate in the study. Based on the composition of this group of minority executives, we then selected a group of individuals from each of the comparison groups: white executives, plateaued minority managers, and plateaued white managers. Our attempt was to make these groups comparable to the minority executive group in terms of functional group representation, educational background, tenure in the workforce, and gender.[11] Each was a paired match to one of the minority executives based on these background factors. The data on the white plateaued managers was used only for comparison purposes in Chapter 3.

We decided to focus on a small group of people we could study exhaustively and to include more minority executives than individuals from the other comparison groups. It is not uncommon in studies such as this to oversample in the group of theoretical interest, especially if they are a small segment of the population.[12] This was also justified because of the ethnic diversity of the minority executive group.

African Americans and men dominated the minority executive populations at each company. Our study population reflects this fact. Thirteen of the minority executives are African American, four are Asian American, and three are Hispanic American. Among the minority managers, two are Hispanic and the rest (eleven) African American. Eight of the fifty four participants are female. We included all the female minority executives at each company who met our criteria.[13] Table I-1 provides the distribution of our study participants across the three companies.

Table I-1   Study Participants

		Acme Industries		Advanced Technology		Gant Electronics	
		Males	*Females*	*Males*	*Females*	*Males*	*Females*
Minority Executives	(n=20)	4	1	9	—	5	1
Minority Managers	(n=13)	4	1	3	1	3	1
White Executives	(n=13)	5	—	4	—	3	1
White Managers[14]	(n=8)	4	1	—	—	2	1
Total	(N=54)	17	3	16	1	13	4

◢ WHO IS A MINORITY?

Our choices for selecting the study participants raise two important issues. These relate to the race and gender composition of our study participants. They bear on the limitations of our approach and its potential contribution to knowledge about race relations in organizations and minority executive development.

What Does It Mean to Be a Racial Minority?

This question is hotly debated in both policy and academic circles. As yet, there is no consensus on a right answer. From the outset, we were interested in the development and advancement of executives who had "racial minority" status. This included people from diverse ethnic backgrounds and phenotypes (i.e., those who were visibly identifiable as racial minorities and those who could pass for white). Our operational definition of racial minority, as represented in our study population, was largely determined by the companies' own definitions of racial minority and the racial composition of their executive groups. We also found that in each instance the minorities in the study self-identified in the interview as a member of the racial group to which we had assigned them.

The fact that the African Americans, Asian Americans, and Hispanic Americans in our study identified themselves as members of a minority group does not answer a question that will exist for some readers: Are these different minority group memberships equivalent in their likely impact on individuals' careers? Research would seem to indicate that while cultural differences between the groups exist, each is underrepresented at the higher levels of management. Our study found that the basic career patterns and social processes that characterize the advancement and development of these minority executives was similar. Therefore, what we report here represents the commonalties of the experiences of racial minorities.

What About the Women?

Just as the career development experiences of racial minorities have been understudied, so too have those of women. Perhaps even more noticeably lacking are studies of the experiences of women of color.[15] A clear limitation of our study is the lack of women included. This largely reflects the scant presence of women of color in the kinds of executive jobs that would have made them eligible for our study.

In the chapters that follow, our focus is on the common and disparate patterns of achievement experienced across race and hierarchical levels. We do not treat gender specifically as a dimension of comparison. In our attempts to identify its influence, we did not observe ways in which the patterns of succeeding to the executive level or plateauing differed for minority men and women. This, of course, is not to suggest that the experience of moving through a corporation was not influenced by gender. We believe it is. Our study design and data, however, do not allow us to establish gender effects.

Our hope is that together with other studies examining gender and, in particular, the experiences of women of color, this study can contribute to a richer and more complete understanding of how race and gender influence careers.

⬛ THE DATA

Our data collection had two major objectives. First was the creation of career biographies for each of the fifty-four executives and managers selected for the study. We spent six to fifteen hours interviewing each person on family background, progression of jobs, development as a manager, experience of race and its effects on career, and the events and relationships seen as critical to current level of career attainment. In addition to interviewing each study participant, we asked each to nominate three people with whom we could speak to get an independent assessment. We specifically asked that one of these persons be a recent boss and another a subordinate. We asked these individuals to share their impressions of the participant's style, strengths, weaknesses, and performance as managers or executives over the time they knew them. In all we interviewed 158 informants in relation to the careers of our 54 study participants.[16] In addition to the participant and informant interviews, we reviewed company human resource records on each participant. These records provided a check on the interviewee's recollection of his or her career progression and whether a move constituted a promotion, lateral move, or demotion.

The second objective of our research process was to develop an understanding of the three organizations, in particular, their cultures, orientations toward executive development, and approach to promoting racial diversity in management. We gained significant insight into these areas from our study participants and the interviews conducted with their bosses, subordinates, and peers. We also interviewed several people at each company whose current positions or involvement with the companies' diversity efforts made them valuable sources of information. Indispensable in this process was the review of internal company documents and publicly available published material on the companies.

The fieldwork for this project spanned three years during which we interviewed nearly 250 people, accumulating thousands of pages of transcripts. In addition to the personnel records of the executives and managers in the study, we were also given access to the promotion records of 554 Acme managers and executives. The conclusions drawn in this book are the result of our analysis of these data.

CAREER STAGES AND THE COMPARATIVE ANALYSIS

To aid us in comparing the career experiences of our study participants, we created a career stage typology that corresponds to their advancement up the managerial hierarchy. Each individual's career was divided into three sequential stages that spanned a specific period of the career, each marked by a significant increase in managerial responsibility.[17]

Stage 1 begins at the start of a person's professional career and ends when he or she reaches middle management. This is roughly the point at which the manager becomes responsible for supervising a complete work unit, with a group of first-line managers (such as front-line production supervisors) or highly skilled professionals (such as senior design engineers) reporting directly to him or her.

Stage 2 is the period from middle management to upper-middle management. Upper-middle managers oversee direct reports who are themselves middle managers. Generally, upper-middle managers reported to a divisional vice president and general manager (VPGM) responsible for an entire business unit or to a senior executive in charge of a function, such as VP of manufacturing. Frequently encountered upper-middle management titles included director of marketing, branch manager, and plant manager. Upper-middle management was the highest level attained by plateaued managers in our study.

Stage 3 covers the period from upper-middle management to executive. As described earlier, we defined executive as a general manager who is either a corporate officer or reports to one, or the leader of a core business function. All of the executives we studied were either line general managers responsible for the running of a major business unit or corporate functional leaders reporting directly to the chief executive officer or to one of his direct reports. The most frequently held title by members of this group was vice president and general manager (VPGM).

Although our total study population included four groups— minority executives, white executives, plateaued minority managers, and plateaued white managers—the focus of our comparative analysis is on the first three. This was proposed from the outset and reinforced by our initial examination of results. Therefore, data for plateaued white managers are presented and discussed only in Chapter 3, the analysis of career configurations. Appendix A provides a detailed description of the study's design and methods.

◢ THE ORGANIZATION OF THIS BOOK

Part I sets the study in context by providing a picture of the processes that produce minority executives and an understanding of the social and corporate contexts that shape these processes. Chapter 1 looks at the challenges that confront people of color as they compete for executive jobs in mainstream corporate America. It also provides an overview of what we discovered as critical to overcoming these challenges. Chapter 2 describes the three companies and the evolution of their diversity strategies in the social and historical context of the 1960s, 1970s, and 1980s. Chapter 3 looks at the structure of competition in the minority executives' career paths and how their trajectories differed from those of white executives. The findings of this chapter lay the contextual frame that we use to analyze the career experiences of minority executives and to contrast them with white executives and plateaued minority managers.

Part II examines the career experiences of minority executives and contrasts them with those of both white executives and minorities who plateaued in middle management. Personal background factors and the developmental experiences of Career Stage 1 are examined in Chapters 4 and 5, while the process and experience of breaking through to the executive level is described in Chapter 6.

Part III addresses the role of organizational processes in bringing about a corporate culture that allowed for more than token representation of people of color in the executive suite. Together, Chapters 7 and 8 detail the unique diversity strategies that guided each company's efforts and the factors that sustained them over a period of time.

Part IV, Chapters 9 and 10, review the implications of this study for corporate leaders who want to develop minority executives more effectively, and for people of color who aspire to successful careers in the corporate mainstream.

SETTING THE STAGE

1

Minority Success in
the Corporate Mainstream

To understand how I got here, you have to understand the challenges. I grew up in a situation where corporations didn't want black salespeople because they doubted whites would buy from them, and they doubted how articulate blacks could be. When we broke that barrier, they didn't want blacks to be sales managers because they didn't think blacks could lead whites. Then at the branch manager level, where you are mixing sales, service, and administration, so you have a little general management, it becomes more complicated. The question was, were blacks smart enough to do that? We had to break that barrier, too.

—BEN RICHARDSON
VICE CHAIRMAN AND CHIEF OF OPERATIONS
GANT ELECTRONICS

THIS BOOK IS ABOUT the making of "minority executives," African American, Asian American, and Hispanic American professionals who reach the executive level in large, predominantly white corporations. Minority executives, like white executives, are products of organizations. The process of becoming a corporate executive has two important ingredients—preparation and opportunity. Careers can be derailed by lack of one or the other. Succeeding at the highest levels of the corporation requires sufficient levels of both. Indeed, the debate about why there are so few minority executives often centers on these two issues—who is prepared and who gets opportunity—irrespective of what one views as the root cause of the glass ceiling.

Ben Richardson is a minority executive.[1] Today, he sits two doors away from the CEO and is a potential successor. His story helps to anchor us in the reality of a climb up the corporate ladder that was both similar to and different from that of his white executive counterparts. On hearing his story, one might ponder what in his experience is universal and what is particular to his being a member of a racial minority? In the end, the Richardsons of the world must meet the same tests and survive under the same scrutiny as white executives, and they must cope with the subtle and not-so-subtle differences that race makes.

◢ BEN RICHARDSON'S STORY

Almost twenty-five years after joining Gant Electronics, Ben Richardson was named Vice Chairman and Chief of Operations, one of the top four jobs in the corporation. In addition to his line responsibilities, the forty-eight-year-old Richardson joined the other members of Gant's executive committee to determine corporate strategy and preside over its implementation.

Ben Richardson grew up in New York City. Both of his parents were college-educated; his father worked as a postal worker and his mother as an elementary school teacher. They provided Ben with a solid middle-class upbringing. After fifth grade, he attended predominantly white Catholic schools. His parents' friends included many professionals and other accomplished men and women of color. Richardson learned the skills and developed the confidence to move effectively between the mostly separate worlds of whites and blacks.

> I grew up bilingual, [living] in a very black, middle-class community, where most of my parents' friends were professionals. After school, that was where I spent all my time, but during school I was in a white environment.... I was growing up bilingual: understanding the majority world but living and gaining confidence in who I was in the black world.
>
> I was fortunate that I always had confidence because my parents, being black and middle class, had very strong values, good educations, and very

high expectations. You were expected to be successful. You were expected to win in sports. You were always expected to excel. So I never had those self-confidence issues or leadership issues. You knew you were supposed to be a proud black person—proud of who you were. You would be able to compete with anybody, black or white, and I kept winning in that environment.

Elected president of his high school class three times in four years, Richardson displayed obvious leadership traits. In college, however, Richardson stumbled. At Cornell University, he had signed up for extra courses while also playing football and basketball and sampling fraternity life. The combination proved overwhelming, and, during his second year, with his grades in decline, he dropped out.

Looking back on this dismal experience, Richardson saw it as one of his first lessons in organizational life:

I realized that some [white] students understood things that I didn't. They learned from their fraternities about how the power structure worked. They learned how to maneuver around the institution. I learned it the hard way because I didn't maneuver. I remember talking to one of my professors, I hadn't done well in his course, and he told me, "If I had known you were getting into trouble, you could have come to me and talked about it." I didn't know that. I didn't know that was part of the rules. . . . I realized that whatever explicit rules there are in the institution, there are also unspoken rules. Whatever objective criteria there are, there are also subjective criteria. So one of the tricks in an institution is to understand not only objective criteria, but also subjective criteria—not only the written rules, but also the unwritten rules.

His first attempt at college also taught Richardson a lesson about himself—a lesson he didn't like:

In the end, I got angry. I said to myself, "Wait a minute. You made yourself fail because you thought of all these reasons why you didn't think you could make it. Therefore, you made a decision which in and of itself meant that you could not win: You took yourself out of the game." Yes, you can make a lot of excuses about why you shouldn't take this or do that, but if you make a decision that you are too good a person to stand for the b.s., and so drop out, that means you cannot win. By definition.

Richardson soon returned to school, this time at New York University in the familiar environs of New York City. To pay his way, he worked nights at a department store, selling men's clothes. This experience proved formative: he loved to sell and was good at it. He also changed his major from political science to marketing.

Armed with his BA, Richardson sought a job in sales and marketing with a big corporation. He found few takers, though, until he began an aggressive campaign to sell himself. Talking his way past wary receptionists and recruiters who were skeptical about the prospects for African Americans to rise to high-level sales positions, he eventually got offers from Xerox, Polaroid, IBM, Gant, and several other big companies. He chose Gant Electronics because it was both a prestigious employer and, among these companies, seemed the most open to the career he imagined.

Richardson's first job at Gant was as a sales representative in the black neighborhoods of New York City. Although the company held out little hope for this market, Richardson quickly distinguished himself as one of his unit's top salespeople. Still, his chance to break into the mainstream of corporate selling did not come immediately. Several times he requested better territories, but to no avail. It took a new manager to get him his first real opportunity. After two years, he ranked number three out of nearly fifteen hundred Gant sales reps nationwide.

> I kept suggesting that they give me one of those rich territories, downtown with all these corporate accounts, one of those real choice ones. They kept saying "no, no, no." Finally this hip white guy, Steven Berg, became my sales manager. He was a Jewish guy who turned out to be from Brooklyn. He gave me the territory I asked for and I crushed them, all the targets. In total, I was third out of fifteen hundred sales reps nationwide. I was number one in my region.

Despite such success, Richardson encountered trouble getting promoted to the next level at Gant. He was passed over for promotion five times. Finally, after four years of selling, he was offered and accepted a sales management position in the white suburbs of Pittsburgh. The extra time as a sales rep—with three years in a row as number one in his region—had given him the expertise and confidence he now used to succeed.

Since this was my first significant management job, the question was, did I really know how to do it? I realized that I didn't know how to do parts of the management job. What I did know was how to motivate people. I knew how to get people to go the extra mile.

I came in and learned about the people—what made them tick. I quickly overcame their concerns about race because normally, if there weren't other issues, I could overcome the black-white issue. I could sell better than most people, and I could teach others how to do it.

This one guy, for example, had only one large sale all year. I told him that I was personally going to do all the proposals. I took home the book on his territory and I picked out what I thought were the plum potential accounts. I did the proposals, and I told him, "You take me out in the car to see these people." That day, we had four big sales, one right after the other: boom, boom, boom, boom. He was shocked. At 5:00, he was all ready to go home. I said, "No. We are not going back. We have one more account to visit, and we are going to get it." We went at 5:30 and sold a fifth one.

In addition to helping individual sales reps with their territories, Richardson also motivated them by setting high goals. When he arrived at the unit, it averaged 30 orders per month and was ranked 38th out of 40 in the region. Richardson fixed 100 orders per month as the new goal and soon exceeded it. Within a year, the unit climbed to number four out of 40, exceeding its target.

However, once again, success did not pay immediate career dividends. Richardson did not get along with his manager, whom he found rude, abusive, and racist. The manager asked Richardson's wife whether he beat her and called him a thief. Blocked from advancement by his manager, Richardson considered leaving the company. Instead, he applied for a program that sent selected Gant Electronics employees to Massachusetts Institute of Technology (MIT) for a nine-month management course. Over the opposition of his supervisor, Richardson was accepted to the program. His appointment was possible because of the relationships he had formed in his previous job in New York and by the support of his former boss and mentor, Steven Berg.

The program at MIT provided another key developmental experience for Richardson because it broadened his knowledge of management while deepening his understanding of interpersonal and organizational dynamics. It also restored his faith in Gant.

After earning his MBA degree, Richardson returned full-time to Gant. By then, the company had recruited about a dozen more young, high-potential black sales representatives. Richardson joined with these new hires to form a self-help group called the Black Network. He recalled:

We started developing black self-help groups. Part of our role was teaching each other this thing called subjective criteria, teaching about spoken and unspoken rules, teaching about managing your manager. It became our learning network and our assessment network. It was a network in which we learned how to lead, a network in which we learned how to talk about strategy. It was a network in which you learned teamwork. It was a network of friendship. It was a network that provided you sustenance to deal with understanding yourself and the system.

Meanwhile, Richardson's career finally began a sharp upward turn—after a momentary pause when he was passed over for yet another promotion he believed he had earned. Shortly thereafter, however, Steven Berg, by then a region manager, named him a branch manager in Philadelphia. After eight years with Gant, he had his first general management job. Once again, he quickly established himself as a strong performer, albeit at the cost of very long hours and ultimately a failed marriage. Behind his business success lay not only competitiveness and drive, but also a philosophy of inclusive coalition management.

I wanted to prove once and for all that affirmative action was not negative. In fact, I wanted to have the number one branch in the country. And that number one branch was going to have a lot of black people and a lot of females in it. Therefore, I became involved in every hiring decision. I wanted to make sure that we got an equitable number of blacks and an equitable number of females. . . . I wanted to prove that we could do this thing.

What I ended up doing was picking people who were talented, but who in my opinion also were not biased. There were white females, for example, who would only promote white females. I was looking for a talented white female who was also unbiased, . . . I wanted blacks who would not think of themselves as only promoting blacks, because they would be brought down. I wanted to pick those white males who were also as close as possible to being unbiased.

You have to put together consortiums of power ... blacks, whites, males, females who can see the world similarly to the way you do. ... To have such a thing, you have to actively help people. I think there is a way to make sure you are helping the right people, to put together a consortium so that they in turn are more prone to hire blacks, females, and whites of similar disposition. That is how you start controlling power. And when you start controlling power, you start controlling and influencing decisions, perceptions, subjective criteria, and how the system works given the unstated rules.

By his mid-thirties Richardson was clearly on a track to the top. His subsequent assignments helped broaden and round out his experience and skills. He had several corporate staff assignments at corporate and bigger jobs in sales and marketing. He described himself as taking each job in sequential order, not missing a single step. Along the way, he internalized still more management lessons about accumulating and exercising power and responsibility, while forging alliances with other key managers, acquiring new skills, developing new perspectives, and building teams of strong people with complementary abilities.

You can't be afraid to have smart people around you. You need them. You have to have the self-confidence to not feel threatened by it. The issue of leadership is of paramount importance. Even if they are smarter than you, they may not be as good a leader. What saved me, frankly, is my people management and leadership abilities and the decision I made early on to go for the smart people and get them on my side, not with the traditional people who show they can run a particular function. What they know is how to run that function, and they can tweak it to death. They are not break-through thinkers. They are not people who see a different system, a different framework.

So this whole mix of diversity that we talked about, race and color, is important, but diversity of thought is truly important to help push a company forward. I was cognizant that revolutions always start with a small group of people and then grow. I wanted to have that diversity of thought. Later on I blew up the five regions I was handed. We had staffs in all the regions. I blew them up. I took levels out. I changed power. I changed goals. I changed how the goals were formulated. I changed the job roles. I changed the system I grew up in.

By age forty, Richardson was in a very important upper-middle management job as head of sales and service for Gant's largest division. Around this time, the presidency of the division came open. While Richardson had developed a reputation for being unafraid to implement new policies and able to lead effectively, he seemed an unlikely candidate for the job because it was several levels above the job he then held. Originally, several other more senior managers were competing for the position; Richardson was near the bottom of the pack. But time and persistence paid off.

> *I got to be president because all of the other players shot themselves in OK Corral–type situations. In the political in-fighting, they all shot themselves—it was amazing. It was like I was back in college, when I was fourth sitting on the bench. In this situation, I was like third on the depth chart. I don't like getting into killing anybody else. That's not my style. I like competing against someone and showing I'm better, but I don't like dirty, in-fighting, political assassinations. That's not in my value system. These guys, it was not against their value system. So I sat there in the dugout watching them kill each other, and when the smoke cleared, they were all gone. It was another lesson: that you can't win in that kind of unethical, unprincipled fight over power. It resulted in the corporation getting hurt because people weren't cooperating.... [W]hen the smoke cleared, people were saying, "Who is open-minded? Who is a change agent? Who are we willing to take a risk with?"*

The executive who appointed him to the division president's job described Richardson's appointment in similar terms.

> *I put Ben in the job because I wanted to change the way the job was being done, change it dramatically. We took the person who was in the job out not because he was not successful, but because he was not doing the job effectively. I chose Ben because he was the best choice that we had, even though he wasn't ready to do the job. It was a high-risk choice. He did not have the background to go into it—it was a big jump for him, probably a three- or four-level promotion when we put him into that job. We also chose him because I thought he would be a change agent, not somebody steeped in the mythology of a headquarters mentality. [Somebody] who could go in with his set of field eyes rather than somebody who has spent a lot of time run-*

ning headquarters and running the bureaucracy, who could focus on the customer and have real empathy for the customer's requirements and turn the place around.

Success at turning around the division and, essentially, changing its business paradigm to be customer-focused with an emphasis on quality put him on the road to his current executive position as vice chairman. From this difficult and high stakes turnaround, Richardson moved to several posts that involved even more responsibility. Seven years later, he was appointed to his current top position.

Ben Richardson's story is one of great success by any standard, regardless of race. But it is an especially remarkable story for an African American of his generation. Richardson is one of the few who have made it to the top. This book is about what it takes for people of color to break through the glass ceiling in large U.S. corporations. Ben Richardson's story illustrates the drive and personal resources that it takes as well as the focused persistence and deeply grounded competence that make a difference. The story also reflects the kind of support and help that he got in a corporate environment that, though not free of racial prejudice, seemed from the start to be more open to people of color than most U.S. companies were at that time.

This book is about identifying and overcoming the barriers that keep minorities from advancing to the topmost ranks of U.S. companies. It is these barriers —visible and invisible—that comprise what we refer to as the glass ceiling. To understand how to break it, one first has to understand what these barriers are.

◢ CHALLENGES TO MINORITY ADVANCEMENT

Other scholars who have examined barriers that block or impede people of color from advancing in predominantly white corporations reveal categories of barriers that seem particularly germane to the study of minority executive development and advancement. Three major categories are (1) the prevalence of prejudice; (2) issues of comfort and risk; and (3) the difficulty of identifying high-potential minorities.[2] When taken together these aspects of race relations form

an important part of the context in which minority managers encounter challenges to upward career mobility. The story of Ben Richardson
as well as others described in this book make clear that these challenges are neither avoidable nor insurmountable.

The Prevalence of Prejudice

Virtually everyone writing on the career experiences of minority
and women managers and professionals identifies race- and gender-
based prejudice as a major—perhaps *the* major—barrier to advancement.[3] Prejudice can be understood as a cluster of negative preconcep-
tions, attitudes, and expectations that people of one group hold about
members of other groups. There are two sorts of prejudice: individual
and systemic. The former is held by individuals about members of
groups other than their own. The latter, systemic prejudice, is a set of
institutionalized assumptions, attitudes, and practices that have a
kind of invisible-hand effect in systematically advantaging members
of more powerful groups over members of less dominant groups.[4] Systemic prejudice, or institutionalized discrimination, does not take
place because of the mean-spirited actions of bigots but rather takes
such forms as culturally biased assessment and selection criteria,
group norms that permit or condone racial or sexual harassment,
lower performance expectations based on group membership, and
collectively shared assumptions that relegate members of certain
groups to particular positions—for example, the common practice of
not assigning African Americans to the customer side of the business
because of perceptions that African Americans do not interact well
with white customers.

As a result of both kinds of prejudice, minorities frequently find
themselves having to disprove the rule of their inferiority. With each
change of job position or department, they find themselves needing
once again to establish credibility and to counter and overcome stereotypes. Meeting such challenges requires time, effort, and mental
energy not required of their white colleagues. A consequence is that
minorities sometimes internalize these negative views of themselves
and lower their own expectations. Alternatively, they become embit-
tered and behave in ways that validate some stereotypes of them as
not being team players or being too confrontational. They may also

withdraw and fail to seek help and build alliances.[5] The net result of any of these reactions is to collude with the forces of prejudice that exist, to take onself as Ben Richardson would say "out of the game."

But prejudice does not account for all of the subtle social dynamics that shape the career experiences of minorities. Indeed, many of the impediments that hinder minorities' progress in companies result from the actions of well-meaning and essentially unbigoted people and in the context of progressive and committed organizations.

Issues of Comfort and Risk

The natural need to be comfortable and avoid risks also creates career barriers for minorities. Many have written about the tension produced when members of different racial groups must work together closely. People habitually seem to prefer working with people who are racially similar.[6] Thus, while superior–subordinate relationships that cross race lines may provide the interaction needed to get work done, they often fail to lead to the close interpersonal bonds that form between mentor and protégé.[7] Without such mentoring relationships, people may develop an overly narrow view of the work, feelings of alienation, and a diminished perception of self-efficacy. As a direct result of this discomfort of mingling with members of minority groups, dominant-group members may be slow to include minorities in social activities and informational and other networks and may be less likely to support them unequivocally when challenged by others.

A similar dynamic involves the risk that is perceived in supporting a person who is a minority. Whites often feel that sponsoring a person of color is riskier than sponsoring whites because minority protégés will be scrutinized more closely.[8] Minority employees, for their part, may also feel that they represent bigger risks to their bosses and potential sponsors because they are aware of the assumptions and prejudices people hold about members of racial or ethnic minorities. They become tentative or overly cautious in making decisions, unwilling to increase the potential discomfort of a boss or sponsor. With risk perceived from both sides, even bosses and mentors who feel socially comfortable with their minority employees may hesitate to push for rapid promotions or high-risk job assignments that might put their minority subordinates on the fast track. Eschewing such

risks avoids not only potential failure for the protégés but also potential damage to the sponsor's own reputation and credibility.

Organizations may also systematically thwart minority progress.
In large companies, promotion decisions are often made by committees. The candidate's sponsor must win the support of others,
including, in most cases, someone who agrees to provide the next
opportunity for the protégé. Many of the white mentors studied
noted that to create the same career opportunity for a black protégé
took more work than for a comparable white protégé. They attributed this to the risk others felt they would be taking in assuming
responsibility for a minority manager. Convincing their colleagues
that their protégé would not be a huge risk often took time and special maneuvering.[9]

The Difficulty of Identifying High-Potential Minorities

Given the realities of prejudice and the challenges of comfort and
risk found in interactions between different races, it is not difficult to
imagine why predominantly white institutions face difficulty assessing minority potential accurately or fairly. Kotter notes that those who
make it to the executive level are usually identified early in their
careers.[10] Companies best known for developing managers, such as
IBM and Bell Atlantic International, attempt to hire and develop high-
potential managers early in their careers, usually before they reach
middle and upper-middle management levels.

People systematically give higher performance ratings to members
of their own racial groups and view members of their own groups as
more promotable.[11] High-performing members of other racial groups
remain comparatively invisible in the selection process. As a result,
one can predict that minority managers are in general more likely to
spend significantly longer than the company average in the same job
or hierarchical level.

The lack of minority representation on selection committees
decreases even further the likelihood that minorities will be identified
as having high potential and promoted. In 1982, Clayton Alderfer and
his colleagues intervened at a company disguised as the XYZ Corporation to test if minorities who met the appropriate performance
criteria were being considered for the company's high-potential man-

agement program.[12] Alderfer and his partners created a selection committee that was balanced in its membership in terms of race and gender and drawn from the same pool of line managers as the other selection committees. It considered candidates from the same pool of individuals as did the company's traditional departmental selection committees that were composed almost entirely of white males. Despite the company's commitment to diversifying its management, Alderfer's heterogeneous committee selected a much more diverse group of high-potential candidates than the preexisting departmental committees. This experience illustrates how the racial and gender composition of decision makers can influence who gets chosen, quite apart from whether performance criteria have been met, even when an organization has an ongoing affirmative action program.

Even when minorities are recognized as outstanding performers and have comfortable relationships with their bosses and peers, their chances of getting placed on an accelerated path may be hindered by the very structure of decision making and the racial and gender composition of the decision makers. Yet it is clear that managers do need a broad array of developmental experiences if they are to become executives.[13] This, in turn, requires that they move to different areas and assume progressively larger and more important responsibilities. Thus losing promotional opportunities through the combined result of individual and systemic prejudice, issues of comfort and risk, and decision-making processes places minority employees in an unfavorable position for acquiring the critical experiences necessary for rising to the top.

This book addresses a set of as-yet-unanswered questions. We examine here the development of African American, Asian American, and Hispanic American professionals who ascend to the executive level and occupy roles that control major corporate resources, possess profit and loss responsibility, and influence business strategy. We have studied four groups (minority executives, white executives, plateaued minority middle managers, and plateaued white middle managers) across three *Fortune* 500 companies. We are interested in articulating the dynamics that allow racial minorities in large, predominantly white firms to penetrate the invisible barrier. Our work was motivated by four broad questions: What are the key career patterns and developmental experiences of racial minorities who make it to the executive level in large U.S. corporations? Are these patterns and experiences different from those of white (racial majority) people who make it? Are their experiences different from minorities who do not make it but plateau in middle management? And finally, but of critical importance, what role do organization-level contexts and processes play in facilitating minorities reaching the executive level?

Different Paths, Same Destination

The single most robust pattern found across all three companies is that the trajectories of minority executives in early career are different from those of white executives. The early career trajectory of white executives can be characterized as *fast and steady*. They experience a fast takeoff to upper-middle management in Stages 1 and 2, followed by a slower and steadier period of testing during their Stage 3 rise to the executive level (see "Career Stages and Comparative Analysis" in the Introduction). By contrast, the movement of minority executives, regardless of their ethnic group, is one of *punctuated equilibrium*. Minority executives move at a significantly slower rate during Stage 1, in their ascent to middle management, at which point their trajectory changes and their pace *accelerates* in the move to upper-middle management during Stage 2. It then levels off to approximately the same pace as the white executives during Stage 3 as both groups approach the executive level. Most noteworthy is the fact that the pace of minority executives' movement to middle management in Stage 1 was roughly the same as whites who plateau in upper-middle management and only slightly faster than that of plateaued minority managers.

This is a fascinating result. Given the equivalent credentials and work experience of our participants at the start of their careers, these patterns suggest that different sets of criteria exist for minorities and whites in gaining entry into the main competition for executive jobs, beginning in Stage 1 of their careers. More specifically:

- Whites quickly emerged or sorted themselves into high-potential and low-potential groups during Stage 1 of their careers. High potentials were given frequent promotions and stretch assignments. Their period of testing occurred during Stage 3 in the path from upper-middle management to executive.

- Minorities, however, were tested twice, first in the early period of their careers during Stage 1 when they repeatedly had to exceed performance standards and expectations in order to gain promotion to middle management, and then again during Stage 3 (as were white executives) with a number of upper-middle management challenges.

These differences are the direct result of the unique challenges that confront minorities in their climb up the corporate ladder. Overcoming them consumed time, thereby slowing down the rate of advancement in the early period. It is also evident that a different set of rules and rewards governs the mobility of racial minorities in this early period. The normal rules of tournament competition for executive jobs do not apply to minorities. Being put on the management fast track early is not a prerequisite nor predictor for becoming an executive, as appears to be the case for whites (see Chapter 3).

◢ INDIVIDUAL RESOURCES NEEDED FOR SUCCESS

One question that emerges out of the findings on mobility patterns is, What is the nature of the early career period for minority executives? Is it a state of limbo in which high-potential individuals mark time and wait for their opportunity? Or, are the minority executives average performers (like the plateaued white managers) whose promotions result from affirmative action policies that dictate placing a few average minorities on the fast track? What we discovered is that the early career period, Stage 1, is *crucial* to what happens later in the careers of minority executives.

In this early period, the minority executives in our study developed three fundamental personal resources that were critical to their later success: competence, credibility, and confidence. These resources were acquired as a result of work experiences during their early career that provided them with a solid foundation. Family background, education, and the experiences of succeeding in multiracial settings were all critical factors on which this foundation was built. Most important, though, was the pattern of their early career experiences and the testing, coaching, and mentoring they received during this crucial period.

Despite moving slowly in the early period, minority executives experienced it as a developmentally rich period that contributed to their competence. Compared with whites in this period, they were more likely to receive an expansion or broadening of their job duties, often assuming responsibilities normally reserved for higher-level managers. (In contrast, the company generally promoted the white executives when they had signaled that they were ready to expand their roles and authority.) Minority executives also tended to have stable assignment patterns in this period; they seldom changed functions or took staff assignments. Such opportunities for expanded roles, and the longer length of time spent in each position, meant that the minority executives developed a deep grounding in the social and technical aspects of the company's work.

Another critical aspect of the early period was the development of mentors and, for African Americans, a multiracial support network. These observations about the nature of minority executives' networks and mentor relationships confirm findings from the first author's work on developmental relationships.[14] The combination of successful track records and well-developed networks of relationships provided them with high levels of credibility.

Confidence, in turn, is the belief in one's own past achievements, current competence, and future ability to succeed. Social psychological studies suggest that minorities may be vulnerable to racial stereotypes of inferiority, which undermine their confidence even as they consciously attempt to defy them.[15] Professional confidence is built on the self-efficacy people bring to work from previous experiences and can be enhanced or diminished by their subsequent experiences at work. Central to gaining confidence in the workplace is the quality of one's relations with bosses and peers as well as succeeding in a *series* of challenging assignments that can be assessed against objective criteria.

One indicator of this pattern's effect on early career development is that in *every* case our minority executives were overprepared for the challenges of their middle management assignments. They exceeded all performance standards as well as some of the specific expectations others had for them personally. This then influenced the subsequent opportunities that provided "breakthrough moments" that set them on the path to the executive suite. Some individuals were able to succeed even in the face of race-based resistance from bosses, peers, and/ or subordinates.

◢ THE ROLE OF ORGANIZATION AND CORPORATE CONTEXT

What conditions within the organization facilitated the ability of minorities to rise to the executive level? Each company began with proactive efforts to hire minorities in the late 1960s. As these efforts yielded results, key leaders saw the need to get beyond simply looking at the number of minorities hired to addressing the role of racial diversity in their organizations. Each company then developed a unique strategy for achieving the diversity results it sought. In all three companies these strategies produced real culture change and resulted in the adoption of racial integration as a core value of the firm.

Each of the three companies succeeded at creating a racially diverse workforce at all levels using its own distinct approach to diversity. This implies that there is no single strategy for achieving diversity. There were, however, a number of commonalties among the three strategies. Foremost, top managers and executives were always personally involved in issues of minority advancement, particularly in supporting the building of an internal supply of minority talent. Furthermore, the essential common element was aligning the company's approach to racial integration with its corporate culture and core values. In each instance, the company's diversity strategy exploited the organization's shared values and *positioned the diversity effort in support of them.* Indeed, in some instances, the approach also exploited major weaknesses in the culture of the organization and, in some ways, strengthened the company's ability to make change. Finally, driving these efforts in all three companies was an ongoing partnership between white executives and diversity champions who took a personal interest in equal opportunity for minorities.

To make this work accessible to a broad audience of academics, senior managers, and people of color who aspire to executive responsibility, we will draw on several cases extensively. Ben Richardson is one of these. Clarence Williams, Nydia Padilla, and José Gonzalez are others. But their experiences are similar to those of Robert Carter,

Emma Sims, Pradeep Gupta, Vicrum Singh, and the other minority executives we studied. Our hope is that these stories bring to life the substantial amount of quantitative and qualitative data and analyses that form the empirical foundation of this work.

In the next two chapters we elaborate on the corporate and historical context and the structure of career mobility that shaped the development and advancement of the minority executives we studied. Without this understanding, neither the individuals' experiences of becoming—nor the organizations' role in producing—minority executives can be understood.

2

Doing Diversity
Three Decades in Pursuit of Equal Opportunity

From 1965 to 1967, there was a war going on in this company. Acme was a White male–driven company and remember, the people who run it own it. The good old boys run the company. And now they were going to share it with minorities?

The group of minorities you are studying all started in the 1960s and early 1970s. They are the people who changed this company.

—WHITE MALE, HR EXECUTIVE, ACME INDUSTRIES

This corporation was a microcosm of the system. It had all the biases of the broader society.... We came of age in a time when most people had not seen people of color in authority. To really understand it, you have to understand the times. When I came, there were maybe fifty black professionals. I never saw any Asians, and most of the Hispanics were undercover. Latino here meant Italian.

—MINORITY EXECUTIVE, GANT ELECTRONICS

THESE QUOTATIONS PROVIDE A WINDOW into the context of corporate race relations surrounding the early career period of our study participants. By the 1990s, the three companies where they worked, Acme Industries, Advanced Technology, and Gant Electronics, led their industries in being racially diverse. They were particularly noted for their ability and success at promoting racial minorities to executive level positions that carried significant authority and responsibility, such as running a line of business or managing a major corporate function such as finance or purchasing. This accomplishment was not the result of their having a better starting point than their corporate peers. Each company, in 1960, had fewer than a dozen minority managers, most of whom were in low-level staff jobs. Like their peers, all three companies had no racial minorities among their corporate officers.

In the chapters that follow we will detail the story of this transformation as it was experienced by the actors. It is possible to explain the rise of these minority executives by their individual character, achievements, and circumstances without reference to their organizational and social contexts, as is sometimes done in studies of career mobility and managerial behavior. But what makes Acme Industries, Advanced Technology, and Gant Electronics unique is not just that people of color have made it to the executive levels of these companies, but rather the large number and wide dispersion of minority executives throughout their organizations. Many companies have one or perhaps two executives of color among their ranks. In most cases, however, these individuals are not running core businesses and functions. Instead, they are frequently in staff functions where they are less likely to influence key decisions about products, processes, and strategy.[1]

Our purpose in this chapter is to set these companies, and their efforts to create a racially diverse management corps, in a temporal and societal frame. Without this perspective, the efforts and success of the companies can hardly be understood. To this end we chronicle the social and political trends that affected these and other U.S. companies, as well as their particular efforts to promote equal opportunity and racial diversity within their organizations. The time frame is the three decades spanning 1960 to 1990. This period corresponds to the height of the civil rights movement in this country, and its evolution from a focus on citizen rights to human rights, which included fairness in the workplace. It is also the era in which the overwhelming majority of our study participants began their careers and achieved their current levels of managerial responsibility.

◢ THE THREE COMPANIES

At the outset of our study, Acme Industries, Advanced Technology, and Gant Electronics were firmly established as major forces in their industries as well as leaders in their diversity efforts. All were multibillion dollar companies. Both Gant Electronics and Acme Industries had successfully regained lost market share, while Advanced Technology had survived a shakeout that destroyed most of its direct competitors, leaving it one of the top three firms in its high-technology segment. As discussed in Chapter 7, the three firms evolved distinct approaches to diversifying their management and, eventually, executive ranks. In each case, the company's approach was one that was consistent with its culture and values. In this section we describe each company's products and services, organization, culture, and affirmative action history. These key characteristics are summarized in Table 2-1.

Acme Industries

Founded early in the twentieth century, Acme Industries is a multibillion dollar manufacturer that dominates its industry and the

Table 2-1 The Three Companies

	Acme Industries	Gant Electronics	Advanced Technology
Products and services	• Production and distribution of price-sensitive products • Just-in-time delivery • Low technology	• Electronic and electromechanical products and systems • Medium tech	• State-of-the-art products and systems • High technology
Customers	• Corporate	• Corporate and consumer	• Corporate
Revenues	• Multibillion dollar • Rapid growth in 1960s and 1970s	• Multibillion dollar • Rapid growth in 1960s and 1970s	• Multibillion dollar • Rapid growth in 1960s and 1970s
Culture	• Strong culture of "Acme Way" • Hands-on; results-oriented • "Marine Corps"; loyalty to company and customers • Low profile; top down; action-oriented	• Quality and customer-focused • Team-oriented (after 1982 action-oriented)	• Engineering and network-oriented • Fluid; unstructured; premium on creativity and environment • Consensus-oriented

market share leader in nearly all of the segments it serves. It was the least technology-driven of the three companies we studied, although it extensively utilized state-of-the-art manufacturing and information technologies. The company is strongly production and distribution focused and operates in product/market segments where quality, cost, proximity to customers, and speed of delivery are critical and have been its traditional key success factors. Over the years, Acme Industries has developed extensive production, engineering, and distribution strengths and a strong customer franchise.

Acme Industries' organization can be described as highly functional. The corporation's operations are organized geographically into strategic business units (SBUs) that are responsible for manufacturing, engineering, sales, marketing, and distribution of Acme's products for a given area. Each SBU is managed by a vice president and general manager (VPGM) who reports to one of a half-dozen senior Acme executives.

The firm's culture was often described to us as pervasive and resolutely meritocratic. It has always had a tradition of promotion from within and has required that most management employees gain first-hand experience as production workers before being allowed to supervise line personnel. It is a very "hands-on" environment. Managers described an explicit "Acme Way" of doing things and values that the Acme culture stood for: hard work, honesty, loyalty to the company and its customers, modesty, results-orientation, and discipline. The company has actively sought people with these qualities from its hourly ranks as well as in its college recruits for promotion to supervisory or management jobs. A history of employee stock ownership, especially among management, is believed to reinforce the strong culture of loyalty and dedication to the company and its customers. Many described the company as having a "Marine Corps" or military-like culture.

Prior to affirmative action, Acme (and the foundations established by its founder's family) had a long tradition of civic and community involvement. Its initial efforts in affirmative action occurred in the 1960s in its manufacturing and distribution operations. Although the minority managers and executives we studied started in different parts of Acme, its production operations were clearly the most fertile source of minorities who made it to executive levels.

Advanced Technology

A multibillion dollar high-tech company, Advanced Technology is one of the three largest firms in its segment of its industry. It manufactures and sells a range of state-of-the-art products and services based on a specific body of technology that it pioneered. Of the three firms studied, Advanced was the most technology-intensive and technology-driven.

Advanced Technology was organized into several major product groups that were headquartered in the United States. For many years, it utilized a product-function-geographic matrix on a global basis, with an industry dimension being added in the early 1990s. For most of its history, Advanced's large manufacturing and sales organizations had served multiple product groups. Product divisions were typically responsible for research, development, and engineering as well as for product and market planning.

Advanced's initial efforts in affirmative action occurred mainly in the late 1960s and early 1970s when it actively sought minorities for professional and managerial positions and built plants in targeted inner-city areas. For this reason, manufacturing was seen as the spawning ground for many of the firm's minority managers and executives. By the early 1980s Advanced was widely acknowledged as the diversity leader in its industry in terms of its aggressiveness and its success in attracting and promoting minorities.

Advanced's culture was described by both respondents and outsiders as one that valued a certain degree of ambiguity and creativity and that required the ability to influence others in order to get things done. It was depicted as an organization in which having informal networks of relationships was critical to achieving results both within one's unit and across other functions.

Gant Electronics

Gant is generally recognized as the leading firm in its industry—an industry that it created in the late 1950s with a series of revolutionary technological breakthroughs. Its products and services were largely based on electronic and electromechanical technologies that were becoming increasingly digitalized. By the mid-1990s, all of its markets had become fiercely competitive. Most of its products, especially its larger and more complex ones, could be described as technologically sophisticated, although the industry itself was no longer viewed as state-of-the-art as it had been in the 1960s and 1970s. Though Gant was much more technology-driven than Acme Industries, most observers considered its products to be less "high-tech" than those of Advanced Technology. It too was a multibillion dollar company.

Gant had grown at a phenomenal rate during the 1960s and 1970s but ran into significant overseas competition in the early 1980s in terms of both cost and product quality. Insiders and a number of outside observers described its 1970s culture as expansive, driven, top-down, and highly political. The culture changed dramatically during the 1980s in what was characterized as a major turnaround and transformation into a culture more focused on quality, customer needs, collaboration, and commitment.

For most of its history, Gant's business had been organized into two interdependent parts: the marketing and sales organization, which sold and serviced products, and the manufacturing and engineering organization, which was responsible for design and production. Both of these organizations were large and complex until the 1980s. In the years immediately preceding the study, Gant had reorganized itself into a number of highly focused product divisions responsible for the design, marketing and product planning, manufacturing, and finance of specific product families.

As a corporation, Gant had been a strong proponent of affirmative action from the beginning and is widely recognized as a model in the area today. Its earliest and most focused recruitment of minorities into professional jobs took place in its field sales organization during the 1970s. The sales and marketing organization subsequently became the most fertile part of the corporation in producing minority managers and executives. In more recent years, the engineering side of Gant has also been the source of several highly placed minority executives.

THREE DECADES OF CHANGING RACE RELATIONS

The 1960s: From Civil Rights to the Workplace

The temporal context for the efforts of these companies at diversifying their management begins in the 1960s, a period of great change and upheaval in America. The decade opened with the election of the nation's first Roman Catholic president, John F. Kennedy. The civil rights movement was reaching maturity behind the powerful voice of Martin Luther King, Jr. War loomed in a small Asian country that most Americans had never heard of, Vietnam. Lagging in the race to explore "the final frontier," America's greatest vision—to put a man on the moon by the end of the decade—took shape.

Early in the decade, few, if any, corporate executives saw the need for change in the racial makeup of their workforces, no less their management staffs. The federal government and the military, in particular, were far ahead of the private sector in their efforts to eliminate discriminatory practices. During the years of World War II, Franklin Delano Roosevelt had issued executive orders mandating nondiscriminatory employment practices in the federal civil services and establishing the Fair Employment Practices Committee. President Truman extended the federal government effort to make equal employment opportunity accepted practice when he issued executive orders to end discrimination in the armed forces. Twenty years passed between the issuance of Roosevelt's fair employment executive order and the passing of the 1964 civil rights bill that included legislation requiring private corporations to provide equal employment opportunity.

In 1960, only 1.7 percent of managers in the United States were black, and 1.0 percent were Hispanic.[2] Most minority managers were employed in government and education. The struggle for civil rights raged in the courts, the legislatures, and the streets. The civil rights movement's purpose was clear: to guarantee the privileges of citizenship, voting rights, housing, and public access to all without regard to race. The workplace was hardly mentioned.

Much in America changed during the decade between 1960 and 1970. A generation rose up to challenge the values and social conventions that the majority of Americans had for so long taken for granted. The Vietnam War became the only one this country had ever fought and lost on two fronts: home and abroad. The civil rights movement, with its multiracial character and focus on integration, gave way to a call by racial minorities for self-determination and empowerment. With this demand came growing impatience and resentment of the inequities in a society whose social organization and stratification seemed based on white racial superiority.

Nineteen sixty-four was the first year of "the long hot summers," so named because of the inner-city riots that came with them, which left entire blocks of cities devastated. Rochester, New York, was the first city to ignite. The physical devastation was only moderate, but the effect on the nation's psyche was large. The next year Watts, California, exploded. Thirty-four people were killed, thousands injured, and hundreds left homeless. The damage estimate exceeded $40 million. Many saw the Watts disturbance as an indication that time had run out for a nonviolent transformation of the racialized society America had been from its founding. Liberals and civil rights moderates called for calm and restraint, while radicals on both sides of the racial divide called for armed self-defense and maligned the idea of interracial partnership. By the end of the decade, almost every major metropolitan area in America had experienced a riot of some sort. Study after study came to the same conclusion about the antecedents of these disturbances. The Report of the National Advisory Commission on Civil Disorders, more commonly known as the Kerner Report, cited

> ... the continuing exclusion of great numbers of Negroes from the benefits of economic progress through discrimination in employment and education and their enforced confinement in segregated housing and schools. The corrosive and degrading effects of this condition and the attitudes that underlie it are the source of deepest bitterness and lie at the center of the problem of racial disorder.[3]

The clear implication was that lack of participation in the economic mainstream of American life had created two societies, racially divided and unequal. The civil rights legislation of 1964 reflected this reality. Title VII of the 1964 Civil Rights Act established the Equal Employment Opportunity Commission (EEOC). The EEOC's oversight and legal jurisdiction applied directly to private sector firms doing business with the federal government with fifty or more employees. Its enforcement powers, however, were quite limited. The agency did not, for instance, have the power to sue companies for non-compliance. In 1965, new civil rights statutes began to reflect this concern. Legislation was written to strengthen fair employment laws and President Johnson signed Executive Order No. 11246, which established the government's mandate that its contractors hire a racially diverse workforce.

To many, it seemed that time was running out for a calm transformation of the country on issues of race. The struggle for voting rights in the South and access to employment and housing in the North fermented the minds of a younger generation of civil rights advocates. The Black Panther Party, a paramilitary organization, was established in Oakland, California, in 1965. The Student Nonviolent Coordinating Committee, the central organizers for voting rights activities in the deep South during the early 1960s, changed from a grassroots multiracial organization into a black nationalist one, with leaders such as Stokely Carmichael threatening to call for violent means of transforming the country. Other smaller and less well-known black nationalist groups organized in various cities and towns. Black trade unionists also became more militant in their demands that African Americans receive equal consideration and protection from labor unions. Even established civil rights leaders and integrationists shifted their focus from citizen rights to economic enfranchisement. Nowhere was the shift clearer than in Martin Luther King's evolution as an activist. By 1968, his focus had shifted from the traditional issues of civil rights such as voting rights, public accommodation, and citizens' rights to those of economic opportunity. His last movement activity was on behalf of striking sanitation workers in Memphis, Tennessee. Following a speech there on April 4, 1968, he was assassinated.

The civil rights movement of the 1960s and the militancy of the latter part of that decade are most associated with the African American struggle for civil rights and fair employment. In fact, the Hispanic and Asian communities were also mobilizing during the late 1960s and well into the next decade. Mexican American farmworkers organized in the West and fought to protest the exploitation of migrant workers. Mexican Americans also organized in urban areas. The Brown Berets, the Denver Crusade for Justice, and the National Chicano Moratorium March in Los Angeles are all examples of urban Chicano activism that were national in scope. By the late 1960s, high school and college students in Los Angeles and Crystal City, Texas, were protesting the lack of Mexican American representation in their curriculum and faculty. In south Texas and Denver, Colorado, Mexican Americans, under the leadership of Reies Lopez Tijerina and Rodolfo

"Corky" Gonzalez, respectively, organized for political rights by forming a Mexican American political party, La Raza Unida.[4] In New York,
Chicago, Newark, and Washington, D.C., Puerto Ricans organized for
political rights. Some of their youth joined the Young Lords, a militant
group that espoused community control and the independence of
Puerto Rico.[5]

The Asian American community, long a silent voice, likewise
became active in struggles to end employment discrimination, such as
the exploitation of garment workers. Asian Americans across the country were involved in community and union organizing, the fight for
bilingual public schooling, and opening up higher education to Asian
Americans. In Chinatowns and Japantowns across the country, community activists developed social services and grassroots organizations to focus attention on the worsening conditions in these ethnic
enclaves. Asian American garment workers were active in the formation of unions and cooperatives such as the San Francisco Chinatown
Coop, a worker-owned garment factory that not only provided
improved working conditions and wages for workers but English
classes and trips to the beach as well.

Asian Americans were also involved in the fight for greater equality
in education.[6] In the 1974 case of Lau v. Nichols, non–English-speaking
Chinese students successfully filed a suit against the San Francisco
Board of Education for failing to provide equal educational opportuni-
ties for all students. This decision mandated bilingual education in the
United States and has had far-reaching effects for many ethnic groups
and immigrants. In higher education, most notably in protests at San
Francisco State College, the University of California at Berkeley, and
the City College of New York (now City University of New York),
Asian American student groups fought for Asian American Studies
departments, ethnic courses, and greater access to higher education.
They also became active in opening the educational institutions of California and the City University of New York to Asian students.

Economically, by 1960, America was the world's largest consumer
of goods and services, its standard of living having risen steadily in
each year of the preceding twenty. The Vietnam War meant that
defense jobs were plentiful. The information age was dawning, though
only the farsighted futurist could imagine that thirty years later people would have at their fingertips more computer power than was

available at most corporations in 1960. While the 1960s were not recession-proof, the economy expanded. Despite the turmoil, the availability of work and opportunity may have helped the push for equal employment.[7]

Acme Industries, Advanced Technology, and Gant Electronics grew phenomenally during this period. Undoubtedly, this situation helped to create a context in which their efforts at promoting equal employment were not seen as an imminent threat to their already employed white majorities. Furthermore, by the decade's end, their diversity efforts were still nascent. In 1969, for example, none of the three companies had named an African American, Asian American, or Hispanic American general manager or vice president. Invariably, the highest ranking minorities were in human resources, looking after federal equal opportunity compliance and community relations.

Pro big-government, liberal ideology dominated the nation's political conversation. In the 1940s and early 1950s, the success of Roosevelt's New Deal and Truman's G.I. Bill had convinced much of the populace that government was not only a friend of the people, but could also solve their problems. Conservatives were saddled with two albatrosses: one, their resistance to civil rights and, two, the excesses of McCarthyism. Lyndon Johnson, president from 1963 to 1969, had a vision for America even though the country was ensnared in the Vietnam War: to achieve the "Great Society" in which racism and poverty would be eradicated. Following the model of the New Deal Democrats who were his mentors, President Johnson's Great Society took the form of a slew of federal government programs and mandates.

This ideology of centrally driven program change had its corollaries in business. America's large companies were governed by centralized bureaucracies. Many employees took for granted lifetime employment and felt assured that their personal interests and those of their corporations were indistinguishable. What was good for the company was good for the individual. When change was needed, the response was most often reasoned, slow, and driven by top management down through the organization. No wonder, then, that companies responded to the call for equal opportunity and nondiscrimination with centralized programs.

Acme Industries, Advanced Technology, and Gant Electronics were not unique in facing the new environment of the 1960s. This was the context for all of America's large corporations, many of which would find themselves signatories to court monitored consent decrees in the early 1970s due to lawsuits brought by minorities and women alleging systematic bias in hiring and promotions.

In reviewing the history of these three companies, two patterns stand out in how they responded to the issues of race and opportunity in this early period. First, each company had at its helm a leadership that believed that their corporation's civic roles and obligations were important. In all three companies this belief was rooted in histories of philanthropic participation and partnership with local government on problems of education, employment, and the quality of civic life. Each company responded to its community's needs for better conditions and opportunities for minorities out of a sense of social responsibility. For example, when riots hit a city where Gant Electronics was one of the largest employers, Gant's president publicly committed the company to providing jobs and funding to rebuild. Similarly, Advanced Technology directed its focus toward improving educational opportunities for inner-city residents.

A second pattern was the three companies' proactive response to the government's call for equal employment opportunity. While these early efforts did not focus on the upper echelons of their organizations, their commitment and success in hiring minorities served to differentiate them from other companies. During this period, Gant Electronics embarked on a major effort to recruit minorities in areas in which it had significant sales or manufacturing organizations. Gant Electronics' CEO made a series of public and highly visible commitments to hiring more minorities, which the company then acted on aggressively. Similarly, Advanced Technology's CEO committed his company to addressing economic decline in the central cities where it was located. This resulted in its building several plants in areas with large African American and Hispanic American populations. At Acme Industries, top management made a quieter but equally concerted effort to recruit minorities for jobs leading to its top non-exempt positions. This process, which took several years to implement, had as its explicit goal the "changing of the complexion of the workforce" so that the composition of employees in these key jobs better reflected that of the local community. Characteristically, this initiative was carried out in Acme's low-profile but no-nonsense, top-down style.

Admittedly, the changes in each corporation did not take place evenly across the entire company. At Acme these changes occurred more quickly in certain parts of the country than others. Manufacturing and sales and service were the easier areas to integrate at both Gant Electronics and Advanced Technology. In all three cases, the initial focus was non-exempt, technical jobs with little customer contact. Yet, in the context of the times, their actions and progress were hopeful examples of commitment.

As a result of their efforts in the 1960s, all three companies had acquired reputations by the early 1970s as being good places for people of color to work. This had the effect of making it easier for them to recruit top minority talent for entry-level positions. In our interviews, a number of the minority executives noted that their companies seemed like better places for minorities in the late 1960s than other, higher-profile competitors. One African American executive at Gant Electronics recalled this period by commenting, "Gant got more than its share of top black talent because it was seen as an open environment for minorities." Many of the other minority managers and executives who joined these companies in the early 1970s cited their companies' reputations as primary reasons for choosing them over other alternatives.

Despite the progress of Acme Industries, Gant Electronics, Advanced Technology, and other U.S. corporations that were committed to equal employment, the decade of the 1960s ended on the opposite note from which it began. It seemed that disillusionment was the order of the day. Reeling in the aftermath of two political assassinations, many Americans despaired over the country's state. In 1968 both Robert F. Kennedy, the leading Democratic presidential candidate, and Martin Luther King, Jr., voice of the civil rights movement, were assassinated within weeks of one another. Vietnam seemed a quagmire from which the country could not extricate itself.

While the rhetoric and metaphor of "equal employment opportunity" resonated with the ideals of the civil rights movement, many minorities felt that something more was needed to spur action. Increasingly, it seemed that the more militant voices of the black power movement and other nationalist groups such as the Chicano movement, the Brown Berets, and the Young Lords represented the sentiments of people of color in America. In the next decade, a new metaphor and rhetoric for mobilizing corporate efforts to ensure equal employment—"affirmative action"—would capture the nation's imagination and its efforts.

The 1970s: Affirmative Action and the Pursuit of Equal Opportunity

The year 1970 marked the height of student protest against the Vietnam War and racial discrimination. National Guardsmen opened fire on student demonstrators at Kent State University. Four students were killed and several others wounded as the National Guard attempted to break up an antiwar demonstration on the campus commons.[8] African American students, armed in some cases, occupied buildings at several predominantly white universities demanding cultural studies programs, admission of more minority students, and the hiring of minority faculty. Tom Jones, CEO of Citigroup's Asset Management Group, was an African American student leader in the takeover of the administration building at Cornell University. He describes the feelings that led many to advocate and act against the establishment in the 1970s:

> [T]he denial of the legitimacy for our need to be educated about ourselves was consistent with the historical denial of the humanness and full equality of African-Americans as part of this country. [We] happened to be part of the generation that the random wheel of history had selected as the generation that was going to say that if we can't be full and equal partners in America, we will resist being less than that . . . the anger that began to really build in the mid-60s, the shift in rhetoric towards black power, the shift in rhetoric towards separatism, the shift in rhetoric towards urban guerrilla warfare. There was an anger that was—it was like 375 years of anger welling up in black America.[9]

In the midst of this turmoil, life for people of color was both changing and remaining stubbornly the same in corporate America. Some companies, or, more accurately, parts of companies, were beginning to open up. However, in the first six years of its establishment, affirmative action was largely a voluntary endeavor. Little effort was made to enforce compliance rules in the legislation. This situation

changed in the early 1970s, and by the mid-1970s the entry of minorities at the lowest levels of the professional and managerial pyramid
was steadily increasing.

Two major trends facilitated efforts to diversify the professional
and managerial ranks of organizations. First, the aspirations of the
civil rights movement had translated for many minorities into the pur-
suit of education and a desire to make it in the mainstream, which to
many meant corporate America. Second, affirmative action got teeth.

For many parents of color, the period of the 1960s had ushered in a
world of possibility for their children that most had not imagined only
a decade earlier. They saw opportunity in the "mainstream" looming
for this next generation. Many of these fathers and mothers were
themselves college educated or self-made business people who felt
underutilized and thought that race had circumscribed their potential
success to a small ethnic enclave. Others were blue-collar workers
with little education, veterans of World War II or the Korean War,
born in the Depression era. They taught their children two lessons.
One was to know they were as good as anybody else, no matter the
color of their skin. The other was to get an education—the one thing
that no one could take from you.

In 1959 only 4.6 percent of the U.S. minority population had completed four years of college or more. Between 1964 and 1975 the number of African Americans attending college increased, from 5.5
percent to 10.7 percent. Comparable figures for Hispanics showed a
growth in attendance to 8.8 percent by 1975.[10] This increase was especially noticeable on predominantly white campuses. Programs such as
A Better Chance and Upward Bound identified promising minority
high school students and worked to prepare them for admission to
college.[11] Admissions representatives from some colleges came to the
inner city and offered scholarships to students with high potential.
Some schools had summer programs that were unofficial auditions for
admission.[12]

The early 1970s was an era of ethnic pride for many people of color.
But some found themselves torn between a desire to help their communities and to attain personal success in a corporation. Many reconciled these two by claiming their goal was to advance minority
progress in the corporation. They would first succeed themselves and
then help others to do the same. Ben Richardson, one of the minority

executives in our study, entered corporate America in 1968, the first African American salesman in his region. He described the shared perspective that he and other African Americans held:

> I chose to make a difference in the corporation, I and others. We had a lot of very talented blacks at Gant Electronics. All of them were leaders. The culture of the black thing at Gant Electronics was you had to perform. You had to show you were better. That was our banner, to say, "You can't fool with us because we are good. We are the best." Personally, I admit, I wanted to prove we weren't inferior.

Not everyone shared this view. Some minorities saw only opportunity for themselves as individuals and race was, in their minds, "other people's problem." And for yet another group, especially those whose parents had gone to great lengths to assimilate them (e.g., by moving the family out of the barrio or inner city to be educated with whites or by forbidding the use of Spanish), this was the chance to enter the world that they had rehearsed being a part of for so long.

Robert Rodriguez, one of the minority executives at Gant Electronics, was from such a background. His father knew the discrimination that Mexican Americans faced in the Southwest. Despite being born in that region of the country, he felt he was treated as a newcomer. The elder Rodriguez worked hard to put Robert and his sister in good schools, and predominantly white ones. He encouraged their full assimilation into the majority culture, not even speaking Spanish with his children. By the time Robert entered college, he felt little association with the Mexican part of his cultural heritage. Aided by his European physical features, he blended relatively easily into the dominant culture of Texas. Only later in his career, at the initiative of others, did he become actively involved in efforts to increase the number of Hispanics in management and professional positions at Gant Electronics and in his industry.

Richardson, Rodriguez, and other young minorities came to corporate America bright-eyed, ready to work, and eager to succeed. During the 1970s a critical factor affecting the opportunities available to them was affirmative action. The term *affirmative action* first appeared in 1961, as part of President Kennedy's Executive Order No. 10925, prohibiting discrimination in government employment and the federal contract program. Johnson reaffirmed it with Executive Order No. 11246. Initially, its meaning was vague, requiring only that companies make a "reasonable" effort to hire a diverse workforce. The term did not take on real meaning until organizations began targeted efforts to ensure that people of color received access to jobs and educational opportunities. The label was applied to a broad array of efforts from focusing on recruitment to special college admissions processes and to establishing quotas for hiring.

The executives and managers in our study varied in the importance they attached to affirmative action as a direct factor in their own job attainment. No one said it did not make a difference. In most cases, affirmative action operated like an invisible hand. It was there, they felt, to correct white bias but guaranteed nothing except the possibility of having a fair shot at proving their value and competence. On some occasions its role in securing opportunity was obvious. Jeff Edwards, an African American in our study, described how he had delivered his resume to his first employer and was rejected. A few days later, after his resume was submitted by an employment agency retained by the company to find minorities, he was hired for the same job.

Whatever affirmative action's indirect or direct role in securing opportunity for people of color, much of the credit goes to President Richard M. Nixon. Though not remembered in history as a champion of civil rights or affirmative action, it was his administration that gave teeth to the fair employment laws. By 1970 it was clear that many large corporations were continuing business as usual, allowing blatant patterns of discrimination in hiring to persist. Nixon's Justice Department went to work on the problem and, in 1972, the EEOC received the authority to enforce antidiscrimination measures by bringing suits against corporations. In addition, the agency received funding to expand its corps of investigators and attorneys.

Over the next several years the EEOC took some of the nation's most powerful corporations to court, including General Motors, Exxon, AT&T, and Sears. Many ended their struggle with the EEOC as signatories to binding consent decrees, obligating themselves to change their practices. By 1975, every large company in America had an EEO compliance officer; in some organizations, these individuals were given broad authority for promoting and hiring people of color.

Affirmative action had a profound effect on the access of racial minorities to jobs. Several studies demonstrate that from 1970 to 1980 corporations subject to review by the Office of Federal Contract Compliance Programs (OFCCP) had a minority employment growth rate that was twice that of firms that were not subject to review.[13] Much of this growth was in professional, technical, and managerial positions. The primary targets and beneficiaries of initial hiring efforts spawned by this governmental pressure were African Americans, but women and other minorities quickly followed.[14] Pressures to comply were not the only reason for this improved employment picture. Collins observes that implementation and oversight of these various compliance efforts created a new category of professional and managerial jobs necessary to provide guidance, oversight, and vision to these early EEO and affirmative action efforts. People of color were attractive candidates for these positions, which included such jobs as affirmative action officer and community relations manager. They were also sought out to manage work units composed predominantly or significantly of people of color. In some instances they brought external legitimacy to their organization's efforts at affirmative action. They also brought knowledge of their respective ethnic communities, which allowed them to build recruiting networks in places that were unfamiliar to whites, such as predominantly African American and Hispanic colleges. Collins maintains that in addition to serving the company's interest, these jobs became primary gateways for people of color to enter and move up in the managerial and professional ranks of America's corporations.[15]

Gant Electronics, Acme Industries, and Advanced Technology were not without their problems or internal inconsistencies in implementing EEO initiatives during the early 1970s. Each, however, avoided the appearance of coerced compliance, and their earlier commitment to ending discriminatory practices in the 1960s provided a solid basis for moving forward in the era of affirmative action. Although the individual actions and initiatives of the three companies differed substantially in the 1970s, it was during this period that all three began major efforts to recruit minorities for management and professional jobs. Until the 1970s, their major emphasis had been largely on hiring minorities into non-management, non-exempt hourly positions. Each of the three companies went about attracting and selecting minorities for professional and management positions in its own unique way; what they had in common was the goal.

Advanced Technology, which was undergoing very rapid growth through this period, began targeting minorities for professional and managerial jobs in the early 1970s. Frustrated by its own inability to locate and hire suitable minorities, it enlisted executive search firms to identify potential job candidates. By the mid-1970s Advanced had also built three manufacturing plants in predominantly African American and Hispanic areas for which it had actively recruited minority management personnel.

In contrast, Acme Industries, which had a strong promote-from-within tradition, took a very different tack. Its top two officers hired a former civil rights activist to join the company as vice president of personnel with the mandate of helping them open up the company to minorities. The new VP quickly concluded that "changing the complexion of the workforce" was not enough to make this kind of change and that Acme needed to begin identifying and promoting minorities into supervisory ranks. These three men formed a powerful partnership, which drove this agenda through most of the 1970s. As part of this process Acme also began identifying senior managers who exhibited prejudiced attitudes. These individuals were relieved of their normal duties for several weeks and asked to do community service work in poor communities to sensitize them to people of different backgrounds. By the end of the 1970s it had become clear that focusing solely on the numbers entering the organization was not enough to ensure equal opportunity; thus, the company was actively identifying, grooming, and promoting minority managers.

Like the other two companies, Gant Electronics had also begun the decade with heavy recruiting of entry-level minorities for its professional and managerial ranks. As a result of an eleventh-hour effort to settle a dispute with a group of African American employees that might have resulted in a drawn-out class action suit, top management became actively involved in efforts to ensure that minorities received fair consideration in assignments and promotions. By the end of the decade, a number of innovations had resulted from these efforts and Gant's top management had begun meeting periodically with representatives of minority employees to mutually assess the company's progress in minority advancement into management.

As the 1970s drew to a close, each of the three companies had made major inroads in recruiting minorities into professional and managerial ranks. Indeed, by the late 1970s, many of those hired had worked their way up to upper-middle levels of these organizations. Some of these would advance even further in the decade that followed.

Near the decade's end, however, one could already hear the undertones of the coming affirmative action backlash. In 1976, sociologist Nathan Glazer published *Affirmative Discrimination*, the first book to propose that affirmative action cheated white males out of their rightful claims to promotions and jobs. The book implied that less-qualified minorities were leapfrogging white men for jobs. Though this message was a harbinger of the attacks that were to come in the 1980s and 1990s, Glazer's major criticism was that affirmative action was flawed social policy. He maintained that it did little to eliminate the basic conditions that led to poverty in the inner cities, a topic on which he was an expert.

Criticisms notwithstanding, both affirmative action and the EEOC's role in monitoring compliance continued throughout the late 1970s, but not without significant challenges, and the response was often ambivalent. The Supreme Court's ruling in the first major legal assault on affirmative action, *Bakke v. Regents of the University of California*, was representative. The court ruled in favor of Alan Bakke's petition that he had been unfairly denied admission to medical school because of a "quota system" that favored minorities. However, it also said that race could be used as a selection criterion in decisions as long as there were no "hard quotas." Depending on one's view, affirmative action had either been mildly amended or ended.[16]

By the close of the 1970s, Gant Electronics, Acme Industries, and Advanced Technology all appeared to have firmly committed themselves to racial diversity in management. Each had realized that ensuring equal opportunity would require more than simply hiring people from underrepresented racial groups. Firmly in place at each company was a core set of practices aligned with the company's culture that constituted a coherent diversity strategy. Interestingly, these strategies differed significantly with regard to philosophy about racial integration and the core strategies on which they relied. We discuss these distinct approaches in detail in Chapter 7. Despite their differences, however, a diversity strategy existed in each of these companies by 1979.

The 1980s: The Reagan Revolution

In 1981, Ronald Reagan came to the White House repeating the promise that had gotten him elected, "to take the government off the backs of the American people." It seemed clear to most political observers that Reagan would not be a friend of affirmative action. To many of his supporters the policy was one more example of overzealous government intervention and social engineering. Furthermore, few among Reagan's constituents had a vested interest in affirmative action. A mere 10 percent of racial minorities voted for him.[17] On top of this, the American economy was in serious trouble, threatening the standard of living of all Americans, regardless of race. Inflation was in double digits and many doubted U.S. industry would successfully respond to the challenge of foreign competition.

Although some ardent critics of affirmative action argue that Reagan missed key opportunities to end it,[18] his early administration appointments and decisions sent a clear signal about his intent. To head the Justice Department, he appointed Edwin Meese, an unambivalent opponent of affirmative action. William Bradford Reynolds became Assistant Attorney General for Civil Rights and worked consistently and tirelessly to end affirmative action as law.[19] Future Supreme Court Justice Clarence Thomas, an African American and opponent of affirmative action, was his choice to head the EEOC. Although their efforts were met with resistance from Democrats and Republican moderates, they had an effect. A clear sentiment developed that the government was relaxing its standards for compliance on matters of equal opportunity for people of color.

The first of many salvos were fired in the attack on affirmative action within months of Reagan taking office. The Administration announced relaxed procedures for affirmative action reporting; only the largest corporations still had to draw up detailed affirmative action plans, and even then, less frequently. The Justice Department lobbied for rules that made it more difficult for minorities who were discriminated against to receive back pay and promotions as remedies.[20]

Though not fatal blows, these actions were used by many minorities and civil rights proponents to conclude that the Reagan Administation was a foe of affirmative action.

The Reagan revolution was certainly about much more than affirmative action. It was about a more conservative ideology and vision for the country. Its key components seemed to stress minimal government intervention, supply-side economics in the context of market capitalism, and individual self-interest as the motivating force in social life. By several objective measures, Reagan was a successful president. He served two terms and swept the 1984 election with over 60 percent of the popular vote. Inflation was under control by the end of his first term, and the financial markets had roared back. Deregulation blurred boundaries, while mergers and acquisitions made investment bankers and traders cultural icons.[21] More important, though, for historians his revolution succeeded in changing the political conversation in America. The nation was now more conservative and had shed its addiction to big government as a panacea.

Despite the improving economy that came with this conservative shift, some worried that race relations in America were in regression. Surveys indicated a rise in racially motivated assaults, as well as domestic violence and attacks on homosexuals.[22] Sociologist John Fernandez surveyed the attitudes of 12,000 managers and nonmanagers at thirteen *Fortune 500* companies in 1986. He asked them a series of questions about their general attitudes toward racial minority and majority group members. Many of the questions were taken from two previous surveys used in 1972 and 1976. Fernandez concluded that employees, regardless of race, felt that discrimination had increased between 1976 and 1986. In contrast, he had found that Americans perceived that discrimination had decreased between 1972 and 1977.[23]

Antagonism and ambivalence toward affirmative action also increased in this period. A number of widely read and cited books and articles were attacking the policy. Their authors were both white and persons of color. Among the whites were Charles Murray, Frederick Lynch, and William Beer.[24] All made claims that white males were being unfairly denied opportunity and that those given preference were less qualified. Unlike their predecessor, Nathan Glazer, they did not premise their arguments on affirmative actions' failure to help the worse-off minorities. Their arguments went to the questions of merit, fairness, and reverse discrimination.

The minorities who criticized affirmative action in the 1980s were led initially by Thomas Sowell, who for a time was a lone voice among intellectuals of color. He was joined by Republican Administration officials such as Linda Chavez and Clarence Thomas. Glen Loury, the Boston University economist, and Shelby Steele, a California State College English professor, entered the fray later, but with powerful and compelling voices. To these individuals, affirmative action may have had some positive impact on minorities, but it had also done them harm. They argued that rather than relieve the effects of racial stigma, affirmative action had made the real achievements of minorities questionable. According to Steele, it had also angered well-meaning whites. Finally, like Glazer, they argued that it had not helped the large mass of people left behind in the ghettos and barrios.[25]

Some of these commentators also pointed out the paradoxes of race relations in the United States. If things were so bad, why did the middle class of these minority groups greatly expand throughout the 1980s? Symbols of this advancement were obvious. Magazines such as *Black Enterprise*, *Ebony*, and *Hispanic Business* regularly featured people of color who penetrated the executive suite in mainstream jobs. Clifford Wharton was CEO of TIAA-CREF, the largest pension fund in the world. Barry Rand had engineered the turnaround of Xerox's U.S. Marketing Group. Frank Savage was a corporate officer at the Equitable Company. Reginald Lewis had completed the leveraged buyout of Beatrice Foods International and served as its chairman and CEO. Many detractors of affirmative action argued that it diminished the real accomplishments of individuals such as these. The counterargument usually pointed out that were it not for affirmative action these opportunities would not have been forthcoming.

Some believed that many companies responded to the Reagan years by reducing their efforts at attracting and retaining a diverse workforce. In a 1986 survey of executives responsible for corporate affirmative action programs in Chicago, 67 percent reported that between 1980 and 1985 their jobs were either downgraded or their influence and authority significantly limited, resulting in a reduced focus on equal employment and affirmative action.[26] By the end of the decade, there emerged a growing perception, supported by some hard data, that corporate America had a "glass ceiling" when it came to the promotion of women and minorities beyond middle management.[27]

◢ WORKFORCE DIVERSITY: A BOTTOM-LINE RHETORIC

By the late 1980s the ideological center of the nation's political spectrum had shifted to the right. To many in the civil rights establishment this seemed like a move toward a colder, less socially responsible stance on racial inequality. A parallel shift toward "bottom-line" thinking had occurred for American executives. The mergers and acquisitions of the 1980s filled companies' balance sheets with debt. Downsizing became a search to achieve the "right size." All corporate activities needed a bottom-line justification. If the government was "going soft" on affirmative action and EEO there seemed little reason for companies to maintain the same level of commitment as before unless there was a business motive.

The business rationale for inclusion came in the form of a short research report produced by the Hudson Institute under the auspices of the U.S. Department of Labor. *Workforce 2000: Work and Workers for the Twenty-first Century* identified the changing gender and racioethnic composition of the workforce as a major trend in the economy. Its conclusion caught headlines: "By the year 2000, . . . only 15 percent of the people entering the workforce would be American-born white males, compared with 47 percent in 1987."[28] It also made for good rhetoric. Others extrapolated from this that managing diversity to effect the full utilization of the workforce had become a bottom-line issue.[29]

One result was a renewed interest in the question of how far American corporations had come in their efforts to create a more inclusive workplace. It was clear by 1987 that people of color had successfully run some of America's largest universities, government departments, and nonprofit corporations. By the end of the 1980s, an African American, General Colin Powell, would be at the helm of the armed forces as they subsequently won the Gulf War. In contrast, no African American, U.S.-born Hispanic, or Asian American was CEO of a *Fortune 500* company. White women had fared little better and the pipeline provided little hope of the situation changing. In 1989, the Labor Department created a panel to study the extent to which socially constructed barriers to minority and female advancement existed in corporate America. Women and people of color, they concluded, were unlikely to reach the most senior levels of their companies, especially positions with line authority and responsibility for profit and loss. The reason was discrimination based on race and gender.[30]

The decade ended with a series of mixed messages. It was hard to find anyone who liked affirmative action or who was for quotas. On the other hand, it was equally hard to find anyone who was against diversity and inclusion.

Despite the pressures of the 1980s that worked against affirmative action, Acme Industries, Gant Electronics, and Advanced Technology finished the decade having kept their commitments to racial inclusion intact. Selected for our study in 1991, each was a leader in its industry in this regard. It is important to note that all three companies maintained their commitments during the 1980s even though their fundamental business models and dominant market positions were being challenged by competitors and market shifts away from their products.

As was the case in the 1970s, the three companies we studied took quite different approaches to managing diversity during the 1980s. Their only commonality was a drive to improve their performance in what were, in all three cases, increasingly competitive and turbulent business environments. So, here too, we see a heightened sense of concern with performance. By 1979, a key member of Advanced's top management had become increasingly dissatisfied with what he viewed as subpar performance of the three "minority" plants and— even more distressing—the fact that the white executives responsible for them were not holding these plants or their managements to the same standards as other plants. This led him to engage an outside consultant who worked extensively within Advanced, initially in manufacturing but later throughout the company, in surfacing issues concerning stereotypes and standards for performance and then in institutionalizing a process for understanding and valuing differences. These efforts resulted in a number of initiatives, one of which focused on raising the performance levels of not just the minority plants but of all operations in manufacturing. Eventually these efforts resulted in a number of minorities being promoted to plant managers of nonminority plants based on their strong performance records.

A second major initiative involved formation of "dialogue groups" in which people of different races, genders, and functions could come together to work through questions of differences. This initiative was sufficiently successful in increasing both understanding and performance that by the late 1980s it had spread throughout the company. Many of the managers and executives (both minorities and whites) that we interviewed at Advanced Technology made repeated references to these dialogue groups as sources of insight into how people of different races and genders saw themselves. These groups also served as vehicles through which managers made close relationships with people of other races. By the early 1990s several corporate officers, a number of senior operating executives, and one of Advanced's top officers were minorities. All of this occurred during a period in which its industry underwent a major shakeout.

The story at Gant Electronics was much more turbulent. Gant's major product markets were besieged by international competitors, and its new CEO knew he had a major turnaround on his hands by 1982. Before becoming CEO, he had been a highly visible champion of Gant's diversity efforts and a strong supporter of its minority coalition groups and their self-initiated developmental activities. Rather than seeing these initiatives as luxuries of a more benevolent era, he touted them as critical sources of energy going forward and as role models of what highly committed employee involvement could produce. Indeed, a vital part of the firm's turnaround was its extensive use of high-involvement, total-quality efforts. Gant's management pressed even harder on its diversity agenda during this difficult time, but with the aim of enhancing performance as well as equity. It was during this period that one of our study's participants was tapped to turn around one of the corporation's most significant entities, a feat he had successfully accomplished by the end of the decade. Gant Electronics' current CEO, who had played a pivotal role in the firm's turnaround, is as avid and outspoken a champion of diversity as were his two predecessors.

Acme Industries, like Gant, faced fierce competition in the 1980s in the form of new competitors with new products in their higher-margin market segments as well as new competition in several existing product markets. It was, in fact, the first time that Acme had ever been successfully challenged in any of its major product-market segments, all of which Acme had traditionally dominated. Acme's top management countered these attacks on several fronts including a push to change the firm's culture so that it was less top-down, more focused on managing through people with less emphasis on managing solely by the numbers. Acme's CEO saw the company's diversity strategy as a key element in bringing about these changes, and he and his top officers increased their pressure on the firm's executives to identify qualified minorities and move them into positions with increased responsibility as soon as they were ready. As at Gant, the motives driving these initiatives were as related to the need to improve performance as they were to questions of equity. These and other initiatives taken by Acme during the 1980s succeeded, and Acme emerged from this turbulent decade as once again the dominant force in its industry.

What is striking about all three companies is that during this difficult decade each one continued to press for the identification and promotion of high-performing minority managers. Indeed, it was during the 1980s, when all three companies were facing their toughest competition, that most of their minority executives were tested—in many cases by fire—and promoted. One of the reasons the companies were able to do this was that their efforts of the 1960s and 1970s had resulted in a cadre of highly committed minority managers who had the potential to rise to the challenges posed in the 1980s. It is also clear that all three of the companies worked hard to ensure that minorities were given the opportunities to meet these challenges.

True values face their greatest tests under adversity. The actions of these companies attested to the strength of their commitments to diversity as well as to the fact that racial minorities in these companies, including the participants of our study, were in positions to add value to their corporations' efforts at a critical time.

On reviewing the history of this thirty-year period, several common characteristics stand out in the approaches taken by Acme, Gant, and Advanced in responding to the civil rights environment of the 1960s and early 1970s and the subsequent challenges of the 1980s. First, each company had taken a strong, proactive stance toward both affirmative action and EEO. Second, all three companies had a history of civic and community involvement, which facilitated their initial efforts to hire African Americans, Hispanic Americans, and Asian Americans into their organizations. Third, all three companies made concerted efforts by the early 1970s to select and recruit minorities for professional and management positions.

Another commonality that no doubt helped these companies integrate their professional and managerial ranks was growth. All three of these companies experienced phenomenal growth in the 1960s and 1970s. This sustained expansion most likely facilitated the racial integration of these companies by allaying the anxieties of whites who might otherwise have felt that they were competing with minorities for a shrinking set of opportunities.

A final characteristic shared by the companies was that all three encountered increased competition and decline in revenue growth and market share during the 1980s. This prompted major reorganizations, shifts in business strategy, and, for Advanced and Gant, significant layoffs as well. Yet by 1990, each company had strengthened its position as an industry leader in both its competitive position and the racial diversity of its management and executive ranks. In fact, it was during the 1980s that over 90 percent of our minority executives were promoted to their first executive post. By the early 1990s, one can safely conclude that the efforts of these companies to racially integrate their management ranks had taken root and were much more than a matter of legal compliance.

3

The Career Tournament and Its Rules

AMONG THE EARLIEST PEOPLE OF COLOR to aspire to successful careers in their companies' core operations, the minorities we studied charted new territory. They began their careers in corporate America in the 1960s and early 1970s, after completing their postsecondary education or military service. They came to their positions with all the right credentials and experience. In this regard there was no significant difference between them and their white counterparts. At Gant Electronics, where the requirement was that new hires have BA or BS degrees, all did. The minorities at Acme Industries had either leadership experience in the military or a college degree, just like their white counterparts. At Acme, they all started in the same job; all potential managers were required to start on the front lines as production workers before moving into production management. Similarly, the minorities hired into professional or managerial jobs at Advanced Technology met all the hiring requirements, as did their white counterparts.

James Rosenbaum has used the metaphor of a tournament system to capture some of the distinguishing features of the competition for career advancement.[1] According to Rosenbaum, managerial careers advance through a series of competitive rounds, where cohorts of individuals with roughly the same hierarchical status and tenure perform against one another for promotions, with the winner advancing to the next round. Each competitive round produces winners and losers. Winners receive promotions faster than others in the cohort.

In Rosenbaum's tournament metaphor, winning a round guarantees only that a contender will be allowed to compete at the next higher level. In order to reach the top, the contender must win at each successively higher level. Fast early promotions make it more likely that a manager will someday gain a top position in the company, but they do not assure or guarantee that outcome.

Losing a round on the other hand, automatically takes managers out of the competition to reach the highest level of the organization. In early career, these managers are placed in a secondary group where they can play for consolation prizes—for example, the privilege of remaining at the company with the tacit agreement that they will never reach the executive suite. Promotions may come to round losers but only to low-visibility or low-impact jobs. According to the tournament model, therefore, early losses affect both future promotions and the final rank or position likely to be attained. The longer a manager remains in a particular position without promotion, the less likely he or she is to move to the next and subsequent levels.

These features of the tournament model, as originally framed, imply that in a study such as ours it should be possible to find managers who rise rapidly and early yet do not reach the top, but not possible to find anyone who rises slowly—that is, loses the early rounds—yet still reaches the top of an organization.

Some of our findings were consistent with the tournament model. Indeed, our data supported the thesis that the pattern of promotions early in managers' careers is a strong predictor of which managers will become executives in later years—but only for whites. By the logic of the tournament model we should have expected to find that the minority executives in our study would have moved just as rapidly as their white executive colleagues and more rapidly than their minority and white colleagues who plateaued in upper-middle management. Instead, we found that most minority executives, when compared to their white executive counterparts, experienced a slower pace of early promotions. It seems surprising that minority executives advanced in spite of not meeting what seems to be a virtual precondition for whites to reach the executive rank. Our data show, however, that during the early part of their careers, minority executives tended to ascend at about the same modest pace as white managers who never made it to the executive level, and somewhat faster than minority managers who plateaued at upper-middle management.

The career paths we observed for minority executives therefore challenge the fundamental principle of the tournament model and put some of its hypotheses at issue. According to the model, slow or below-average upward movement early in a managerial career should reduce the chances of reaching the top. Instead, we found a sizable cohort of minorities who had moved at a modest pace early in their careers, yet nevertheless became executives. Perhaps, then, the tournament model applies only to whites, or the rules governing tournament play somehow differ for minorities and whites; perhaps it is simply the wrong model for the phenomenon. We found that the different career patterns of white and minority executives can be well described in terms of *two* different tournaments, one for whites and one for minorities—a model we will return to in greater detail as we explore these observations and explain why they occur.

◢ TOURNAMENTS AT THE THREE COMPANIES

We arrived at our conclusions by studying the career trajectories of both minority and white executives and managers at Acme Industries, Gant Electronics, and Advanced Technology. We then compared the average rates of movement for each of these groups from the start of their managerial careers through the three career stages: start to middle management (Stage 1), middle management to upper-middle management (Stage 2), and upper-middle management to executive (Stage 3). We reconciled differences in job titles and the number of management levels by applying a common set of criteria across the three companies, permitting cross-company comparisons of the career trajectories of our participants.[2]

◢ CAREER MOVEMENT THROUGH THE ACME HIERARCHY

Acme Industries is the best illustration of the general pattern of our findings. All twenty of our minority and white participants joined Acme's management ranks as supervisors or the equivalent, such as industrial engineers.[3] Figure 3-1 illustrates the management hierarchy of Acme. Supervisors are usually responsible for a production group of ten to twenty hourly employees and report to a middle manager, called a unit manager. Unit managers have oversight of an entire production process or operation, sometimes an assembly operation at a large facility, a satellite location, or a small functional group (such as a customer service group). Some units operate twenty-four hours a day, and in those cases the unit manager is responsible for all aspects of the operation. Unit managers report to an upper-middle manager, who is responsible for an entire production operation or department or divi-

---

Figure 3-1 Acme's Organizational Hierarchy

Job Title and Responsibility	Management Level	Career Stage
Corporate Officers	Senior Executive	
Vice President/General Managers *Manage SBU (Full P&L responsibility)*	Executive	*Career Stage 3*
Division Operations Managers or Department Managers *Manage multiple units*	Upper-Middle	*Career Stage 2*
Unit Managers *Manage entire production process or operation*	Middle	*Career Stage 1*
Supervisors *Manage production team*	Entry	

sion. These upper-middle managers, in turn, report to an executive in charge of a strategic business unit (SBU), who typically carries the title Vice President/General Manger (VPGM). Worldwide, there were about 100 people at this level during the period of our study, with profit and loss responsibility for business units generating yearly revenue of $100 million to $500 million. These executives report to one of a group of eight corporate officers.

Within the Acme organization, there is a striking pattern of movement through the three career stages we have called Career Stage 1, the period from entry to middle management; Career Stage 2, middle to upper-middle management; and Career Stage 3, upper-middle management to the executive level (Figure 3-2).

Compared to white and minority managers who plateau, white executives experience a quick takeoff followed by a steady ascent toward upper and upper-middle management, and then a gradual

---

Figure 3-2   *Acme Industries: Average Career Trajectories for Each of the Study Groups*

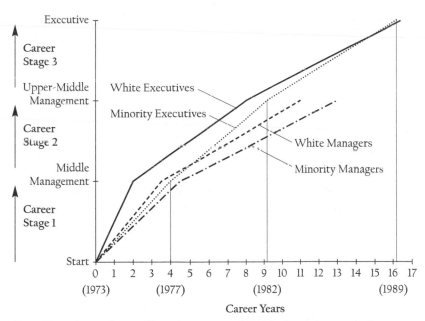

Note: Years in parentheses refer to the mean year Minority Executives reached promotion levels.

leveling off during the period from upper-middle management to pro-motion to executive level. In contrast, the careers of minority execu-tives show a pattern of punctuated equilibrium: moderate or slow rise to middle management, followed by a steep ascent to upper-middle management. From there, they rise to the executive level at almost the same speed as white executives.

Despite the large time lag in Stage 1, the difference in the promo-tion rates of minorities and whites who make it to the executive level begins to lessen considerably by Stages 2 and 3. In fact, at Acme, the trend actually reverses: minority executives were promoted more quickly than white executives during these periods. At Acme, it took minority executives 4.2 years on average to move through Stage 2, compared with an average of 4.9 years for white executives. The aver-age time to move through Stage 3 was 8.3 years for minorities and 9.6 years for whites.

Table 3-1 displays the pattern of movement for all twenty study participants at Acme and reveals the specific differences between minority and white study participants. For white executives, the pre-dominant pattern was fast, fast, slow. Fast movement in Stage 1 was followed by fast movement through Stage 2. They then experienced a slower rise through Stage 3 to the executive level. White executives who experienced only an average rate of movement in Stage 1 did not move faster in Stage 2.

In contrast, the most common pattern for minority executives was to experience average or slow movement in Stage 1, followed by a faster rate of movement in Stage 2. In other words, slow or average movement in the early stages of career did not decrease a minority executive's chances of making it to the executive level, contradicting tournament theory predictions. For the minorities in this sample, the most important signal of future career movement was not so much their early speed to middle management as how quickly they made it from middle to upper-middle management. Those minorities whose relative speed increased over this second stage were more likely to make it to the executive level.

For the minority managers who plateaued at upper-middle man-agement, the most frequently observed pattern of movement is slow, slow. On balance, the minority managers were also somewhat slower than their white manager counterparts in Stages 1 and 2.

Table 3-1 Rate of Career Movement at Acme

	Career Stage 1 Supervisor to Middle Manager	Career Stage 2 Middle Manager to Upper-Middle Manager	Career Stage 3 Upper-Middle Manager to Executive
Minority Executives			
Person A[a]	Slow	Average	Fast
Person B	Slow	Fast	Fast
Person C	Average	Fast	Fast
Person D	Fast	Slow	Average
Person E	Average	Fast	Slow
Minority Managers			
Person A	Average	Slow	N/A
Person B	Slow	Average	N/A
Person C	Slow	Slow	N/A
Person D	Slow	Slow	N/A
Person E	Fast	Fast	N/A
White Executives			
Person A	Fast	Fast	Slow
Person B	Average	Slow	Slow
Person C	Fast	Fast	Slow
Person D	Fast	Fast	Slow
Person E	Average	Average	Fast
White Managers			
Person A	Fast	Fast	N/A
Person B	Slow	Average	N/A
Person C	Average	Slow	N/A
Person D	Average	Slow	N/A
Person E	Average	Fast	N/A

Note: Fast moves occurred at least one year sooner than the average, while slow moves took one year more or longer.

[a] The letters indicate the matched pairing with the corresponding minority executive. For example, White Executive A, Minority Manager A, and White Manager A were each selected as a match for Minority Executive A.

Intrigued by these findings, but aware of the limitations imposed by the sample size of our interview study, we set out to see if this pattern could be observed in the larger population of the corporation. Figure 3-3 summarizes career-movement data for 554 Acme managers and executives, both minority and white, who occupied positions in 1991 that were identical in title and description to the managers and executives who participated in our interview study.[4] This larger group included 11 minority executives, 85 white executives, 63 minority managers, and 395 white managers. Analyses on these data using linear regression reveal that the elapsed time for minority executives to reach supervisor and middle management levels is statistically indistinguishable from that of either minority or white managers, but significantly longer than that of white executives.[5] Their relative patterns of movement are almost identical to those we found among the participants in our interview study at Acme.

To test further our hypothesis that the rules that govern tournament competition for whites do not apply to minorities, we performed an event history analysis—a common technique for analyzing job

---

Figure 3-3   Acme Industries Average: Career Trajectories for the Total Population of Executives and Managers

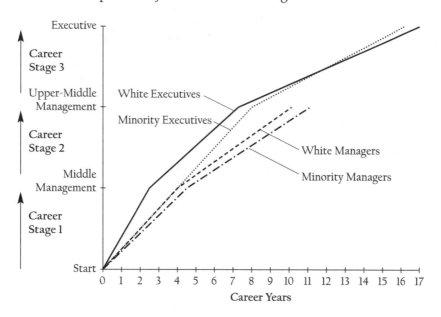

mobility—to examine the effect of early promotion rates on the likelihood of plateauing or attaining an executive position.[6] Our results confirmed the hypothesis that two tournaments or different sets of rules govern white and minority career attainment. Fast early promotion rates significantly increased the likelihood of a white reaching the executive level, while no such relationship held for minorities in the sample. These results hold even when we controlled for education level, which was not significant, and generational differences (see Appendix B).

◢ CAREER MOVEMENT AT GANT AND ADVANCED

The pattern we have described at Acme is also found in the career trajectories of managers and executives we studied at Gant Electronics and Advanced Technology (Figures 3-4 and 3-5). A plotting of the

---

Figure 3-4   Gant Electronics: Average Career Trajectories for Each of the Study Groups

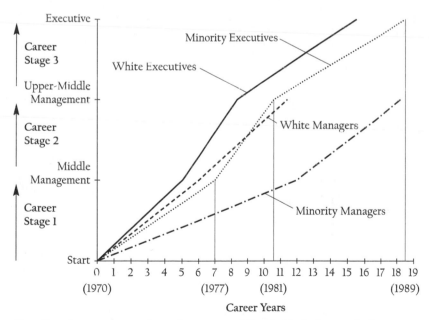

Note: Years in parentheses refer to the mean year Minority Executives reached promotion levels.

career trajectories of each company's study groups replicates the pattern found at Acme for Stage 1, in which white executives quickly ascend to middle management while minority executives move more slowly, more similar to the experiences of both white and minority managers who plateaued in upper-middle management. At Gant as at Acme, minority and white executives took about the same amount of time to go through Stage 3, to executive level.

At Advanced Technology we see the same pattern except that minority executives also lagged behind white executives through Stage 2, but the two groups made it through Stage 3 in almost equal time. The pattern of results at Advanced may differ from Acme and Gant because all of the minority managers and executives that we studied there began their careers elsewhere and were recruited to Advanced during its rapid growth in the 1970s and 1980s.

Figure 3-5   Advanced Technology: Average Career Trajectories for Each of the Study Groups

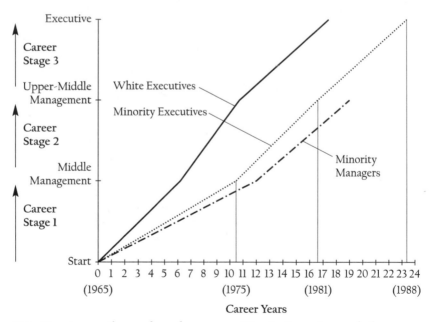

Note: Years in parentheses refer to the mean year Minority Executives reached promotion levels.

What do the differences in the career movements of our study groups at Acme, Gant, and Advanced imply about career mobility in general and in terms of race? Turning to career mobility, analysis of the career trajectories of white managers and executives reveals significant support for Rosenbaum's tournament model of mobility, in which promotion rates in the early part of a manager's career are predictive of a manager's later career attainment. White executives in our study did rise to middle management much more rapidly than their white manager counterparts who plateaued at the upper-middle management level. This pattern supports the idea that, among whites, a process of sorting and "sizing up" begins early in their careers.[7] The promotion patterns that resulted from this early sorting process strongly predict the individuals who are likely to reach the executive rank and those who will plateau at upper-middle management.

The tournament model, however, did not predict the careers of minority executives. Their early career movements most resembled the early career configuration of white managers, not white executives. Put another way, a white person who followed the early career pattern typical of minority executives in the sample would be unlikely to become an executive later in his or her career.

◢ EXPLAINING THE DIFFERENCE

Time in the Bull Pen: A Tax on Minorities

Everyone who has reviewed the differences between the career trajectories of the white and minority managers and executives in our study has been alarmed, though not always surprised. Why are the minority executives in the sample the only ones whose career trajectories do not behave according to the tournament model? Our understanding of the significant challenges minorities face leads us to hypothesize that they might follow a different path than whites to the same executive position. Racial prejudice, whites' need for comfort and avoidance of risk, and the apparent difficulty of identifying minorities as high potential each constitute major hurdles to the career mobility of minority managers. Overcoming them is possible, but it places the equivalent of a "tax" on minorities in the form of time, no matter whether one pays it willingly or begrudgingly, with or without awareness of its existence.

Despite their relatively effective performance at moving minorities into executive level jobs, we have no indication that these barriers were absent from the cultures at Acme, Advanced, and Gant. Half of the minority executives' success comes from the organization's own commitment to ensuring equal opportunity. The other half depends on the individuals themselves and how they manage their careers and overcome barriers, often with the assistance of peers, bosses, mentors, and sponsors.

How do successful minority managers deal with the negative racial stereotypes? What happens when prejudice is codified in operating assumptions about minorities' business sense, work ethics, or ability to manage white staff? Initial successes in achieving goals or performance measures are called flukes or are attributed to the support of others. Overcoming these silent objections requires proving themselves over and over again in order to gain the credibility that is given to whites with the benefit of the doubt. Our minority executives told us again and again that for them, race meant that they had to be better and do more than their white peers. They view overachievement as the only response to the unstated questions of whether or not they deserve all that came to them. For them, it's not enough to be the best once. They have to—need to—prove themselves every time they start a new job. The tax of prejudice is time.

Likewise, time is often the solution to the risk aversion and discomfort that potential supporters might initially feel about minority managers—time to get to know the minority as a person and time to form the necessary bonds to effectively support him or her. Even when this is done, persuading others to take the risk or leap of faith to support the individual in getting important developmental and promotional opportunities can take extra time.

Another factor that added time to the early career paths of the minority executives was the effort it took to get themselves in the right flow of opportunity. Due to a combination of naïveté and racial steering, some discovered that they were working in areas of the company that did not have the best opportunities. At Acme Industries, for instance, several minority executives were initially promoted to supervisory jobs in customer service and personnel, despite having started in an operations or other line function. They then had to lobby to get back into line operations, where the real opportunities lay. Interviews with black executives in the Boston area in a follow-up study confirmed that minority managers were very likely to gain their early supervisory promotions in nonoperational support areas. Many of the minority executives we studied were fortunate to find their way rather quickly into the mainstream and out of entry-level support areas, unlike many of their counterparts who never made it to the executive level.

The challenges of race and the strategies required of minorities to meet them help to explain why there is a time lag in the early careers of minority executives in comparison to their white counterparts. It should be pointed out, however, that a strict application of the tournament model raises the question of whether promotion standards were lowered for minorities. After all, to reach the executive level, a white manager would have to have a more spectacular rise early in career than was typical of the minorities who made it to the executive level.

An alternative to a "lowered standards" explanation is that the standards of admission to the executive suite are actually *higher* for minority managers. Our data suggest that minority executives must hold up under a longer proving period and under more scrutiny than is typically the case for whites. This interpretation would suggest that the criteria that govern promotion to the next level are more rigorous for minorities, and the requirements seemingly take them longer to fulfill, or for organizations to recognize, in early career.

The process that a strict tournament model interpretation would suggest—a setting aside of the tournament rules for minorities in middle management in order to integrate the executive suite—is not consistent with this interpretation. We found that the central reason that the career configurations of minority executives deviate from those of white executives is that the separate requirements for potential minority executives produce anomalous career configurations.[8] That is, they perform at a very high level and attain a deep grounding in early career, but this is curiously combined with only modest rates of promotion up through middle management. This beginning is followed by increasingly more responsible and challenging assignments, but only after they have established a deeply based foundation that is earned more slowly than their white counterparts. This is consistent with the finer-grained data we will present in the next several chapters.

Affirmative Action Effect or Not?

An alternative explanation is that there is an affirmative action boost that advances the careers of some, though not all, minorities as they move through the organization. In this explanation, the tournament's rules would be the same for minorities and whites. Minorities lag behind whites early in their careers because, for whatever reasons, they do not perform as well. Race is irrelevant. Since the career configurations of minorities who later become executives are essentially indistinguishable early in their careers from those of their minority and white counterparts who never make it to the top in the early career period, they must have been given these promotions because of some outside intervention, such as affirmative action quotas. In this way, "average" minorities have an advantage over "average" whites.

But let's ask some more questions. Don't the organizational costs of promoting underqualified managers increase with the manager's level of responsibility? So why did the companies wait to apply affirmative action to minorities who were already in the middle of their careers, already responsible for major operations?

Furthermore, almost all of the minority executives we studied were promoted to the executive level during periods of significant business and market pressures. During the 1980s, as we discussed in Chapter 2, Advanced faced an industry shakeout, Acme was under fire from new competitors, and Gant pulled off a company turnaround. Such times and events are not generally accompanied by a generous doling-out of high-impact assignments—general management and senior functional roles in critical areas such as sales and marketing, manufacturing and engineering, and finance—to underperforming managers. For all these reasons, it does not seem likely that the minority executives we studied spontaneously and suddenly began receiving promotions as a result of affirmative action policies irrespective of qualifications and performance.

But we know that the three companies we studied did develop during the 1970s—and maintained over the period of our study—

strong, proactive responses to the government's equal opportunity/ affirmative action mandate. Perhaps diversity and fairness initiatives at the three companies did spotlight minority managers who were not on the promotion fast track but who nonetheless had developed good track records as middle managers. That is, the companies' affirmative action commitments may have served to level the playing field for slow-starting but high-performing minority managers. While truly average minority players remained plateaued in middle management, the strongest minority managers got the chance to prove their worth as middle and then upper-middle managers, in other words, to stay in the tournament.

Are there, then, organizational and racial dynamics that might slow down the career movement of minority managers who are otherwise strong performers? Let's step outside the confines of our study and consider the career movement of a well-known figure, former Chairman of the Joint Chiefs of Staff, General Colin Powell. His credentials and his performance, both early and late in his career of national service, are well known. Less well known are the particulars of his ascent through middle to top management. They will serve as an example.

In 1977, during President Jimmy Carter's term in office, Secretary of the Army Clifford Alexander asked the Army Chief of Staff for a list of senior officers with the potential to become generals.[9] Alexander received a list that included not a single minority candidate. Alexander told his Chief of Staff that unless the Army's top brass were prepared to publicly state that no military officers of color met their selection criteria, then the list would be rejected: no list, no promotions to general for anyone. Whether unwilling or unable to declare that there were no qualified minorities, the brass developed a new list, which included the name of Colonel Colin Powell. Colonel Powell had served two combat tours in Vietnam, amassed a chest full of decorations for valor and service, held an MBA, had spent a year as a White House Fellow, and had completed assignments key to national security including several in the Pentagon. Colin Powell, of course, ultimately went on to become the youngest Chairman of the Joint Chiefs of Staff, under Presidents Bush and Clinton, before he retired from military service in 1995.

This story, as told by Clifford Alexander, resonates with the career experiences reported by our study participants in terms of their companies' approaches to affirmative action. Essentially, targeted efforts were applied to put minorities who met or exceeded the standard on the list of players in the "mainstream tournament." Operative before Powell's promotion were a number of changes in the military to remove barriers to the opportunities that could prepare Powell and others to compete for these top positions.[10] Likewise, as we discuss in Chapters 7 and 8, the organizational efforts of Acme, Advanced, and Gant facilitated these executives' ability to enter the main tournament for executive jobs.

◢ Two Tournaments, Separate but Unequal

Turning back to the tournament model, Rosenbaum's theory tells us that fast early moves send an important—and closely watched—signal to superiors, peers, and subordinates that the individual is someone in whom to invest. Since the white executives in our study did not level off until they reached upper-middle management, the executive testing ground, it seems that for white managers the handwriting is on the wall somewhere between their fifth and seventh year: "If you are not a middle manager by this time, you won't make it to the executive suite." The signal is clear.

But the signals weren't so clear for our minority executives. What was going on? Maybe it is simply that persistence pays in spite of any theoretical tournament. There is, however, a theoretical explanation that provides a close fit to the data. The early careers of minority managers and white managers are played in two parallel, but distinctly unequal, tournaments.

When the career trajectories of all four groups are analyzed together, it becomes abundantly clear that, as a whole, both minority executives and managers move more slowly early in their careers than do their white colleagues. But this discrepancy between the racial groups may overshadow the sorting process that simultaneously takes place among minorities as well: a comparison of the trend lines for the two groups of minorities reveals that, in their early years, minority executives reach middle management faster than minority managers, although the difference in rate is not as dramatic as that between white executives and white managers. These results suggest that some kind of sorting of minorities by potential does occur early, although neither the winners nor the losers among the minorities are rewarded with the same rate of promotion as white winners and losers.

So, are there two different tournaments, one that determines the career mobility for whites, the other for minorities? We think that this is exactly the story of Gant, Advanced, and Acme.

In the white tournament, people with high potential get fast promotions into middle and senior management and will emerge as winners. Rosenbaum's model explains how fast, early promotions send powerful positive messages to the individuals and others in the organization about managers' relative standing in the competition for upward movement. People who see the signals then revise their expectations upward, affecting their decisions to make personal investments in those managers' careers. Others become willing to act as mentors and to provide developmental support and even access to social networks. Even resentment toward such perceived fast-trackers may be tempered by the perception that the individual is well connected to powerful mentors and sponsors.

The rules of the minority tournament differ. Specifically, the signals sent to winners take another form: instead of fast promotions, it is the willingness of others to invest personally in minority winners. Winning the minority tournament means that people may be willing to serve as mentors or sponsors and help their minority protégés obtain challenging assignments in which they can prove their technical skills and leadership. Mentoring relationships show the rest of the organization that the protégé is worthy of an extraordinary investment. Beyond their value as organizational signals, mentoring and sponsoring aid the protégés' personal development, work satisfaction, and organizational power.[11]

◢ THE RULES OF THE TWO TOURNAMENTS

What makes the two tournaments different is that the rewards to those who are recognized as high performers in each successive round of competition in early career are different for minorities than for white players: whites who perform exceedingly well and show potential are rewarded with a promotion to the next level, while high-performing minorities are sometimes rewarded with a promotion but other times with enhanced resources, challenges, and the chance to play again at the same level. The tournaments, however, do not involve noncompetitive separate pools. Minorities and whites do compete against one another; the difference is that minority managers who perform better than other similarly situated managers—whites as well as minorities—may end up staying in a position for, say, an additional two or three years. It is the different rewards given to minorities and whites for winning rounds that make the tournaments distinct.

In terms of our tournament theory, whites and minorities therefore appear to be playing two parallel, but distinct, early career tournaments—parallel in that, in both cases, winning early is an important characteristic for later becoming an executive. They are distinct in that, as we have hypothesized, the two tournaments are tacitly structured by different sets of rules about the winners' rewards.

Analyzing the careers of the people we studied at Acme, Advanced, and Gant allows us to understand more completely the racial currents flowing beneath the surface. It is not that we find negligence, obstinacy, or insensitivity. The three companies we studied are indeed and by any standard true leaders in the identification and development of their minority employees. But still we see patterns in the career movements of the men and women we studied that show systematic inequity as a result of race. We've also learned, however, that the ceiling is not impenetrable. With enough of the right factors in place, high-performing minorities can, and do, make it to the top. Why? What is the mix of individual strength of character and organizational process that produces success? What is it like for individuals who do go all the way? What can we learn from their stories? Finding answers to these questions is the challenge we take up in the rest of the book.

We will return to the particular paradox represented by these findings. Minorities are not placed on the fast track in Career Stage 1, but also do not find their chance of reaching the executive suite eliminated by it. This raises an interesting policy question about the desirability of actively promoting a two-tournament system.

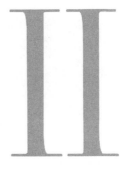

THE EXPERIENCE OF
BREAKING THROUGH

4

The Early Years

Family, Education, and Racial Encounters

IT WAS OBVIOUS TO US by the time we completed our fieldwork that the personal resources for minority executives to succeed began taking shape long before these individuals entered the competition for executive jobs in corporate America. These resources alone were not sufficient to create a solid foundation to support them throughout their entire career; equally important was the nature of their early career experiences. Their early life experiences, however, were the ground on which the foundation was built.

In combination, their preprofessional experiences and their pattern of development in Career Stage 1 provided minority executives with the essential individual resources of self-confidence, competence, and credibility needed to succeed in their business careers. Here we explore the early developmental experiences of our minority executives and, where useful, contrast them with findings from other studies and the two primary comparison groups in this study—white executives and plateaued minority managers. The next chapter will explore our minority executives' early career experiences and give precise definition to the three elements that form this foundation for success.

◢ THE LINK BETWEEN PAST AND PRESENT

Sociological research on executive succession and managerial mobility has long acknowledged the importance of education, family background, and social class.[1] These factors contribute to employees' human and social capital in the workplace. Experiences and credentials that communicate people's potential value as employees demonstrate human capital. Social capital consists of the resources available through an individual's social networks and affects the individual's ability to connect with others. The better or higher status one's credentials and connections are, the more likely one is to have an advantage in the competition for jobs.

Clinical and social psychological studies of leadership and managerial development confirm the importance of family history, social background, and education in the lives of executives, though they do not relate their findings to race or ethnicity. Kotter noted in his classic study of general managers that most of them grew up in upwardly mobile households, with at least one parent who had a two- or four-year college education. Their fathers were in business or were working as managers in nonbusiness settings. The men also reported a close relationship with at least one parent.[2] Similarly, Harrell found that executives had great drive and dominance derived in part from their relationships with their parents.[3] Research in this tradition suggests that background influences a person's disposition and behavior in ways that affect one's likelihood of success.

Family circumstances have also proved to be important in the little research that exists on the backgrounds of minority executives. A study by the Executive Leadership Council surveyed fifty-five African American executives with regard to their education, parental relations, and socialization experiences. It found that 87 percent grew up in two-parent households. Ninety percent of these executives listed a mother or father as the person who most contributed to their professional success, primarily through the values and expectations they instilled. Two-thirds of these individuals considered participation in sports to be important to their preparation for corporate life. Almost universally college-educated, 82 percent had a graduate degree.[4] They tended to be better educated than white executives in comparable samples, but from more varied social class and occupational backgrounds.[5]

Clarence Williams, like Ben Richardson, is an executive at Gant Electronics. When he reflected on the factors that accounted for his corporate success, he responded:

> I think one of the things I had as an advantage was growing up in a very secure background racially. I did not truly understand Northern racism until I came to Boston for college. I was born and raised in a middle-class environment in Philadelphia, so there was no doubt in my mind that black people could do anything because my doctor was black, the lawyer was black. I mean, we had black professionals all around us … that was just a natural part of life to me. Going to Boston, I discovered that people had these misconceptions that blacks couldn't do things. So I had to deal with that in my undergraduate education and professionally in the co-op experiences at IBM. So I think by the time I got to Gant I had a lot of survival skills I had cultivated over the prior five years. [I]t was not necessarily any magic. It's just that I understood the people I had to work with a lot better than they understood me because I had the benefit of being in their culture a lot more than they had the benefit of understanding my culture and background, et cetera. So I was able to more or less adapt to what their expectations were because I understood them. I also had gone to the same engineering school that a lot of the people here had gone to. Education wasn't a factor. I had a high enough GPA that it was clear that I did not coast through school. And it was not like there was anybody carrying me so, you know, I had the appropriate credentials. I was always confident in my abilities.

Nydia Padilla is one of the few Hispanics or females in the top 150 executives at Acme Industries. She too saw the link between her past and present success.

> My family was moving up to better neighborhoods and schools each year. My parents stressed that we should never be content with the status quo. You should always strive to make things better. That stuck with me and continues to influence my thinking.... Another thing that stayed with me is the ability to adapt to different people and different cultures. That's crucial for someone with my background in an environment like Acme.

◢ BACKGROUND OF THE MINORITY EXECUTIVES

In creating our sample of minority and white executives, we focused on work experience, tenure, and functional background. We found, however, that the individuals in the samples shared much more in common. In fact, they are quite similar with the exception of the ways that race influenced the perspectives they had on the world. Whites generally did not experience their racial identity as an important or salient aspect of their early experiences. Compared to minorities, whites placed less weight on their growing-up experience as an influence in their later career success.

In contrast, our minority executives felt their early family backgrounds helped prepare them to succeed. In describing the effects of background, it is useful to examine specific dimensions of their experiences such as education, social class, and the specific nature of socialization experiences that shaped their identity as members of a racial minority in predominantly white settings.

Education

Educationally our minority executives had similar backgrounds to our white executives. At Acme Industries, however, there was a significant difference in the education level between white and black executives. In the 1960s, Acme did not require its managers to have a college degree. Only one minority executive had a college degree when he began his professional career at Acme (though four of the five minority executives had completed at least one year of college). In comparison, three of the five white executives we studied had college degrees.[6]

In contrast, it was the minority executives at Gant Electronics who had more formal education. Two-thirds of the minority executives we studied there held graduate degrees while only half of the white executives did. Several of these minority executives completed their graduate work after entering the workforce. In our interviews, minorities were more likely than whites to tell us that their educational preparation contributed significantly to their career success by providing them with important training or qualifying credentials.

Social Class

The most common indices used for social class in the United States are parents' education, occupation, and income.[7] In each company, all of our participants had a similar range of social class backgrounds. At Acme, with its grassroots, self-made culture, few of our study participants came from the upwardly mobile families typical of most U.S. executives. Instead they hailed from blue-collar backgrounds, the children of manual laborers or career military fathers and stay-at-home mothers.

At Gant, on the other hand, most executives came from middle-class backgrounds, with college-educated parents whose occupations and economic circumstances made them comparable to the executives Kotter studied. Among Gant's minority executives, two-thirds had at least one parent who was a college graduate. This pattern was similar to that of the white executives we interviewed at Gant, who all reported growing up in economically comfortable but not well-to-do families with at least one college-graduate parent. In contrast to the minority executives in the study, three-quarters of the minority managers came from blue-collar or working-class families in which neither parent attended college. In two instances, the parents had not completed high school. White managers, however, tended to come from the same middle-class backgrounds as white executives.

Eighty percent of our minority executives grew up in two-parent households. This was also the norm for the minority managers and the white executives and managers we studied. Not surprisingly, being from a broken home was associated with coming from a working-class background. While being from a two-parent home does not differentiate minority executives from non-executives, it likely does influence who has access to the preparatory experiences that make a corporate career viable. Sociologists make the point that the stability of a two-parent household influences the economic resources available, such as the ability to pay for college.[8]

Family Expectations

Parents' education, family circumstances, and social class are all correlated with achievement in U.S. society.[9] This is in part because these indicators may be predictors of family expectations about education and performance. However, high expectations are not the exclusive province of the well-educated or upwardly mobile. Indeed, a common theme among the overwhelming majority of our minority executives and managers, regardless of social background, was the emphasis their parents placed on education, achievement, and the importance of hard work.[10] Lloyd Simmons, an African American manager, described the message he received from his parents.

> *I grew up in Pittsburgh, went to public school there. I am an only child. My family was economically on the low end of middle class, hard working. Both my parents worked all of their lives. They were very frugal people who, although not well-educated themselves, believed very strongly in the value of education, perhaps to the point of being naive in terms of its pure value. They pushed very hard on that subject. I did very well academically in those early years. I went to college on an academic scholarship, and majored in chemistry.*

Emma Simms grew up in a single-parent household and today is one of the highest-ranking African American female executives at a *Fortune 500* company. Asked if there was anything about her childhood that helps explain her corporate success, she immediately mentioned her mother.

> *Well, I had a great mother, quite an amazing woman. Very, very focused— managed to raise three children by herself on an unbelievably low salary. I*

grew up on the South Side of Chicago during the time when gangs and her-oin had become pretty popular. But it didn't really affect our family at all because my mother was a very focused, strong, decisive individual who didn't have a lot of room for messing around. She had very high expecta-tions for my brother, sister, and me. I can tell you a little story. When I was applying to colleges, I had decided to apply only to the most competitive schools. Harvard, MIT, Princeton, and West Point were all on my list. And so I was sitting down with my mother, telling her where I was going to apply to school. I remember saying to my mother, "you know, it's really risky to do this because these schools, they get thousands and thousands of applica-tions, and they accept a few hundred people." I was really sweating this, and thinking maybe I should apply to a local college. And she said to me, "Emma, I always tell you, you should not worry about the 999 other people who probably won't get in. You should be very focused on you, who will def-initely get in and succeed." I remember thinking about that later, after I actually got into school. And basically what she said to me was, you make sure that you succeed. You make sure that you do well. You do all the things that you can do to do well. Everything else, everybody else, is out of your control. You should make sure that you focus on the things that you need to do to be successful. And that's been the story forever. She is a very good woman. Amazing woman.

Simms's feelings were not unique among our minority executives and managers, regardless of socioeconomic background. In addition to the inspiration and drive instilled by parents, they were also role mod-els who taught lessons about the world of work. Robert Rodriguez's father—a skilled craftsman who moved his family from a poor inner-city barrio to the middle-class suburbs—was his role model. At age 47, Robert was very aware of his enduring legacy.

My father was a skilled craftsman in the aircraft industry. He was a pattern designer and the production [supervisor]. I guess the best way to describe him is that he had a very strong work ethic. He had it right up to the moment he passed away. The last evening he was alive he was somewhat delirious, but thought he was back at work giving instructions to people . . . work was a big part of his life. That very strong work ethic is clearly something that influenced me early on. It was more by example than anything explicit. He very much was a role model. I still think about it sometimes.

Early Exposure to Predominantly White Settings

Numerous scholars note that members of racial groups in the United States tend to grow up in segregated communities.[11] Entering the predominantly white world of corporate America can require a significant amount of cultural and social adaptation in order to become bicultural and comfortable with oneself as a racial minority in the corporate context. Prior exposure to predominantly white contexts can be advantageous. Likewise, the experiences of our minority executives and managers suggest that exposure to predominantly white settings prior to the start of one's career can be advantageous.

For some minorities in our study, school was such a setting. In addition to the credentials it provided, schooling often gave our minority executives and managers early lessons in how to cope and maintain confidence in a predominantly white world. Others gained similar skills and perspectives from living in predominantly white neighborhoods or spending time in the racially integrated military. Interestingly, these experiences did not lead all of our minority executives and managers to the same conclusions about how to behave, the significance of race in their self-definitions, or their expectations for relationships with whites.

Schools and Neighborhoods. It is interesting to note that five of the six minority executives at Gant attended parochial schools, the majority of which were predominantly white. All of those born in the United States grew up in predominantly white neighborhoods, attended high schools where they were one of only a few minorities, or both. Similar patterns were evident among the minority executives we studied at Acme and Advanced. Forty percent at both companies attended predominantly white elementary or secondary schools. Even minorities reared outside the United States went to private high schools run by Europeans.

Attending integrated schools seems to have made our minority executives and managers comfortable in predominantly white settings, as many of them told us. It often gave them a heightened awareness of their racial identity and confidence in their ability to cross racial or ethnic boundaries.[12] For example, Emmett Hines, an African American executive, developed both comfort and a consciousness about racial identity and crossing these boundaries from his early experiences in white schools. Asked to reflect on the aspects of his early childhood and adolescence that shaped him as an adult, Hines's first thought was about the impact of growing up in "two worlds" and the skills he developed crossing from one into the other.

> *I think there are two things. One is how to deal in two worlds, how to deal in a black social world and how to deal in a majority white world where there are different rules, different biases, different values. And if you have early experiences you have an earlier opportunity to form a very clear picture about who you are. And that is important because [you have] to have your own set of principles, your own set of values, that can sustain you in crisis situations. Because in the end the trick is, how do you maintain your persona, how do you maintain being your own person, but still recognize how to maneuver in different worlds. I think that early experience led me to be confident as I crossed from one world to another.*
>
> *I see a lot of people who are very talented, but they get swayed one way or the other and they don't know who they are, why they are being swayed, what the issues are. Do I try to act white? What do I do? Do I try to push away from the black culture, act like it doesn't exist, go into this white world and just live in the white world? They don't know who they are. They are trying to adjust to what are alien systems, alien environments, where there are biases and prejudices, but they don't know if it's them or the system.*

The parents of John Maldonado, a Mexican American executive, deliberately moved their children to an all-white, Anglo environment to ensure their assimilation. Maldonado developed a deep sense of comfort and acceptance within the white majority world of his schools and jobs, but, as a result, grew up distant from his Hispanic heritage and culture: "[A]s a result of growing up outside the Hispanic community and my parents not wanting us to speak Spanish at home, I didn't have any particular association with the Hispanic community, even when I went to college."

Maldonado lived his life as a fully assimilated white-skinned Hispanic until well into his career.[13] Apart from his immediate family and relatives, he had minimal involvement with the Mexican American community inside Gant or the communities where he lived. He was totally at ease in a predominantly Anglo environment and tended not to identify himself as a Mexican American. Indeed, it was not until he was an upper-middle manager that he became personally involved with the company's Hispanic management association and in mentoring other Hispanics.

The stories of Hines and Maldonado demonstrate that early exposure to whites *as equals* helped them become comfortable in predominantly white settings. However, its influence on racial identity was dependent on the social context created by interactions with peers and authority figures as well as the influence of the family's perspective on the desirability of assimilation. Hines described several incidents in his youth when racial prejudice was directed at him. His parents supported the development of a strong black consciousness, perhaps unavoidable in the context of black–white relations in the 1950s. Maldonado's experiences were at the opposite end of the spectrum. His parents worked at minimizing their racial and ethnic differences so that their children could assimilate into the majority Anglo culture.

The minorities we studied had further opportunities to develop their confidence and comfort in white environments. College and graduate school experiences were important in this regard. All but two of the college-educated minority executives attended predominantly white colleges or graduate schools. Most considered themselves successful in these environments and, as a result, they gained comfort operating as a racial minority.

Military Service. Half of the minorities we studied had served in the armed forces. Only at Acme did a comparable number of whites have military experience. Military service was often a credential in hiring employees at Acme, with its culture of top-down management, respect for hierarchy, and performance-based meritocracy. Military service sent the same kind of signal at Acme that college degrees did at Gant and Advanced.

In all three companies, minorities discussed military service as helping them to succeed in their professional careers. One of the most frequently mentioned benefits of enlistment was the opportunity to lead whites in an integrated context. Most of those who had military experience rose to become either commissioned or noncommissioned officers with responsibility for overseeing others' performance.

Ralph Martin, an Acme executive who grew up in a predominantly black setting, spoke to this point in his interview:

> *My experience in the Air Force was really tremendous. I ended up getting promoted every time I was eligible. The height of my experience in the Air Force was having 100 civilians working for me. Some of them were as high as GS-9s and 11s in significant salary grade levels in the Federal system. That experience demystified my whole notion about white folks, because it gave me the opportunity to look at [whites] who I had been conditioned to think about as being, you know, "superior to me." You come to find out that, no, they're not the smartest people in the world. That they are not infallible. And in some cases they were lazy. [Laughter.] You really discover all this stuff. And you also discover that in that environment, while there was prejudice and bigotry, people were more apt to accept you. In the military they were more apt to accept you than in other parts of the society.*

◢ CONCLUSION

Perhaps the major headline from this chapter is that minority executives and white executives were from structurally equivalent backgrounds, especially with regard to education and social class. There is every reason to believe that these men and women entered the corporate arena as prepared to succeed as their white counterparts.

The difference between the minority and white executives revolved mostly around the significance of race and the emphasis they place on their preprofessional experience as a positive factor in their development. In most cases minorities' experiences of being a racial minority in integrated settings were positive, even if stressful at times. They developed confidence in their ability to effectively perform and work with whites. In addition, they gained comfort and experience with being bicultural.

The comparison of minority executives and managers is also marked by the lack of distinguishing features in the backgrounds of these two groups. Social class was the only dimension along which there was a clear divide. Minority executives tended to come from families that were more affluent. The groups did not differ in whether they came from a two-parent household or, more important, the values

instilled at home. Thus it seems that minority managers and executives entered their corporations as equivalents. Each had the rudimen-
tary preparation in education and experiences required to build a
foundation for success; we see little in the preprofessional experiences of these groups to differentiate them or account for their level of
career attainment. In the next chapter, we explore the period of the
career in which the real differentiation of these groups began, Career
Stage 1.

5

Early Career

Developing Competence, Credibility, and Confidence

W E LEARNED IN CHAPTER 4 that the early life experiences of minority executives and of plateaued minority managers—as well as of white executives—were remarkably similar. The first significant distinctions began to emerge only during these individuals' early careers. In the words of the minority executives in our study, their unique experiences during these years "laid the foundation" for future success. Ironically, it is during these very years that race featured most prominently as a potential barrier to progress. And indeed, the early careers of minority executives did move forward slowly compared to their white fast-track peers, as our discussion of career tournaments in Chapter 3 underscores.

The minority executives we studied were far more likely than the other study groups to attribute the later course of their careers to their early work experiences. Researchers have identified the early career as a critical stage in both the personal and professional development of managers in general.[1] This is when the fit between individual and organization is tested; managers are socialized into company norms, mutual expectations set, and full admission granted to those managers who meet them. Unhappy experiences in this early trying ground—poor work relationships, problematic performance, or dissatisfaction with the work itself—can derail people, leading potentially valuable contributors to leave the organization or to demotivate those who stay. Our work highlights these years of trial and testing because of their disproportionate significance in the careers of racial and ethnic minorities, a feature which has been understudied.[2]

In this chapter, we'll focus on the psychological characteristics that contributed to pivotal career decisions, as on assignments and work relationships that distinguished the early careers of minority executives. By the end of this period, a composite portrait of our future minority executives shares three important features, which we characterize as *competence*, *credibility*, and *confidence*. These personal resources form the foundation for the subsequent success experienced by these individuals. Later in the chapter, we'll develop these definitions more precisely in terms of how these people of color were perceived and characterized by their white and minority colleagues, as well as by themselves.

A good place to begin is with the story of Clarence Williams. Today, he is a division vice president and general manager at Gant.

◢ CLARENCE WILLIAMS'S EARLY CAREER: SOLID BEGINNING

I joined Gant right out of college as a newly minted engineer. When I walked into the lab on my first day, my technicians were already at work. As the new engineer, I thought I knew what to expect. These veterans would think, "Here is this new college greenhorn who doesn't know what he is doing, et cetera, et cetera. I have been on this bench for ten years and this kid is going to tell me what to do." There is tension between non-exempt technicians and engineers. I was prepared for that through my experiences working summers as an intern. I was not prepared to walk into the lab and see a banner probably as long as that wall, saying George Wallace—the prosegregation, former governor of Alabama—for President. That's when I knew it was an uphill battle. There were a lot of diehards in that lab.

When he recounts the story Williams is relaxed, even amused. Clearly, whatever resistance he encountered from this group of subordinates did not undermine his ability to succeed. Yet that day remains vividly imprinted in his memory.

Williams grew up in the African American section of Washington, D.C. His father was a college-educated engineer whose career ambitions were greatly curtailed because of his race, and his mother was a homemaker. Education was a central value espoused by his parents. After high school he attended one of the nation's leading engineering schools, working each summer as an intern with IBM. He graduated with a B+ average and a bachelor's degree in engineering. Williams interviewed for positions in engineering and got an offer from Gant, but decided instead to complete his military service.

In the Army, Williams worked as an engineer. While there, he was exposed to many aspects of engineering and found that a childhood of Saturdays spent fixing engines with his father had given him a real love of the work. He also discovered that he enjoyed supervising others and helping them with the work he loved so much. When his military service was up, Williams joined Gant Electronics as a design engineer, working for Nathan Barrett, the white man who had offered him a job out of college.

Working for Barrett was a stroke of luck for Williams. A senior design engineer with responsibility for a technical group, Barrett was looking to expand his own horizons. He therefore gave Williams both resources and responsibility, in the form of funding, subordinates, and room to expand. Barrett also provided advice and counsel on how Williams should negotiate the organization. Williams described the situation:

Now, in reflection, I would have to say that that period was a key to my success. I was fortunate to work for Nathan. He wanted to go do some other things and therefore did all he could to bring me along as his back-fill. He really gave me a lot of responsibilities and leeway. I assumed more and more of his responsibilities.

Why did Williams ultimately succeed when other minorities stum-bled or turned aside? Williams clearly attributed part of his success to his relationship with Barrett:

I think there are some minorities who have not been in the right place at the right time. Initially, I could have been under a supervisor who was out to hammer me, instead of Nathan. Had I been, I could have been disillusioned very early in my career and gone to a different company or profession.

By the end of his early period Williams had developed additional supporters, including Barrett's boss and several white peers who, when they were promoted to manager before Williams, vouched for him with their colleagues or recruited him for key assignments.

Williams also took an active part in managing his own career. Although it took longer to reach middle management than he thinks was necessary, he concentrated on becoming as technically proficient as possible.

During the early years, I was focused on trying to be a good engineer. So in addition to doing my assigned job, I took a lot of in-house courses and sem-inars to stay technically current and competent and to branch out into other areas. So in addition to my specialty, I had a pretty good background in other things.

He also chose his assignments judiciously, consciously avoiding being tracked into staff or nontechnical jobs.

As an aspiring engineer, it was my observation that black people in engi-neering did not get the real design engineering assignments. In the best cases, they got design support assignments. So I always focused on having pure design work with accountability for the assignment. That was not a random chance, that was my focus. I selected my assignments not for how they could advance my position at Gant, but how they would round me out and contribute to my development.

In retrospect, I might have had opportunities to get into management earlier if I had not been insistent on maintaining and demonstrating a high level of technical competence at the beginning of my career.

With a reputation as a technically proficient performer who could deliver, Williams gained the cooperation, respect, and sometimes the friendship of whites who were initially either resistant or hesitant to work with him.

To cope with being one of only a small number of African Americans in the engineering and development organization, Williams participated in the black self-help group network formed by African American employees at Gant. The opportunity to talk with others going through similar experiences was invaluable. In addition to offering him social support, the group also expanded his company network beyond engineering.

After seven years as an engineer, Williams began to consider seriously whether to remain in a technical role or to move into engineering management. He finally concluded that while he loved engineering, greater challenges awaited him in management. To facilitate that transition, Williams decided to get an MBA while continuing to work at Gant in engineering and design assignments.

This brief description of Clarence Williams's early career illustrates a number of Career Stage 1 experiences characteristic of and unique to minority executives. Let's turn now to the story of Roosevelt James, a minority manager whose career has stalled.

⬛ ROOSEVELT JAMES'S EARLY CAREER: A CONTRAST

The career of Roosevelt James, a plateaued minority manager at Gant, provides a sharp contrast with Clarence Williams in many respects. Despite similar backgrounds in electrical engineering, their experiences in Stage 1 were vastly different. These differences give us a number of early clues about why one eventually made it to the executive level, and the other did not.

Unlike Williams, whose early career was spent building a deep and solid expertise in design engineering, James had worked in no fewer than seven different functions before being promoted to middle management, including engineering, quality, first-line manufacturing, industrial engineering, facilities management, project engineering, and affirmative action. In total, James had twelve different assignments (nearly all lateral) in seven different functions before reaching middle management level.

While Williams was motivated by a deep interest in engineering and held out for job assignments in design engineering, James was motivated by the prospect of getting into management. He saw his early assignments as stepping-stones to a larger goal. It is not surprising then, that lacking Williams's intrinsic love of the work, James became bored in his early assignments and sought one transfer after another, trying out different jobs while accepting small lateral promotions.

One of James's assignments in this period seemed a real plum—to serve as project manager for the technical operations of an international start-up facility. Unfortunately, this high-visibility project failed—and with it vanished any goodwill toward James on the part of several senior executives.

During these years, James had only one real mentor, an early boss who initially seemed to be "an out and out racist" but who later ended up "turning around" his attitude and actually taking a deep interest in James.

Ultimately, James's career stalled in middle management while Williams's has continued to grow and flourish. What accounts for these differences? Let's start with an analysis of the psychological characteristics that seem to be at work in these two individuals and, more generally, that seem to have differentiated minorities who reached the executive level from those who plateaued in middle management.

▰ PSYCHOLOGICAL CHARACTERISTICS

How does slow or moderate career movement affect the spirit of ambitious managers? What are the psychological consequences of slow or moderate early career mobility? How do the most successful minority executives withstand these psychological challenges?

Barbara Lawrence has shown that employees' sense of being ahead, on time, or behind an apparent promotion schedule can affect their psychological orientation toward their work. Those who believe that they are moving slower than the norm feel less optimistic about the future and less satisfied with their jobs than those who think that their careers are moving at average or fast speed. Lawrence has also shown that these norms about promotion timetables are shared within an organization, which confirms the tournament model's use of promotions as signals of winning or losing in tournament rounds.[3]

Researchers Claude Steele, Jeffrey Howard, and Floyd and Jacqueline Dickens have each described how encounters with racial prejudice can lower the performance of otherwise high achieving minorities, who may cease to put in as much effort.[4] When asked to reflect on other minority colleagues who did not achieve the success he did despite their preparation and capabilities, Raymond Jones, an African American executive at Advanced Technology, observed, "The crucial difference is they gave up early. They stopped wanting to be the best." The most successful minority executives possessed two traits that helped them overcome these psychological challenges: a passionate commitment to excellence and an inherent and unshakable love of the work itself.

Commitment to Excellence

Internalizing excellence is a key aspect of sustaining performance and drive in the critical early career period. Ben Richardson's colleagues at Gant told us that Richardson had always been focused on getting results and being number one. Richardson described his attitude: "I focused on each assignment, excelling at it and broadening myself. I could only assume that performance would eventually count. I always wanted to be the best for myself, no matter what else happened."

It took Greg Jones, an African American executive at Acme Industries, six years to become a unit manager. His unit was number one in his operating group in each of the next two years. Jones then pitched in as acting plant manager when his boss was out for an extended leave, but was passed over when the post later became vacant. For Jones, this was the low point in his career. When asked how he coped with this disappointment, he said, "I resolved to be the best unit manager in this company." This persistence and performance was later rewarded. When the promotion finally came, Jones "hit the ground running. Everything took off. . . . We got all kinds of recognition. We had the number one operation in the country after being the worst before I took over. I got up full of fire every day. It was fun."

Some people lose hope if their performance seems to go unrewarded. Our minority executives experienced more than their share of disappointment, especially in Stage 1, but they viewed their performance in personal rather than external terms. Their commitment to excellence led them to learn new skills. Many of these individuals went back to graduate school or took nonmandatory training courses to enhance their knowledge base as well as their qualifications for future opportunities. Both Clarence Williams and Ben Richardson are examples of this behavior.

Loving the Work

The minority executives in our study consistently reported that their vocational interests and aptitudes matched their functional area of work in Stage 1; some of them even changed jobs once they perceived a mismatch. Minority executives described making early career choices in order to be at the leading edge of the work they liked. They were most enthusiastic about the work itself, and less so with how quickly—or slowly—they were promoted. In contrast, minority managers who subsequently plateaued were more likely to describe choosing the company or organization for fast-track career opportunities to management rather than for the work itself.

Butler and Waldroop maintain that intrinsic motivation is critical to achieving and sustaining job satisfaction.[5] Kotter describes the fit between an individual's interests and strengths with the work and context of early career as being essential to building a power base of competence and credibility.[6] This type of alignment may be even more critical for minorities since the strategy of choosing work solely because it is the gateway to bigger and better things may not be enough to sustain the energy required to be successful over the long career haul, especially during their slower pace of advancement in Stage 1.

Bill Parsons is an example of the problems that can beset those who fail to find motivation in the work itself. An African American trained as a chemical engineer, he initially joined General Aviation, a leading aircraft manufacturer, because he felt its training program would put him on the path to general management. He did well on all of his assignments, but became quickly bored with them; he was looking for an opportunity to get on the fast track. Although he encountered no overt racism, he felt race to be one of the limiting factors in his progress and failure to get better assignments. After four years, Parsons went to Gant Electronics, where he made a series of career decisions based on what he thought would get him into top management. Later, he found himself stuck in an assignment that he had seen as just a stepping-stone. With little intrinsic interest in the work, Bill became frustrated. One result was a poor relationship with his boss, which led him to transfer into a business unit whose product was peripheral to Gant's core business. His career never recovered from this decision.

Another difference between the minority executives (e.g., Clarence Williams) and the plateaued minority managers (e.g., Bill Parsons) that we studied was that in order to fulfill their ambitions for upward mobility, the plateaued managers were more prone to take salary and title change promotions that offered little real increase in management responsibility. As a consequence, some prematurely left the line of opportunity that was most likely to lead to the executive suite. Indeed, this pattern may account for plateaued minority managers at Gant and Advanced Technology receiving, on average, more promotions than minority executives during their early careers, but then not achieving the same success as minority executives later in their careers. In striking contrast to this pattern, two minority executives at Acme Industries actually took demotions to get themselves out of staff jobs and into operations, where they saw a better match with their skills and the greater opportunity for professional growth. For these minority executives, these were more important than losing a job title or status.

JOB ASSIGNMENTS AND OPPORTUNITIES FOR DEVELOPMENT

We saw in Chapter 3 that the careers of minority executives moved more slowly up to middle management than did those of white executives. Clearly, minority executives must miss out on some of the benefits of fast movement, especially the advantages of being publicly perceived as having high potential and being consequently rewarded with opportunities for additional, immediate career growth. But since our data show that a moderate pace of movement on its own does not preclude minorities from reaching the executive suite, are there perhaps some compensating benefits to a moderate rate of career advancement?

In fact, studies of executive development do seem to show that rate of movement may be less important in the long run than the total content of the experiences. Work by researchers at the Center for Creative Leadership (CCL) suggests that moving too fast can lead to career derailment, especially if the accelerated early career does not provide adequate preparation for meeting future challenges.[7]

We can find another potential solution to this puzzle by looking at the early career experiences of the three study groups in terms of overall career content as well as upward career mobility. The first clue is found in the pattern of Stage 1 job assignments.

Job Assignments

Table 5-1 shows the relative frequency of different assignment types that white and minority executives received during the early

Table 5-1   Relative Frequency of Assignments in Career Stage 1 for
Minority Executives and White Executives

Type of Assignment	Minority Executives ($n = 20$)	White Executives ($n = 13$)	Paired Comparison ($n = 13$)[a]
Department change	.4	.4	ns
Lateral assignment	.7	.8	ns
Line to staff move	.1	.1	ns
Involved in start-up	.1	.1	ns
Promotions (within level)	.7	.8	ns

Note: Average frequency of assignment per participant per period.

[a] In order to get a more stringent comparison that could control for variations across organizations, we conducted paired comparisons for thirteen of the minority executives with their matched white executives and plateaued minority manager counterparts.

Significance test for paired comparisons: $^{*}p < .10$. $^{**}p < .05$.   ns = not statistically significant.

career period. Very few differences emerge: the two groups were equally likely to change departments or make lateral moves; they received similar numbers of within-level promotions, and were equally unlikely to move from line to staff jobs or to be involved in a start-up operation. In short, while minority executives took longer to reach middle management, the content of their resume matched that of their white counterparts.

A very different pattern is found in a comparison of minority executives and plateaued minority managers. Minority executives advanced to middle management only slightly faster than minority managers but with much greater job continuity. Table 5-2 reveals that minority executives were significantly less likely to change departments, make lateral moves, or move from line to staff positions, as highlighted in the contrast between the careers of Clarence Williams and Roosevelt James, for example. Surprisingly, we discovered that minority executives actually received, on average, fewer within-level promotions in Stage 1 than did the plateaued minority managers. On close inspection, however, minority managers' promotions were typically smaller and offered little real expansion of responsibilities as compared to

Table 5-2   Relative Frequency of Assignments in Career Stage 1 for Minority Executives and Minority Managers

Type of Assignment	Minority Executives ($n = 20$)	Minority Managers ($n = 13$)	Paired Comparison ($n = 13$)
Department change	.4	1.1	*
Function change	.5	1.1	ns
Lateral assignment	.7	2.0	**
Line to staff move	.1	.5	**
Location change	1.2	1.5	*
Promotions (within level)	.7	1.9	**

Note: Average frequency of assignment per participant per period.

[a] In order to get a more stringent comparison that could control for variations across organizations, we conducted paired comparisons for thirteen of the minority executives with their matched white executives and plateaued minority manager counterparts.

Significance test for paired comparisons: $^*p < .10.$ $^{**}p < .05.$ ns = not statistically significant.

those of the future executives. Furthermore, these promotions frequently involved moving out of line positions to staff roles, often taking plateaued minority managers out of a key function into a support
role—the very kinds of promotions that Clarence Williams avoided
and that led to Bill Parsons's derailing. The career narratives of the
plateaued minority managers further corroborates the characteriza-
tion of their careers as relatively fragmented and unfocused.

Opportunities for Development

A second clue to the benefits of the moderate career pace of our
minority executives can be found by considering how their assignments helped develop their technical skills, managerial skills, and
organizational clout. Morrison as well as Bray, Campbell, and Grant
have noted that demanding assignments usually offer more learning
opportunities, increase the rate of learning, and increase self-confidence for the incumbent. They have also observed that incumbents in
challenging positions remain more motivated than those who hold
more limited jobs.[8]

The specific developmental experiences we studied were those
jobs that involved participation on task forces; responsibility for turning around a previously failing project or unit; assumption of a stretch
assignment requiring skills and perspectives beyond those already
demonstrated; taking on additional responsibility or expanded scope
beyond the current job, but without a promotion; and eye-opening
experiences—opportunities that came with a big "aha!"

Task-force assignments often provide technical managers and
first-line supervisors with a broader general-management perspective
by exposing them to views outside their own technical specialty.[9]
Managers on task forces can develop the skills of persuading and getting commitment from a diverse group of stakeholders. Such assignments also put managers in front of senior people from different
departments. Good performance on a task force can be showcased
across the company. Turnaround situations provide some of the same
benefits and, in addition, the opportunity to innovate and lead. They
also come with a high level of external visibility—whether the result
is a success or a failure. Taking on additional responsibility can also be
developmental if it involves assuming duties normally reserved for

higher-level managers or increasing the scope of current duties. Such assignments, even if they don't involve a promotion, can help managers develop skills needed to manage at higher levels.[10]

Minority executives for the most part enjoyed developmental opportunities broadly similar to both white executives and plateaued minority managers. They did tend to receive more responsibility without promotion than their white counterparts and to serve on fewer task forces. But the biggest distinction was that the minority executives had a high frequency of experiences that they told us had "opened their eyes," by giving them new insights into managerial decision making, the importance of company culture, or their own potential impact on the lives of others in the organization.

Again and again in our interviews, minority executives told us that their early career assignments had helped them gain a personal perspective on the organization and on their own careers. We rarely heard about such a shift in outlook from either white executives or minority managers. Ben Richardson, for example, talked about being passed over for promotions in his early years as a lesson in the subjective aspects of corporate life.

> *[Getting passed over] was a lesson that even if you were the best objectively, there might be a couple of people who did well enough. But why does one person get the job and not the other? What is the objective here? What is the political thing that happens? It is an issue of how you are perceived. [I learned] I had to manage that as well.*

Similarly, the positive experience of filling in for his manager compelled Clarence Williams to stop and assess whether to stay as a senior engineer or go into engineering management. Other minority executives decided during this period to leave other companies and move to Gant or Advanced, once they became aware that their goals were out of sync with their employer.

A final, critical difference in the early careers of the three groups is the quality of their developmental experiences. Minority executives were less likely than their white counterparts to report a significant failure during these years in their career, and far less likely—in fact one fifth as likely—than plateaued minority managers to report such a failure (Table 5-3). Some studies highlight the value of what are called constructive failures as sources of learning, but this may very well not be a common outcome for minorities. In terms of their own self-definition, minorities may feel that failure is unacceptable given the extreme scrutiny they are likely to endure. Others have noted that poor performance of a minority is likely to be attributed by others to the actions of the individual, whereas the same performance by a member of the majority will be attributed to an inherently difficult situation.[11] Thus, highly visible mistakes, as in the case of Roosevelt James and the failed international start-up, may shut minorities out from being sponsored for another good opportunity.

Though it took a longer time for minority executives to reach middle management than white executives, their pattern of developmental experiences suggests that their early careers provided them with deep technical grounding and personal learning in place of the fast-track series of assignments that white executives experienced. During their early career, the minority executives were deeply exposed to a range of core business issues within their own original functional or technical expertise. Table 5-4 summarizes the similarities and differences between minority executives and the comparison groups.

MENTORS, SPONSORS, AND SOCIAL NETWORKS

Minority executives attributed much of their later success to the presence of developmental relationships with bosses, other superiors, and peers. Of course, having mentors and sponsors did not make them unique—all of the executives and managers we studied, both whites and minorities, reported forming these important ties. What distin-

Table 5-3   Major Failures or Successes in Career Stage 1

Event	Minority Executives	Minority Managers	White Executives
Major failure	.1	.5	.3
Major success	.3	.3	.2

Note: Average frequency per participant per period. Reference group is Minority Executives.

guished the minority executives from the other groups, however, was that they had had many more such relationships and with a broader range of people, especially in their early careers.

Table 5-5 presents the average number of developmental relationships experienced by minority executives and the comparison groups. On average, minority executives reported more than twice the num-

Table 5-4   Key Differences in Career Stage 1 Job Assignments and Opportunities for Development

	Minority Executives	White Executives	Minority Managers
Rate of hierarchical progression	• Moderate rate to reach middle management • Few, but large promotions	• Fast, steady rate to reach middle management • Few, but large promotions	• Moderate, but slightly slower than minority executives • Many small promotions
Assignment patterns	• Focused, continuous pattern of assignments largely within one function • Few line-to-staff changes • Few lateral moves	• Focused, continuous pattern of assignments largely within one function • Few line-to-staff changes • Few lateral moves	• Fragmented pattern of assignments with frequent moves • Frequent line-to-staff changes • Frequent lateral moves and location changes
Developmental experiences	• Frequent instances of added responsibility without promotion that are stretch assignments • Several eye-opening experiences • Almost no failure experience	• Same pattern as minority executives, but far more task-force and turnaround assignments and fewer instances of added responsibility without promotion that are stretch assignments • Few eye-opening experiences • Few failure experiences	• Same pattern as minority executives except for more task-force assignments and fewer instances of added responsibility without a promotion • Few eye-opening experiences • Many more failure experiences than either minority or white executives

ber of significant developmental relationships than did white executives during Career Stage 1.

Early Career Mentors

As Table 5-5 suggests, minority executives tended to build developmental relationships early in their careers; within the first three years, over 90 percent had experienced at least one such relationship, usually with a boss or a boss's boss. These early relationships provided the job assistance needed to perform effectively in the short term, along with support in moving up the career ladder. In addition, these relationships provided our minority executives with more enduring feedback about personal and social choices and, very important, about potential career decisions. In contrast, minority managers described their early relationships as providing merely job support and help in landing the next job. Conversations between mentor and protégé, in the cases of future plateaued minority managers, were generally limited to work-related issues and lacked the breadth and rich texture that seemed to typify exchanges between future minority executives and their early mentors.

Specifically, the mentors of our minority executives contributed four critical kinds of support during these early years. First, they

Table 5-5   Relative Frequency of Forming Developmental Relationships for Three Study Groups

	Career Stage 1 Start of Career to Middle Management			Career Stage 2 Middle Management to Upper-Middle Management			Career Stage 3 Upper-Middle Management to Executive Level		
	Min. Mgrs.	*Min. Execs.*	*White Execs.*	*Min. Mgrs.*	*Min. Execs.*	*White Execs.*	*Min. Mgrs.*	*Min. Execs.*	*White Execs.*
Acme Industries	0.8	2.4	0.6	0.8	1.8	1.4	1.0	3.0	2.2
Advanced Technology	2.8	0.7	0.8	2.0	3.3	2.0	0	2.3	1.7
Gant Electronics	0.8	1.8	1.0	1.0	2.0	1.5	0.3	2.0	2.0
Average for entire sample	1.4	1.8	0.8	1.2	2.3	1.5	0.5	2.5	2.0

opened the door to challenging assignments and expanded responsibilities that allowed these future executives to grow professionally. Second, by putting their protégés in high-trust positions, these mentors sent a message to the rest of the organization that they were considered high-performers and important to the success of the operation, thereby helping develop or reinforce these future executives' self-confidence and credibility with others.

Ben Richardson, for example, was greatly aided by his early mentor, Steven Berg. Richardson had been working in a territory that encompassed only the African American and Hispanic parts of New York City, which was not considered a prime business account territory, until Berg gave him the chance to sell in the central business district:

> Ben had been assigned a territory [by the previous manager] that was outside the central business district of the city. Twenty years later I still remember his territory. It was the black section of Manhattan and the Bronx. When I became his manager, I moved him from that territory to a downtown central business district. He more than deserved it. It's just that nobody else was willing to give him the opportunity at that time.

Berg went on to point out that Richardson's stellar performance in that high-visibility territory started his "rise to stardom." On the other hand, any failure might have damaged Richardson's career prospects and reflected poorly on Berg. Berg felt comfortable giving Richardson the assignment not only because he saw that Richardson had the skills of a great sales representative but also because he and Richardson could talk with each other openly and honestly. Berg noted that others might not have felt so comfortable: "I could talk to him in a way that others would not have done, even about race. They were worried about being perceived as racist. Some probably still called him a negro."

Berg's support of Richardson sent clear signals to the rest of the sales group. Berg observed that Richardson "emerged as a leader amongst the team members. People were looking to him, because I would put more and more of my confidence in him."

Third, these mentors provided career advice and counsel that, in many cases, proved critical to keeping the individual on a track that might eventually lead to the executive level. Steven Berg, for example, counseled Ben Richardson to pass up several jobs that were offered to him after he completed his MBA, believing them to be dead-end situations that would take Richardson out of the real action. Other minority executives were counseled by their mentors to sharpen skill areas, return to school while working, or get exposure to other areas of the business. In a couple of instances, future minority executives learned from their mentors that their starting points in the company did not put them in the best position to move up later, and so were persuaded by them to change areas. Such insights were critical for these novice managers, many of whom were initially naïve about the factors that would tend to produce opportunities for advancement.

Finally, these early career mentors often became powerful sponsors later in the minority executives' careers, recruiting them again and again to new positions. The careers of the three highest-ranking minority executives in our study illustrate this point. In their first three years at their firm, each developed a mentor with whom they worked later, either directly or indirectly, on at least three different occasions before reaching the executive level.

Social Networks in Career Stage 1

Minority executives' constellations of relationships expanded quickly beyond their initial mentors to include peers and people below them in the hierarchy. These networks tended to be full of redundant ties (i.e., of people who knew each other) and often mirrored the initial mentor's own relationships. Maintaining these networks over the relatively long time spent in Stage 1 served to create a strong social consensus within their immediate group or organization about their abilities, performance, and potential to succeed, lending them credibility and developing their professional reputations.

Emma Simms, an African American executive at Gant, is an excellent example of someone who developed an effective network of mentors and sponsors early in her career. Simms initially joined the company as a graduate student engineering intern, when she was helped by fellow engineers to learn not only the job but also Gant's culture. Most significant was the mentoring relationship she developed with a mid-career research engineer. He was one of the few African Americans in research and development at the company. Feeling good about the company and her personal connection to it, she ventured to Gant after graduation as a staff engineer.

Having relationships already in place smoothed her transition. The environment seemed open to her. A critical moment came eighteen months into her first job when, in a meeting, she challenged a senior executive's views on issues of gender. To her surprise, he later followed up with a call. This executive, Ray Fletcher, quickly became a significant mentor. And, despite the known obstacles to cross-race and cross-gender mentorships, the two developed a close bond.[12]

Taking some of Fletcher's advice, Simms opted for a stint in strategic planning, an early move out of her core discipline. As it turned out, it was an excellent broadening experience, in part because the head of the planning group, an African American male, also became a major supporter. Little did Simms know that her initial mentor, Fletcher, had personally asked the director of planning to hire and develop her. We discovered this fact only as the result of interviewing her former boss in the planning assignment.

With strong ties in engineering, Simms had no problem going back to the engineering group as a middle manager. She soon demonstrated both her technical ability and her managerial effectiveness and interpersonal skills. Her next stop was a multilevel promotion as chief of staff for Fletcher.

◢ COMPETENCE, CREDIBILITY, AND CONFIDENCE: FOUNDATION FOR SUCCESS

We have now described the characteristics and patterns that typified minority executives and their experiences in early career. These include a strong commitment to excellence and an intrinsic love of the work they had chosen, both of which served to keep them motivated and engaged during a period of slow movement and infrequent promotion. These psychological characteristics combined with their highly focused patterns of job assignments and the critical support they received from their early-career mentors contributed to a focused and deep expertise in one or two core business areas. Figure 5-1 summarizes the most important formative experiences of the early careers of the minority executives in our study.

Let us now evaluate more closely the portrait of minority success we outlined at the beginning of the chapter—the distinguishing features of competence, credibility, and confidence.

Competence

Competence has two components relevant to executive development: deep grounding in one or more areas of expertise and continual mastery of new and broader skills. For the minority executives we studied, deep grounding was acquired in the functional area in which they began their managerial career and was demonstrated through consistent, excellent performance over time. Deep grounding is gained cumulatively, applied in different work contexts, and developed through the recurrent execution of tasks that present various degrees of both familiarity and difficulty. This grounding allows managers to develop an intuitive sense of how disparate elements of their

Figure 5-1   Formative Experiences of Minority Executives

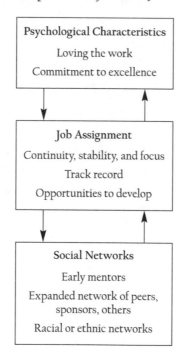

organization's business operations are interconnected, and it enables them to bridge the knowledge gap when they are faced with stretch assignments. Later in their careers, minority managers and executives with such expertise draw on it to overcome resistance from unresponsive subordinates. The depth of their competence helps to compensate for being left out of white peer networks and lets them work around unsupportive bosses. The minority executives in our study had developed and honed these skills to a high degree.

The second dimension of competence is the capacity to reflect and learn from experience and ongoing feedback. This component requires developing self-awareness about one's own motivations and a desire for sustained learning. For minorities, this ongoing mastery also means learning to manage the complex interplay among race, racial identity, and the managerial role.

In Stage 1, white executives were rewarded with promotions that exposed them to new operational areas and challenges. Minorities, on the other hand, used this period to gain extra competence, defined here as deep grounding and ongoing mastery.

Credibility

Extreme competence can compensate for the absence of strong social networks, as it did in the case of many of the minorities we studied. But their experience also suggests that demonstrating competence was not enough for minorities to succeed; they also had to gain organizational credibility.

Credibility depends on a manager's reputation for successful performance, integrity, and impact on the core business. In situations perceived to have high organizational or business risk, critical assignments are more likely to go to highly credible people. Kanter defines credibility as competence plus power, with power, in turn, arising from access to social networks and to important job assignments.[13]

Early relationships with key bosses and peers, when combined with demonstrated performance, directly influence credibility. People invest in the careers of others precisely because they view them as creditworthy or credible. During the early career, the reputation a minority develops is crucial. The more positive the regard in which one is held, the more likely the person is to have credibility with others.

After Ben Richardson placed first in sales for the third year in a row, his accomplishments were seen as a result of his own hard work and skill. In contrast, one of our minority middle managers at Gant commented that she chose not to stay longer than a year as a salesperson in order to gain more exposure in the larger organization. But when she subsequently tried to gain a leadership position back in the sales organization, she was seen as lacking credibility where it was needed—in the sales function.

Credibility tends to give weight not only to the specific recommendations managers make but also to the way they frame the issues. Credible managers are widely believed to come through in a clutch situation. A person's credibility tends to rise and fall according to the quality and authenticity of the information circulating about them in the organization.

Wells and Jennings argue that there are threshold positions at which real opposition to minority advancement begins suddenly and in earnest, such as the promotion from middle to upper-middle management or from upper-middle management to executive.[14] The stakes suddenly get raised and stereotypes may be invoked to challenge the candidate's competence. As a result, minorities usually need sponsorship and support at critical moments, especially when the risk that they might fail is perceived to be high or when their responsibilities expand beyond functional boundaries.

Confidence

Confidence, or self-confidence, may be the most important of the required personal resources, yet is perhaps the most intangible. Confidence includes belief in one's own past achievements, current competence, and future ability to succeed. It tends to have the impervious quality of appearing self-evident to the beholder. Confidence is experienced as a sense of internal security that bolsters one's capacity to ward off doubts, to withstand attacks on one's credibility, and to maintain a self-concept that is relatively immune to the self-fulfilling effects of stereotypes. Minorities typically need an extremely high level of confidence to rise all the way to the executive level, as we learned in our study.

*Formative Experiences and Personal Resources in Minority
Executive Advancement*

Figure 5-2 brings together the common early life experiences of
our minority executives that we considered in Chapter 4 and the pattern of early experiences we discussed in this chapter. It also shows
the link between all these experiences and the personal resources they
developed in the form of competence, credibility, and confidence.
Inevitably, each formative experience has an effect, direct or indirect,
on the development of these personal resources.

To begin, family, school, and other early life experiences can
establish—or fail to establish—the confidence and drive needed to
fully engage in the job, to resist doubt, and to take appropriate risk.[15]
Minority executives generally had experiences similar to those of
white executives during these formative years. We believe these early
experiences also help foster the psychological characteristics that will
be needed to navigate the corporate environment.

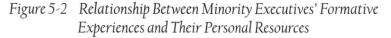

*Figure 5-2   Relationship Between Minority Executives' Formative
Experiences and Their Personal Resources*

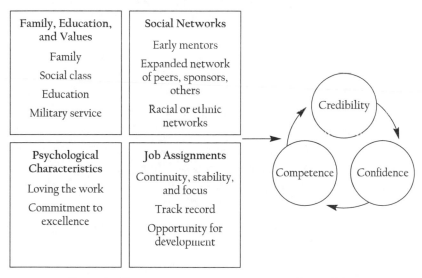

The psychological states of loving the work and possessing an internal standard of excellence facilitate not only persistence, but an orientation toward ongoing mastery and continuous improvement. Research on learning supports this link: Bandura and others have demonstrated that learning is a motivated activity influenced by the intrinsic motivation that an individual holds.[16] Steele's extensive research demonstrates that minority performance and underperformance on a task is influenced by the extent to which a person is positively identified with his or her task.[17] Where we find individuals who love their work, who are oriented toward excellence, and who are able to continuously improve, we can safely conclude that they are motivated in relationship to their work.

When slower movement in early career is coupled with expanded responsibility, stretch assignments, and a developmental relationship, all the elements of competence, credibility, and confidence are reinforced. The result of this pattern of assignments is a track record of performance that sets the individual above the norm.

Developmental relationships that have formed early also raise a minority manager's credibility. We found that people's reputations are supremely important during the early career. When individuals are held in high regard among those who know them well, the opinion of those seniors and colleagues will carry weight with others in early career.

Job assignments and early career movement also influence credibility. Having a more stable and continuous set of assignments allows relationships to deepen and be tested. As a result, others become more confident in their assessments and are more likely to attribute strong performance to a minority's skills and talents rather than situational factors. Experimental research has shown that people are more likely to attribute excellent performance by a majority group member to the majority person's own efforts and abilities. In contrast, the same level of performance by a minority is more likely to be attributed to the situation or the efforts of others.[18]

The personal resources we have described are interrelated and mutually reinforcing. Competence tends to give a manager greater credibility with bosses, peers, and subordinates, thus boosting the individual's confidence and further enhancing the person's motivation and capacity to reach new levels of skill mastery. At the same time, an attack on one element means that the other two are likely to suffer.

The point here is not to suggest that minority executives differ from white executives in needing or possessing these personal resources—they are essential characteristics for anyone who aspires to the upper reaches of a corporate hierarchy. What we did find, however, was a distinct pattern of early career experiences that enabled minority executives to acquire and build on their preprofessional foundation, despite many opportunities to become discouraged, especially by the slow takeoff of their careers relative to white executives. This is a typical predicament of the minority tournament that often triggers a sense of disappointment over not receiving the kinds of rewards that the rules of the *main* tournament lead one to expect for a given level of achievement and potential. Unlike others who become discouraged or lose focus, their lack of rapid promotions in the early years of their careers seems to have driven them to build a particularly robust foundation of competence, credibility, and confidence—inner resources on which they could rely in times of testing and adversity.

6

Breaking Through

Pathways to the Executive Suite

WHEN OUR MINORITY EXECUTIVES reached middle management, they still had another ten to fifteen years before they made it to the executive level. As people of color, many were pioneers in the management ranks of core business functions. How far they would be able to climb in the corporate hierarchy was yet to be determined. To understand their rise we conducted extensive analyses of their advancement and development in Career Stage 2, the period from middle management to upper-middle management, and 3, the period from upper-middle management to executive. We also compared these observations with those of their white executive counterparts and the plateaued minority middle managers in our study.

We have already noted that most of our minority executives reached middle management highly prepared for the challenges of their first job. Credibility, competence, and confidence developed in Career Stage 1 form the foundation for the success in the next two periods. Recall the case of Ben Richardson who was able to move his unit from the bottom of the performance rankings to number three in his region despite an unsupportive boss. Many of our minority executives had similar stories. Their success in these early–Stage 2 assignments paid dividends by allowing them to demonstrate their potential and extend their credibility within the larger organization. Without exception, minority executives vividly recalled these initial middle-management jobs as being critical to their learning and eventual success. In contrast, few of our white executives mentioned these early–Stage 2 jobs as particularly significant, perhaps because they did not regard them as "big breaks" or chances to prove their readiness in the same way that our minority executives did.

Two distinct patterns stand out in the data from Stages 2 and 3. In 80 percent of the cases, we found that our minority executives grew into their first executive assignments by the end of Career Stage 3 as a natural extension of their prior assignments. In these instances the individuals had amply demonstrated the competencies needed for the executive job and had established a strong track record in their organizations. Thus, they conformed to the criteria for promotion to executive on almost every dimension.

The careers of the other 20 percent took a different path. They were promoted at a faster than average rate through at least one of the two later periods (Stage 2 or Stage 3), which then culminated in a promotion to the executive suite that required a "leap of faith" on the part of the sponsor. While the individuals had demonstrated outstanding performance up to this point, they had yet to prove that they possessed all of the skills and experience considered necessary for their first executive jobs.

Despite the differences between these patterns, both groups shared a common set of developmental experiences that once again differentiated them from the plateaued minority managers. Not surprisingly, these experiences even further deepened, broadened, and extended the career foundation of competence, credibility, and self-confidence.

In the rest of this chapter, we'll look at the career stories of three minority executives. We'll then consider the pattern common to their careers. Finally, we'll contrast the careers of the minority executives and their two comparison groups, white executives and plateaued minority managers.

◢ SUCCESS PATTERN 1: GROWING INTO THE JOB

Clarence Williams's career, introduced in Chapter 5, is an excellent example of the pattern of growing into the job, as well as of the key developmental experiences of Stages 2 and 3. Recall that Williams spent almost nine years in Stage 1 before being promoted to his first middle management position. In spite of—or perhaps because of—this long Stage 1, he finished this period with a high level of competence and an especially deep grounding in engineering. By the end of this stage he had also established considerable credibility within Gant Electronics' development engineering function, as well as a solid base of self-confidence in his technical and managerial abilities as a senior design engineer.

Career Stage 2. Two years after deciding to move into management, Williams enrolled in a demanding executive MBA program with sponsorship from Gant. Midway through the first year of the MBA program he was promoted to project manager, his first middle management job and the start of Stage 2 of his career. His new assignment was evidence of his growing reputation within Gant's development engineering community. Williams was responsible for developing a new product vital to one of Gant's core lines of business. Eight of his sixteen-person team were seasoned engineers. Such an assignment was not normally given to novice managers, but Williams, while new to management, knew the Gant technical organization well. Nonetheless, Williams found it a real challenge to tackle both the new job and his MBA studies. His successful completion of both served to enhance his credibility and to bolster his self-confidence, both as a manager and as a technologist.

With his MBA complete and the design of the new component nearly finished, Williams began to look for an assignment that would draw more directly on his business training:

> It was in this transition period that I felt the influence of somebody that I would truly consider a mentor, Tom Lucy. Tom ran an organization that basically was a super-program management function. Now, I did not know Tom that well. When I first met him [six or seven years earlier] he was three levels above me in the organization.... Although I had ... little contact with him, he did remember me and knew who I was and knew a lot more about me than I had recognized. So after finishing the MBA, he gave me an offer to come work with him in the Engineering Program Office....
>
> I went from a pure development role to what was a combination of a business and technical one. I became the reliability program manager. I had to coordinate the reliability activities from engineering, manufacturing, and the field service organization for what was to become the Omega product family. It was a significant product for the corporation.... This job was a real stretch and a challenge. I was suddenly cast into this matrix management role where everything was in tension, there were no clear lines of authority.

Williams described this job as critical to his later success at Gant. First, it provided him with a much-needed broadening of perspective and an experience working with other parts of the company. Working in the matrix organization also required that he learn to lead without formal authority, and the job led to his developing a strong and powerful mentor in Lucy. Next, the assignment broadened his network of contacts and reputation beyond the narrow confines of development engineering. Finally, the assignment deepened his confidence in himself as a manager able to make decisions and succeed in Gant's fast-moving environment.

Before reaching upper-middle management, Williams had one more middle management job as an assistant engineering program manager. This assignment rounded out his business exposure because it included contact with sales and marketing as well as engineering, manufacturing, and service. In a short four-year period, Williams had created two successes which both broadened and deepened his management skills. Critically, his successes were built on the technical know-how he had developed in Stage 1. As a result, his rate of upward mobility increased substantially.

Career Stage 3. Williams began Stage 3 with the first of several promotions that would eventually lead to the executive suite. After briefly working on a task force specifying a new product, he was promoted to the challenging position of engineering program manager, which required leading the turnaround of a failing project. Again, Lucy was central to his receiving the assignment, though by this time Williams also had other supporters among the executive leadership at Gant. And again, he succeeded.

Williams had several more opportunities to broaden and deepen his expertise as a manager during this period. In particular, he assumed another turnaround assignment involving the development of a new product as a critical learning experience. He likened it to being asked to take over a start-up. Even though the project was eventually scuttled because of marketing problems, Williams had proved himself capable of stepping into a crisis situation and bringing order and productivity to it.

Another key opportunity came when Williams was assigned to work temporarily in strategic planning. He described it as a powerful broadening experience; in some respects this assignment marked the completion of his business education.

> I had to plan a replacement for one of our product families, one I had started working on as reliability program manager [the Omega]. I was working on the business implications and requirements of this product replacement which enabled me to get into an analysis of the competition, understanding the market segment, understanding some of the feature function benefits of the products, the economics of replacing one product with another and the life strategies. . . . That forced me to pull together a lot of things I had been exposed to in various program management assignments, but had never really focused on.
>
> The candidate replacement product was produced by our Japanese affiliate. So I had to work much closer with the Japanese than I had up to that point in my career. I had had some incidental contact with them over many years in engineering, but this was really getting in and negotiating with them and understanding some of their processes and business plans. I

was also introduced to a whole host of new people that I hadn't really worked with before.

It was during this time frame that Williams's mentor, Tom Lucy, left Gant. By now, however, Williams had broadened his networks sufficiently and shown himself to be a valuable performer and team player. Soon after, Williams began to express a desire to get back into product development when another big opportunity came his way.

I was getting antsy to get back on the line. I really enjoyed and I guess I liked the pressure of product development. I got a call from Jeff Loomis. I had never worked directly for him, but he knew of me through some of the relationships I had in engineering. He said he had a great opportunity and was really looking for someone to manage the systems engineering activity on this new product we were developing. It was a radically new product called the Nova Systems unit and it turned out to be the major product we sell today. The job meant working for Jeff in a dual role as systems engineering and program manager.

[The project] had been underway for about a year but hadn't gotten far. It was still in the concept stage at this point. It was truly a fascinating assignment, a lot of technology challenge, and the breadth of my responsibilities was quite large. In addition to the systems engineering part of the job, I had to develop a program structure to deliver this product. I became the implicit number two person in the organization. Whenever Jeff was out, I was the guy in charge.

The assignment came with a tremendous amount of challenge and external scrutiny. Asked about his learning from this assignment, Williams noted:

The learning was in terms of several things about myself, about how far I could really push the limits, where the limits really were. It was a whole new level of, let me say, political environment, for lack of a better term. The pressures were substantially different. We, the Nova System, were making a radical departure in terms of technology. We were essentially pushing on every boundary within the corporation. There were very few people outside of our team who really understood it. We were suddenly cast under the spotlight. We were doing something counter to the culture of the corporation. We forced changes in many areas of the corporation that were totally resistant to change. It was just growth and learning in so many areas.

An important by-product of this period was that Williams developed a sponsor in Jeff Loomis, a white executive in charge of the project. Loomis recognized Williams's skills and put them to maximum use in key management roles. Williams (and others we interviewed about him) believed that his work for Loomis was crucial to his eventually reaching the executive position he holds today.

As Loomis's number two person, Williams's responsibilities continued to grow, significantly. After several major additions to his responsibilities, Williams assumed Loomis's position as chief engineer of the Nova System, his first executive-level job. Two years later, while still reporting to Loomis, he was put in charge of the development of a major new product, the Omni System, and was subsequently responsible for its successful launch. "I believe the highest moment of my career was the day we launched Omni. That was years of hard work, and to see the recognition and the awe in people's faces was the highest moment."

Williams received two more executive promotions. The first brought him a vice president's title and resulted in the expansion of his duties as chief engineer to include oversight of other important development projects. Following a major reorganization, he was chosen to run one of Gant's business units and was promoted to vice president and general manager, a coveted position with profit-and-loss responsibility.

When reflecting on the factors that accounted for his success, Williams initially listed the jobs that provided him with important opportunities in Stages 2 and 3 of his career. Chief among these was the first assignment offered by Tom Lucy to be a reliability manager and the five-year period working for Jeff Loomis. Williams's comments also highlighted the importance of the foundation he had built in Stage 1: "In the early days, I was able to move because of my track record of success. I got assignments because I was able to demonstrate achievement and get results. A lot of it was luck. I had a senior engineer who wanted to develop me so he could do other things."

Regarding race, Williams had the following reflections:

I believe there are some racial barriers for blacks and people of color in general. They are the same in the outside world. Fortunately, we have the umbrella of a very progressive corporation. People cannot do blatantly racist things here and get away with it. So, unlike some other companies where those things are happening, things were better here.

Clarence Williams's rise illustrates the dominant pattern of minority succession to the executive level, one in which a steady progression of jobs provides the cumulative experience and positioning through which they grow into an executive assignment.

This pattern involves an evolutionary broadening and deepening of managerial skills and exposure during Stage 2 that builds on the foundation established earlier. Characteristically there is at least one important mentor who provides opportunities and developmental experiences. We see a similar progression in Stage 3, with at least one intentionally broadening assignment involving a planning or task-force assignment which is typically followed by a series of increasingly responsible (but incremental) jobs in high-stakes assignments. This progression is invariably "tracked" and often facilitated by one or more high-level executive sponsors, including the individual's immediate boss.

Variation of Growing into the Job Pattern

Sometimes promotions to high-visibility upper-middle management jobs in Stage 2 or Stage 3 came about because the individuals took the initiative to get others to recognize their track record and potential for succeeding in a high-profile job. Often they were not even being considered as potential candidates until they were able to persuade others to give them the opportunity. In these cases, the three personal resources—the individual's credibility in the organization, their demonstrated competence, and their self-confidence—came together at a critical juncture and decisively changed the trajectory of their careers.

José Gonzalez, a Hispanic American executive at Gant, is an excellent illustration. In Stages 1 and 2, he moved at a moderate but steady pace. Along the way he amassed an impressive track record of performance in planning and finance, and acquired several mentors and sponsors. After working on the planning phase of a major development project, he asked to be put in charge of its start-up operation. Others had not thought of him as a candidate, but once he put his name up for discussion, any objections raised were satisfactorily answered, and he won the assignment. Gonzalez performed well in the job. As a result, he enhanced his reputation and gained new supporters higher up in the organization. This move ultimately put Gonzalez in line to become vice president and general manager of a related business unit. Without this opportunity, he most likely would have remained a functional manager with a much smaller possibility of making it to the executive level.

◢ Success Pattern 2: Leap-of-Faith Promotions to the Executive Suite

A small group of minority executives we studied diverged in their pattern of promotion to the executive level. Instead of growing into their executive jobs through a sustained sequence of preparatory assignments like Clarence Williams, their first executive-level promotion entailed a leap of faith on the part of their managers. The career of Nydia Padilla, a Hispanic American executive at Acme Industries, illustrates the "leap-of-faith" pattern.

When we interviewed Padilla, she had just finished her first year as an executive at Acme Industries. She was vice president and general manager of a division with 3,800 employees, including 600 management and professional personnel and 10 direct reports. She had launched her career at Acme seventeen years before, while working as an hourly employee to put herself through college at night.

Padilla stayed on at Acme after receiving her degree, eventually becoming a manager in a manufacturing division. Like many minority executives, Padilla had a long Stage 1 as an entry-level manager (9 years compared to the 3.6-year average at Acme). She worked in almost every frontline supervisory post in her plant before taking a lateral move to become a supervisor in human resources (HR). Padilla then worked her way up to division employment manager, thus moving into middle management.

Career Stage 2. Padilla recalled her first Stage 2 assignment as an exciting time:

> *The employment manager's job was a lot of responsibility, but I was not apprehensive. It just sharpened my skills. I became a lot more conscious of my conduct and appearance, because now I was representing the company at a higher level. I enjoyed this position very much. A few months after my promotion, my boss was assigned to a special project for six months. I became the acting head of HR. So for six months, I worked directly for the division general manager, Bill Kennedy. He became my strongest mentor in terms of level in the company. I respect him highly. I accompanied him to high level meetings and observed. I was able to sit and listen, watch how he managed people. I began to make a list of do's and don'ts. I think that's what helped me develop my management style—observing what worked well, the reactions, body language after a particular executive would say something. Through mere observation, I learned a lot.*

Padilla performed well both as employment manager and as acting department head. She attributed this success to her long experience doing the jobs of those she was supervising. As acting head of HR she was exposed to highly sensitive personnel matters involving middle and upper-middle managers.

Padilla was in this position only a year before she made an important move out of HR and into one of the division's key distribution centers. Her mentor, Bill Kennedy, advised her that it would be good for her to spend some time running an operations facility if she really wanted to make a mark at the company. Kennedy remembered something that Padilla had previously told him, "I'll take however many assignments you give me, but I want to make a contribution. I don't want to be just a statistic."

Padilla found that being a unit manager back in operations involved a steep learning curve. Padilla emphasized to us the stretch in skills the job required of her. The VP, Bill Kennedy, provided a complementary view, focusing on the challenge of the assignment itself:

> *We put her into a distribution center, where we had another high-potential manager. We had someone talk to the other person about Nydia coming in. This manager came across that "oh, this would not be any problem," but as*

it turned out, the person really didn't take well to this whole thing and was not cooperative in the sense of helping Nydia assimilate into this job. The other manager was very highly regarded by the mostly male population at that facility. As it turned out, we put Nydia in a [difficult] situation where, looking back, I would not do it again, but Nydia was able to run the facility and get people on her side in spite of the other person's [lack of cooperation].

She made some mistakes, because she did not have the background you need for that kind of job, and she didn't have the support of the key supervisor in the center. However, she was able to learn from the experience, fix whatever the mistake caused, and at the same time, not create an impression that she didn't know what she was doing. Overall I thought it was a very good experience and a very good test.

Kennedy elaborated on the impression Padilla's handling of the assignment had made on him and other senior managers:

I thought that succeeding at the assignment was a great feather in her cap because after we saw what was happening, our first reaction was we had made a mistake, maybe we better fix it. But that, of course, would have been really harmful to her self-confidence. I think that she would have felt that we didn't have confidence in her. She did well. It was like that in most of the jobs she did. In Nydia's case, she was probably being asked to grow more quickly than perhaps a male would because at the time we were still trying to promote minority females and get to a position where the workforce and the management team were representative of the population.

Padilla's stint in the operations job was short. Just as she settled in to make a long-term go at running the unit, she received an offer to go to a different division as its director of HR. The promotion came as a surprise since little more than two years had passed since Nydia had reached middle management. Her career was moving much faster than it had earlier, faster than the norm for Stage 2 managers at Acme.

Like her mentor, Kennedy, Padilla believed that her development was influenced by the company's genuine commitment to promote minorities and women, especially on the part of its leadership. For her, Kennedy embodied this commitment. Her parting comments as she left for her new position communicated her deep respect and gratitude for her mentor.

> *[They] set up a farewell type of reception for me, and quite a few division management people attended. I had written my ... farewell speech. Bill kind of teased me, because he said "Nydia's never lost for words." And I made mention of how I was a true example of the company's philosophy of affirmative action. If they needed an example, I was a prime example of that. So I think Bill appreciated hearing that because it was an extension of his practices, his commitment.*

Padilla was quick to point out then as she did several times in the interview that she received no "preferential treatment on the job." Like almost all of the interviewees at Acme, she felt she had been treated and judged on the same meritocratic basis as others.

Career Stage 3. Padilla moved to Texas to assume her new role as head of HR for a small division. The promotion represented a big stretch and a vote of confidence. Padilla was both pleased and challenged by the job. Frequent turnover in general managers had contributed to a high incidence of personnel problems, specifically to a heavy backlog of unsettled EEO complaints. Turnover at the division VP level continued during her stint, with several general managers coming and going in less than three years. With an already tense local labor market, personnel problems threatened to undercut the division's ability to increase production and revenue. Padilla's role, therefore, was critical to the performance of the general managers as individuals and to the division as a whole. With this role, Padilla gained a strategic perspective of the operation of a division. She also coached the division's senior management team on how to handle difficult personnel issues and avoid crises in the future.

Padilla also took on the role of internal change agent as part of her job. Over the preceding several years, Acme had begun to change its culture, placing more value on HR issues such as workforce diversity and empowerment, initiatives that the division's managers had actively resisted. Padilla began to find ways to introduce these changes to her new division, both adapting her own actions and influencing the division's norms and attitudes.

After two-and-a-half years, Padilla was reassigned to one of Acme's largest divisions, headquartered in Michigan, as the division's director of HR. This was nominally a lateral move, but with a huge expansion of responsibility and staff. Here she became much more involved in working with line managers and in changing personnel practices. Again, she was successful in helping the division change its culture and in significantly reducing a severe turnover problem.

During this period Padilla continued to build a reputation for dealing well with difficult situations. Her division VP asked her to consider a move back to operations. His successor, Jonathan Logan, also approached her with the idea. Padilla remembered both the challenge and the fun of her earlier stint as manager of a distribution center and looked forward to tackling another stretch opportunity.

Padilla was offered an upper-middle management position as head of a medium-sized operations group with several production managers reporting to her. Over the course of her two years there, Logan became both a mentor and sponsor, sharing his wealth of experience while giving her detailed coaching and feedback on her progress. After her initial success in running this medium-sized operation, he put her in charge of one of the division's most complex manufacturing and distribution operations. Once again, she grew into the responsibility and performed exceedingly well.

Two years later, to her surprise, Padilla was promoted to vice president and general manager of a medium-sized division headquartered in the Northwest. It was clear to her that this was largely due to Logan's support, but by this time she had established an impressive track record in four upper-middle management assignments, including two in production. She also had other supporters in the corporation, including the group VP to whom Logan reported. The combination of her nontraditional background and the short time she had spent in operations made her appointment stand out. Padilla noted, "By any standard this is a key position in the company and I am sure many people were surprised to see a female, and someone of my temperament and race, achieve it in the time frame that I did."

Asked what factors influenced her success, especially as the only woman of color at divisional general manager level, she replied:

Actually I thought to get this position, you would have to spend a lot of years in operations, and all the staff functions would be just an enhancement. I've achieved the reverse. But I think I was able to do that because the company had enough confidence in my ability [to take a risk on me]. There's

*a lot of people that think I got this job because they want females and His-
panics. I can argue with them, but I don't because I know what I did to get to
this point: great work ethic, high commitment, the desire to do well, and not
being complacent but consistently aspiring to do better.*

She mentioned the mentoring she had received from Kennedy and
Logan as a critical factor in her success and elaborated on the importance of having focus and the persistence to deal with adversity:

*If things don't seem to go well, I learned very early on that you don't retract,
you don't withdraw. You just keep plugging away. Regardless of how bad it
looks out there, you have to give the appearance that it's no big thing. It can
be worse. So besides the internal fortitude, there is a tolerance level that you
have to have [to withstand] the heat of battle one month after another, time
and time again.*

That Padilla would end up successfully running the largest manufacturing operation in one of Acme's largest divisions might have been
unimaginable to her colleagues at the time she became a middle manager. Her career would not have been possible without the support,
on-the-job coaching, and career advice of her two very capable mentors. She also had the support of key executives at the corporate level
who acted on Kennedy's and Logan's recommendations. Because of
Padilla's outstanding performance, especially in earlier stretch assignments, her superiors believed she could handle a line executive assignment, despite her limited management experience in production. Not
surprisingly, Padilla succeeded once again and is now managing an
even larger operation than she was when we talked with her.

Finally, Padilla's story reveals an important characteristic common
to those who received leap-of-faith promotions; namely, that most
were quite junior when they were promoted, in both age and seniority.
A generational effect seems to be at work here. Those minorities who
started their careers after 1974 when the three companies were well
along in their efforts to achieve diversity may have benefited from the
results of their companies' early efforts to integrate their workforce
and management. By the time they reached middle management, there
were already minorities in positions of power who had established

credibility and could act as role models and mentors. With few exceptions, minorities such as Padilla who received these leap-of-faith promotions to the executive level got their break after a number of other minorities had already paved the way, including many in our study. The trail had already been blazed, making it easier for people like Jonathan Logan to take risks and offer such promotions to a next generation of potential minority executives.

◢ CAREER STAGE 2 AND 3 DEVELOPMENTAL EXPERIENCES

The stories of Clarence Williams, José Gonzalez, and Nydia Padilla exemplify a pattern: They all broadened and deepened the career foundations they had laid in Stage 1 and then were able to accelerate their careers in Stage 2 by exploiting their hard-won competence, credibility, and self-confidence. Soon they found themselves in active competition for executive assignments.

Career Stage 2: Breaking Away

Stage 2 (middle management to upper-middle management) is where the career trajectories of most minority executives turn sharply upward. Clarence Williams's and Nydia Padilla's careers are both characteristic of the predominant pattern: moving slowly in Stage 1 while acquiring a deep grounding in a core functional area and then accelerating in Stage 2 in ways that exploit the competencies, self-confidence, and credibility gained in Stage 1.

Deepening Their Functional Knowledge. Stage 2 is characterized by several key developmental experiences. First, minority executives continued to deepen their functional knowledge. The positions they assumed most often required applying existing skills to complex situations in addition to leading others. Here they benefited from their deep grounding in the functional or technical aspects of their job. Much of their ability to influence subordinates who might otherwise be resistant came from their personal connections with them and their sheer technical or functional competence. Clarence Williams's case illustrates how his technical skills and knowledge proved invaluable in his initial middle management assignments.

Developing Deeper Managerial Skills and Judgment. The second developmental experience in this period is the acquisition and development of deeper managerial skills and judgment. This includes learning the interpersonal skills needed to manage subordinates, supervisors, and peers. They had to learn how to work through others, provide leadership, and influence others without authority. In essence, they were expanding their set of managerial competencies while still relying heavily on the functional or technical grounding they had acquired in Stage 1—as Padilla did while serving as acting head of HR.

Continuing to Build a Track Record of Success. The third characteristic of this period is that minority executives continued to build a solid track record by providing successful results. Clarence Williams, for example, was successful in each assignment during Stage 2. Each assignment allowed him to see it through to a conclusion that would allow others to affix praise or blame to him. This series of assignments provided him the opportunity to establish credibility within the larger organization and to experience a growing sense of mastery, which is an essential part of continuing to build one's self-confidence.

Extending the Network of Relationships. Finally, Stage 2 is a period of building the network of relationships beyond the boundaries of the original functional area(s) in which the person began their career during Stage 1. This process is facilitated by the opportunity to work in key roles that require spanning organizational boundaries and interacting with managers and superiors in other parts of the company. Williams had several assignments during this period that allowed him to work with other areas of the corporation, gaining an understanding of how they operated and developing working relationships with key people in other functions.

A critical element in the expansion of their network was the acquisition and help of mentors and powerful sponsors. By the end of Stage 2, all of our minority executives had at least one mentor relationship with an influential executive. At this point, many were highly regarded by several executives who had acted to support their careers during this stage or earlier; for example, Nydia Padilla's career was boosted by Bill Kennedy and other more senior executives during this stage.

Career Stage 3: Breaking Through

Stage 3 (the climb from upper management to the executive level) is a period of preparing for and proving executive potential. Three developmental experiences are critical to the deepening of the executive's competence as well as the enhancement of credibility in the greater corporate context.

Broadening the Experience Base. The opportunity to broaden beyond an original functional background is a key developmental experience in Stage 3. In some cases this process had already begun in some form in Stage 2, but it is critical that it happens no later than Stage 3. Here, people take on issues specific to working across functional boundaries and learn to think and act more strategically and politically. Often this exposure is augmented by a task-force or provisional assignment in strategic planning or is the result of a function change. We see examples of this functional broadening in Williams's task-force and planning assignments.

Achieving High-Consequence Successes. The second critical factor in this period is the need for highly visible successes. Clarence Williams played a critical role in the development and launch of a product line that helped to redefine Gant's position in the marketplace. It is important that these successes be related to the company's critical strategic contingency, as this influences one's credibility in the larger corporate context. Many upper-middle managers, both white and minority, continue to build track records of performance during Stage 3, so that at this level, there are many managers with strong performance records. A promotion to executive level often requires one or more widely visible and high-impact achievements which serve to distinguish the individual from the many other qualified candidates.

Gaining the Support of Important Sponsors. The third critical element of Stage 3 is the maintenance and development of highly placed mentors and sponsors. The individual's relationship with the executive boss becomes crucial. For each minority executive we studied, the immediate executive boss played a central role in creating the opportunity, as did Jonathan Logan for Nydia Padilla.

This pattern of preparation and opportunities in Stages 2 and 3 brought each minority executive to the point of an executive-level job candidacy. By this time, the minority executive had established a track record of success, attracted high-level sponsorship, and developed a network of supporters. Underlying and driving this process was the continuing development of competence, credibility, and confidence.

◢ A CONTRAST WITH WHITE EXECUTIVES

We'll begin contrasting the career experiences of minority and white executives by exposing a feature they share—namely, that their career experiences begin to converge in Stages 2 and 3, becoming increasingly similar in their experiences, assignments, and pace of advancement. The most obvious illustration of this is the speed with which these two groups progressed through Stages 2 and 3. Figures 6-1, 6-2, and 6-3 document for each company the average number of years it took to rise from the first middle management job to upper-middle management (Stage 2), and then upper-middle management to the executive level (Stage 3). Only at Advanced did a significant advantage still accrue to white executives. Whites at Advanced reached the executive level almost six years ahead of minorities. But even at Advanced, the pace of minority executives picks up significantly in these later stages, with minorities taking, on average, only six months or more than whites in Stage 3.

At Acme, the advantage actually accrues to minority executives in Stages 2 and 3. The result is that the Stage 1 differences are eliminated, and minorities and whites make it to executive level at about the same time. Examination of the larger data set from Acme on 554 minority and white executives and managers shows a similar pattern. The Gant data also follows this pattern. Minority executives move almost as fast as white executives in Stage 2 and are promoted to executive level

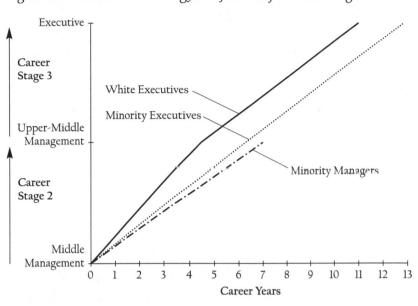

Figure 6-1   Advanced Technology: Trajectories for Career Stages 2 and 3

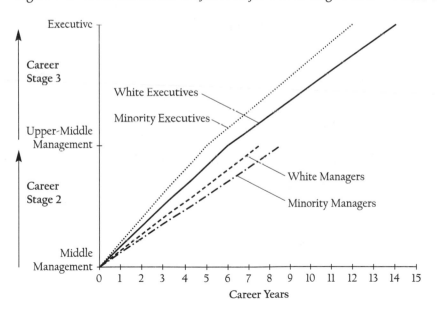

Figure 6-2   Acme Industries: Trajectories for Career Stages 2 and 3

slightly slower than whites. The net result is that minorities reach the executive level three years behind their white counterparts, calculated from the average start of their careers.

An important lesson of Chapter 5 is that rates of movement alone do not tell the entire story. In terms of their content and form, the Stage 2 experiences of the minority and white executives were in most respects comparable. However, there were several notable differences. Compared to minority executives, white executives in Stage 2 were

- half as likely to change functions;
- half as likely to take on special projects or task-force assignments;
- one-third as likely to take a turnaround assignment;
- almost half as likely to change locations; and
- one-fourth as likely to report a big success.

Along some dimensions these differences are a reversal of what occurred in Stage 1, when white executives had markedly more turnaround and task-force assignments than did minority executives.

Figure 6-3   Gant Electronics: Trajectories for Career Stages 2 and 3

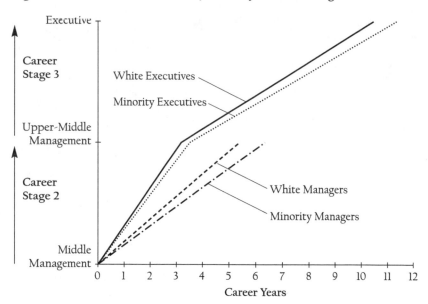

What these differences highlight is the "breaking away" pattern of minority executives in Stage 2: strong success in their initial Stage 2 assignment followed by a series of increasingly greater challenges in which the minority executives prove themselves. The differences reveal the relative acceleration of activities undertaken by minority executives in Stage 2 as compared to the slower pace and stability of their Stage 1. In many respects these differences reflect the "catching up" that occurs in this stage.

Another interesting area of comparison is the formation of important developmental relationships with mentors and sponsors. Our data indicate that the two groups are similar in the overall average number of developmental relationships they reported for Stage 2. The one major difference between them is that minority executives were more likely than white executives to report having had powerful corporate-level executives as sponsors and mentors during this period. In reviewing their careers, minority executives commonly described a senior person who had been watching their progress without their full awareness.

By Stage 3, the period of movement from upper-middle management to the executive level, minority and white executives have comparable experiences. Indeed, they have even fewer differences than in Stage 2. With regard to developmental relationships, the executive groups exhibited similar patterns. Clearly, it was impossible to make it to the executive level, regardless of race, without sponsorship from an immediate boss and at least one other key sponsor or mentor in Stage 3. As was the case in Stage 2, minority executives tended to have a higher proportion of their developmental relationships with senior corporate executives than did white executives.

Why did this pattern appear in all three companies? One explanation is that senior corporate officers, who would not ordinarily be involved in tracking middle and upper-middle level managers, made it a point to do so for people of color because of their company's commitment to identifying and developing minorities. A complementary explanation is that even in companies as enlightened as these, it is not possible for people of color to make it to the executive level unless they have the added support of very senior officers. We will discuss in Chapter 8 the explicit work the companies did to ensure that talented minorities were considered for key upper-management and executive jobs.

As was the case with minority executives, the dominant path to the executive level for white executives was to "grow into" the executive job. In comparison to minorities, however, white executives were somewhat more likely (30 percent compared to 20 percent) to receive leap-of-faith promotions. The same underlying pattern of calculated-risk promotions applied to whites who received leap-of-faith promotions as did to minorities. Again, the only difference is that whites did not require the same level of sponsorship from senior executives as minorities did in order to receive such promotions.

By the end of Stage 3, however, the experiences, track records, and rates of advancement were largely similar for white and minority executives. Table 6-1 summarizes the principal similarities and differences between minority and white executives in Stages 2 and 3.

A Contrast with Plateaued Minority Managers

You will recall from the tournament discussion in Chapter 3 that minority executives and plateaued minority managers moved at simi-

Table 6-1   Comparison of Minority and White Executives' Career Experiences in Stages 2 and 3

Career Stage	Similarities	Differences

Stage 2 Middle management to upper-middle management	• Pattern of stretch assignments
	• Pace of advancement
	• Number of developmental relationships with mentors, sponsors
		• Minority executives more likely to have:
		    Change in function
		    Task force or special project
		    Turnaround assignment
		    Location change
		    Major success
		    More senior executives as mentors or sponsors

Stage 3 Upper-middle management to executive	• Pattern of assignments • Exposure to broadening and strategic assignments • Number of mentors and sponsors	• Minority executives more likely to have: More senior executives as mentors or sponsors

lar paces in Stage 1. Stage 1 differentiation lies in the content and structure of their career experiences, not in their speed.

Career Stage 2

Beginning in Stage 2, the differentiation between plateaued minority managers and executives becomes starker. Stage 2 is clearly the takeoff point for minority executives. As in Stage 1, minority executives receive fewer promotions on average during Stage 2, but they reach upper-middle management in less time than minority managers. The difference is that minority executives' promotions are bigger and more significant.

A second important difference between plateaued minority managers and minority executives is that the Stage 2 assignment patterns of minority managers continue to be more fragmented and unfocused. As was the case in Stage 1, minority managers report more job changes along almost all dimensions. Compared to minority executives, minority managers were significantly more likely to experience

- a departmental change,
- a function change,
- a change from a line to a staff job,
- a location change,
- turnaround assignments, and
- promotions (although they were less significant than the minority executives' promotions).

One might infer from these data that movement on its own is bad, but, in fact, minority executives were actually much more mobile on each of these dimensions in Stage 2 than they were in Stage 1. But such Stage 2 movement almost always led to greater breadth, challenge, and extension of credibility and reputation. While minority managers received more promotions, the promotions tended to be small in terms of increased responsibility. Sometimes the promotion came with a move from a line management job to a staff job, resulting in no real increase in management authority or experience. Case by case, assignment patterns of minority executives are markedly less fragmented and discontinuous than those of minority managers, suggesting that while some change is fine, too much change is not. The pattern we see in Stage 2 for minority managers may be representative of problems that began in Stage 1.

The greater frequency of turnaround experiences for minority managers in Stage 2 is also interesting. Minority managers tended to serve in "fix it" roles and take over a failing area. The problem was that these turnarounds involved the same kind of challenges over and over without opportunity for acquiring new skills. Those minority managers who fell into this pattern had little idea that they were becoming boxed into a role that would ultimately limit them, but instead expected career rewards would follow what they understood was good performance. Lack of good mentoring and counsel from their superiors certainly contributed to their incomplete understanding of their career progress. In many instances, getting stuck in a rut reflected the manager's inability to grow beyond the skill set developed in Stage 1.

The case of Carlos Amado, an upper-middle manager at Acme, is a good illustration. By the end of Stage 1, Amado had established a deep grounding in manufacturing and a reputation for taking problem units and making them the best in their division. He did this by sheer dint of his technical competence and with the brunt of his powerful personality and hands-on style. This approach worked exceedingly well in early career and resulted in his attaining a high degree of credibility as well as great confidence in his ability to deal with tough situations.

These abilities continued to be useful to Amado as a middle manager early in Stage 2. However, although he accomplished several turnarounds in this period, he failed to develop other operational skills such as delegating, developing his supervisors, and using division support staff effectively. He was seen as being effective as long as he was in situations that allowed face-to-face contact, and thus his assignments began to take on a routine fix-it quality. After being passed over several times, he was finally promoted by a highly supportive boss to upper-middle management, where he entered a long period of difficulty and stagnation, leading to increasing frustration, disappointment, and loss of self-confidence. His "turnaround" formula failed at this level of the organization because he had not acquired the skills needed to manage staff indirectly. The operation was now too big with too many interdependencies. Amado received the lowest performance evaluation of his career during this period. Only when a divisional VP began to work closely with him and coach him did his performance improve. But by then, he had already plateaued.

Amado's story stands in sharp contrast to Nydia Padilla's fast takeoff in Stages 2 and 3, especially in her ability to continually develop new competencies, learn from mistakes, and gain high-quality coaching and mentoring.

Career Stage 3

By this stage, it is clear that the executives are in the ascent and the minority managers have plateaued. Minority managers are given no turnaround or stretch assignments in this period. Stretch and turnaround assignments at this level are usually strategic or involve a major new corporate initiative. Success can make careers, and failure can easily break them. Compared to minority executives, minority managers in Stage 3 report fewer

- assignments of additional responsibility,
- start-up assignments,
- promotions, and
- department changes.

Minority managers report more

- moves from a line to a staff job,
- lateral moves,
- major career setbacks, and
- assignments to task forces or special projects.

A comparison of the developmental relationships of these two groups is revealing. Nine of thirteen minority managers developed no new developmental relationships in Stage 3. They essentially ceased to expand their network of senior-level supporters. Several also report developing fairly powerful detractors in this period. In comparison, minority executives report developing at least two new relationships, on average, with executive-level individuals. Only one minority executive reported a major detractor in this period, but this was offset by the development of several very senior-level sponsors.

Compared to minority executives, plateaued managers seem deficient in broadening their network of supporters. Several found themselves lost when a major mentor left the organization or was unable to continue to affect their career positively. Their lack of other relationships left them vulnerable to what Monica Higgins and Nitin Nohria have coined the "side-kick effect," in which early attachment to a significant mentor actually undermines one's ability to develop later sponsors and to be successful in the organization.[1]

Rushton Barnes, an African American manager at Gant, is a prime example of the liabilities associated with not expanding one's network of relationships. After a highly successful rise through middle management into a key upper-middle level general management job, his career began to derail when his powerful, but sole, sponsor left the company. At the behest of his new VP, he took a job running a troubled unit, which he was led to believe would be a temporary assignment. When it became evident that the new VP wanted him to remain and turn the organization around, he felt betrayed and, in a pique of anger, took a lateral transfer to a less central part of the company, earning the enmity of the VP and several other highly placed executives. At the time of the study, he had been platcaued for thirteen years. In retrospect, he is convinced that had he had a mentor or sponsor in place, he would have been advised not to act rashly or to leave the core part of the business.

The racial diversity of the networks also mattered, especially for African Americans. By the end of Stage 2, minority executives had other minorities in networks that often extended across the company, giving them access to information that might not otherwise have been available to them. At Gant Electronics, these contacts were facilitated by the existence of a formalized African American employees group, the focus of which was peer mentoring, information exchange, and advocacy within the corporation. At Acme Industries, these relationships tended to be opportunistic, as people of color ran into each other in the normal course of business or sought out younger managers whom they counseled or mentored. At Advanced Technology, this networking was facilitated by the fact that many of the minorities in the company either had worked in or had contacts with one of two inner-city manufacturing sites. As individuals began to take positions outside of these plants, a natural and far-flung network developed. The company's diversity efforts also emphasized the need for dialogue and exploration of differences. Minority employees came to know each other and whites in these "dialogue groups." These experiences formed the basis for many long-term relationships.

A telling difference between our sample's African American executives and plateaued African American managers is that the latter tended to have less diverse networks. They either relied almost exclusively on members of their own ethnic group for key developmental support or they had only whites for such support. By contrast, those who reached the executive level, especially the most successful among them, built genuine, personal long-term relations with both whites and other African Americans.[2]

Two other factors were also likely to contribute to derailment or plateauing in Stage 3. One is the continued pattern of rapid movement or instability in Stage 2 that began in Stage 1. The individuals never firmly root themselves in a functional specialty or become identified with consistent results. In some instances, this is due to restlessness. Poor advice from mentors and bosses regarding career options is also a problem.

Table 6-2 summarizes the major differences between the minority executives and the minority managers. Our comparative data clearly demonstrate that by the time most plateaued minority managers reached upper-middle management, they were no longer on the executive track. In many instances, the individual never recovered from the lack of deep grounding and strong foundation that the minority executives acquired in Stage 1. Frequently, because the individuals had not actually failed in their jobs, they had no inkling of this deficiency. By the time individuals reach Stage 3, most are not viewed as having executive potential. Several of our plateaued minorities were struggling with reversing this perception when we interviewed them. They felt something was missing, but were not sure what the key was.

In summary, it is during Stages 2 and 3 that the careers of minority executives become clearly differentiated from those of plateaued minority managers, and it is during Stage 3 that the career trajectories and experiences of minority and white executives finally converge. They become increasingly similar in assignment patterns, developmental experiences, and types of mentoring relationships. Both of these patterns define the experience of "breaking through"—through the glass ceiling and into the executive suite. In the following chapter, we will look at the organizational contexts that supported these minority executives' advancement and development.

Table 6-2   Comparison of Minority Executives and Plateaued Minority Managers' Career Experiences in Stages 2 and 3

Career Stage	Similarities	Differences
Stage 2 Middle management to upper-middle management	Both continue to have developmental relationships with mentors or sponsors	Minority managers are more likely to experience less continuity and more changes in: • Department • Function • Line-to-staff • Location Minority managers experience more: • "Fix-it" assignments • Within-level promotions • Line-to-staff changes Minority executives experience more: • Developmental relationships with mentors and sponsors and with more senior people
Stage 3 Upper-middle management to executive	Few, if any, similarities in assignment successes or developmental experiences	Minority managers have fewer: • Assignments of additional responsibility • Start-up assignments • Promotions • Department changes Minority managers report more: • Line-to-staff changes • Lateral moves • Major career setbacks • Assignments to special projects or task forces Minority executives have more: • Extensive networks of supporters • Same-race and other minorities in their networks • Mentors and sponsors Minority executives have more: • High-consequence successes • Stretch assignments • Strategic and broadening assignments

ENABLING MINORITY ADVANCEMENT

7

Diversity Strategy

Three Approaches to
Enabling Minority Advancement

THE PREVIOUS THREE CHAPTERS have described the process of personal and professional development and advancement that characterized the experience of minority executives in our study. However, the making of minority executives does not depend only on individual development. Organizational context played a major role in creating the conditions and opportunities for these executives to reach the executive level. Just as these individuals labored to penetrate the barriers of race, their companies were working to diminish those same barriers. In essence, the making of minority executives and the creating of racial diversity were as much about organizational change and transformation as about personal resources and effort.

Chapter 2 described the actions taken by these companies during the three decades prior to this study and how they dealt with the challenges of equal opportunity, affirmative action, the "bottom line" rationale for diversity, and, very important, the competitive challenges all three faced during the 1980s. Table 7-1 provides a summary of their major actions during the three decades as reported in Chapter 2.

What is clear from this chronology is that by 1990 all three companies had reemerged as dominant leaders in their markets while also integrating their management and executive ranks. By 1990, each of the three companies had also developed a distinct approach to managing diversity that had enabled these outcomes.

In trying to understand their success in achieving this diversity, three aspects of their strategies stand out. The first is that the approaches they took were quite different from each other. Acme Industries used what is generally known as an assimilationist approach; Advanced Technology implemented a pluralist approach; and Gant Electronics took a hybrid of these two approaches, which we have labeled "intergroup negotiation." Second, despite the great differences in their approaches (which we will describe shortly) each was successful in creating contexts conducive to the development and advancement of minorities. This suggests that there is more than a single approach or paradigm that can be effective, provided it is appropriate to the circumstances and is well implemented. Third, each company developed an approach that was aligned with the grain of its corporate culture and core values, which enhanced the diversity initiative's effectiveness and implementation.

This chapter will describe in some depth the nature of each of these approaches, their underlying paradigms, and how each of their diversity strategies evolved over time. The chapter will conclude with a discussion of the change process implied by each strategy and of the conditions necessary for them to work. Chapter 8 will discuss explicitly the role of aligning diversity strategy with corporate culture in bringing about change.

◢ THE ROLE OF CONTEXT

To understand the critical role of the organizational context, we first identified what the managers and executives in our study saw

Table 7-1 Evolution of Company Diversity Efforts

	Acme Industries	Gant Electronics	Advanced Technology
1960s From civil rights to the workplace	• Rapid growth in revenues • Recruit racial minorities into *production and distribution* • "Change complexion of workforce"	• Rapid growth in revenues • CEO commits publicly to hiring more minorities • Recruit racial minorities into *production, sales, and service*	• Rapid growth in revenues • CEO commits company to building plants in inner-city areas • Recruit minorities into *manufacturing, sales, and service*
1970s Affirmative action and EEO	• Rapid growth in revenues • Major effort to recruit minorities into professional and supervisory jobs mainly in *production and distribution* • CEO and COO hire new VP of HR to develop programs to open professional and management jobs to minorities	• *Very rapid growth in revenues* • Major effort to recruit minorities into professional and supervisory jobs mainly in *sales and service* • Top management recognizes and begins meeting with representatives of minority employees	• *Very rapid growth in revenues* • Enlists search firm to identify minorities for *manufacturing and engineering* • Builds three plants in inner cities; recruits minority management personnel
1980s Criticism of and retreat from affirmative action as policy; Diversity: bottom-line rhetoric	• Fierce competition in high-margin segments; competition on delivery and cost • Growth rate levels off • Top management initiates changes *and* culture change • CEO says diversity key aspect of culture change • Major effort at identifying and developing minority executives • By 1990s reestablished as industry leader	• Besieged by foreign competition; loss of market share • Major turnaround in 1980s • CEO touts minority coalition groups as model of high-involvement groups • African American chosen to turn around major operating group • Major effort at identifying and developing minority executives • By 1990s, Gant's turnaround succeeds; reestablished as worldwide industry leader	• One of three firms to survive major shakeout in industry by 1990s • Engages consultants to focus on problems of "minority" plants, leads to: Diversity/performance initiatives Creation of "dialogue groups" • Dialogue groups spread through company • Major efforts to identify and promote minority executives

as significant in their organization's ability to develop a cadre of minority managers and executives. We then interviewed a broader group of individuals with important perspectives on each company's efforts to promote racial diversity. We were also aided by the written materials developed by consultants and others who have examined these corporations' diversity efforts.[1]

Initially, we thought that the success of these companies in enabling minority advancement might lie in a few specific programs or actions on the part of corporate leaders. Instead we discovered that each company had developed its own systematic approach to changing its culture of race relations and to creating contexts that were conducive to minority achievement.

◢ DIVERSITY STRATEGIES

By the late 1970s, each company had begun to move beyond a simple focus on numbers to develop a distinct approach to advancing diversity. These diversity strategies were not well articulated in the beginning, but emerged as the central promoters of these efforts began to find ways to implement their vision of equal opportunity and racial diversity, all within their organization's essential operating principles and values.

In the evolution of their strategies, each company's approach was implicitly based on a different model of diversity. Sociologists have developed two distinct models: assimilationism and pluralism.[2] *Assimilationism* proposes that discriminating behavior can best be eliminated by diminishing the salience of race and ethnicity. The assimilationist approach is based on sociologists' observations of how European immigrants assimilated into North American culture. Under the assimilationist model, people shed their ethnic or racial identity over time and assimilate fully into the dominant culture. Some refer to assimilationism as a "color-blind" approach.[3] We discovered that Acme's diversity strategy shared many characteristics of this approach.

In sharp contrast to Acme, Advanced Technology's diversity strategy embodied many of the basic tenets of *pluralism*, which maintains that it is unnecessary and even undesirable to abandon racial or ethnic identity in order to integrate. Pluralism is based on the premise that different identities actually enrich a society or institution. The belief is that if salient group identities are suppressed or devalued, people become resentful and alienated. The pluralist task, then, is to create a context in which both shared and unique characteristics can be recognized and valued. Contemporary examinations of the corporate responses to diversity have called this approach "valuing differences."[4]

On initial inspection, Gant Electronics represents a hybrid approach to diversity that includes elements of both the assimilationist and pluralist approaches. However, a closer examination suggests its approach is driven by a process of intergroup negotiations. A necessary condition is that representatives of both the minorities and the corporate leaders recognize each other as legitimate parties in addressing the issues of minority advancement and development. Race is salient and recognized, but the emphasis is on changing the system so that members of racial minority groups compete with the majority group members on a level playing field. This model emphasizes systems and incentives, not attitudes, as the levers for change. We refer to it as an *intergroup negotiation model*.

The strategies and implicit models of the three companies varied fundamentally along several key dimensions: premises, principal targets of change, motivating rhetoric, and core tactics, which we will examine in the sections that follow.[5]

◢ ACME INDUSTRIES: A MELTING POT

In the 60s and 70s the culture here was white, male, perhaps Irish Catholic. Certainly, blue-collar roots were a positive attribute to have at Acme.

—WHITE EXECUTIVE, ACME

I think when I started my career at Acme white males definitely had a better chance than anybody else. It was a white male dominated company. I think we've gone beyond that now.

—WHITE EXECUTIVE, ACME

I don't think I could honestly say race has ever held me back, or any other black person I know at Acme. A lot of people can't say that at other companies. I think it comes from the corporate level. That kind of discriminatory

*conduct would not be condoned. I can remember that at least three CEOs
ago [antidiscrimination] started to be enforced and pushed.*

—AFRICAN AMERICAN MIDDLE MANAGER, ACME

These statements capture the story of how Acme Industries, an admittedly white, male-dominated organization with working-class roots, openly transformed itself to be inclusive of people of color at all levels of its hierarchy. In 1960, fewer than 1 percent of its management and none of its executives were racial minorities. Employees and managers held much of the company's stock, so integrating people of color into the management ranks meant not only hiring them as employees but also making them shareholders. Opening the company to minorities was not an easy task. One interviewee described the early years as a "war."

Yet by 1992, when we began conducting our interviews, the major sentiment of Acme's minority managers and executives was that race had not been a major barrier to their advancement. Even when they made reference to racially motivated incidents, they inevitably saw them as stemming from an individual who possessed the wrong attitudes and not a systemic problem with Acme's culture. The Acme system had worked for them.

The Assimilationist Model

Sociologist Robert Park used the term *assimilation* to describe the process by which minorities shed their ethnic identity as the result of being integrated into the majority culture. Park reasoned that over time and through contact with mainstream institutions of the society, immigrants would develop the taste and sensibilities of the native-born majority. Ultimately ethnicity becomes an irrelevant and, preferably, nonsalient aspect of identity. The result is a blending of these ethnic identities into one commonly shared identity defined by the dominant group culture, an idea represented by the "melting pot" metaphor.

The experience at Acme suggests an organizational corollary to the assimilation model. The diversity strategy employed there focused on creating a racially diverse workforce in which racial or ethnic differences were not seen as being relevant to the workplace or to how people should be perceived and treated. Race was to be addressed as an organizational issue until it simply ceased to matter. People at Acme were fond of saying that "everyone here can have green blood" (the color of Acme's logo) regardless of the color of their skin. Rhetorically, issues of race and the interest of the organization were linked by the belief that racial differences prevented people from being fully enfranchised and thus from contributing fully to the organization. The implicit premise was that the problem was caused by individual prejudice. If prejudice could be eliminated by creating a "color-blind" organization, the problem would be solved.

Opening the Company to Minorities

The story of the transformation of Acme's culture begins in 1965 when its leadership committed the firm to affirmative action hiring. They quickly realized that in order to implement affirmative action measures, they had to change the culture of the company. Acme's management cadre was a loyal and performance-oriented group with strong meritocratic values that had benefited upwardly mobile, hard-working white males from working-class backgrounds, like themselves. Although many minorities were hired as operators, few were in management. Racial minorities were not considered part of the Acme "management family." Because of Acme's "promote from within" policy, people of color would have to make it up the ranks in order to succeed at Acme, and progress was slow.

To symbolize their commitment to opening up management to minorities, the CEO and the president of the company took an action in 1968 that was considered dramatic at the time—hiring someone from outside the company into an executive position as the VP for human resources. The company's current VP of human resources commented on the unprecedented nature of this move and its centrality to racial integration of the company:

The critical factor was that [the then CEO] brought Ned Bowman into the company from outside. That was radical. He reported to the president as head of HR. [His mandate] was to implement change and affirmative action no matter what it took. They [the CEO and the president] really supported him. Ned raised the consciousness of everyone in the company. We could say the three of them did it together, but Ned had the vision and made it happen.

Ned Bowman, a white male, had significant experience working on economic development and employment initiatives in the African American and Hispanic communities of large cities. He also understood Acme's working-class cultural roots. To him the similarities between blue-collar whites and blue-collar minorities outweighed the differences.

Leading Change from the Top

Leveraging the visibility of the CEO and president's commitment, these three senior executives began to change the composition of Acme's workforce. It was a top-down process, with Bowman setting hiring targets and, in one instance, even agreeing with the federal EEOC to hire 25 percent people of color and women into its open operators positions. Operators were the heart of Acme's production operations and formed the link between the company's product and its customers. Most of its production managers were hired from this pool. Since these jobs required no postsecondary school training, finding qualified people was not difficult.

Opportunities were also being created as the company expanded its operations into new markets and territories. Bowman's recruitment strategies were aimed at identifying pools of minority candidates who had the best chance of blending into the Acme culture. In particular, he focused on African American churches as a conduit for potential hires, knowing that this was where he could find working-class men with families, strong work ethic, and, oftentimes, military experience—characteristics shared with the white males who succeeded at Acme.

Changing Employee Attitudes

Once minorities were hired, the next step was getting them accepted on an equal basis, a daunting challenge. Though the president and the CEO continued their vocal support of the need to integrate the ranks of Acme, Bowman and the company's president soon realized that they needed to address employee attitudes. They believed that Acme should be able to include anyone, regardless of race, who was willing to adopt the Acme way. Their task was to convince Acme's employees that this was true.

One of their first steps in addressing racial prejudice was to establish an antibias immersion program. White managers who had executive potential but who lacked sensitivity to racial minorities were sent to work in communities of color on special projects. The goal was to have them realize the commonalties between racial groups. The hope, and the result, was that these white managers would have greater ability to "treat people as people."

Bowman also implemented proposals designed to educate the company's current and future leadership. He developed a speakers forum in which civil rights and minority community leaders addressed the opinion leaders in the company. All this was aimed at heightening company leaders' consciousness about race, opportunity, and fairness. These early efforts began to pay dividends as many of the company's up-and-coming leaders started to convey the message. "Fair and equal treatment" became the catch phrase.

A Culture of Equality and Fairness

By the early 1970s, concrete evidence existed that this attitude had infiltrated the culture. Reflecting on this period of their careers, the minority managers and executives we studied reported feeling very much supported by white superiors when they were challenged by white subordinates or encountered resistance by customers. Milton Farmer, an African American manager, reported an event that was symbolic for him:

> Some customers let it be known that they did not want [blacks] to come into their establishments. I had to deal with that. Customers would call my white superiors and say they did not want me to service their account. But all my supervisors told them, "We are not removing him. He is our representative in your area." In other words they would not take the customer's side when it came to the racial thing. ... I felt I had come to a company that was really dedicated to helping minorities. By the company backing us [employees of color] or backing me, it reinforced my belief in Acme and its policies.

This kind of support seemed particularly important to these executives and managers, many of whom had known the effects of discrimination firsthand. Even while working on assignment for Acme, some encountered racial bias when attempting to secure adequate housing for themselves and their families. Today, such support of minority employees would seem expected and unremarkable, but at the time it provided a potent force in shaping Acme's psychological contract with employees of color. Even if they were not accepted by every company employee, they would be accepted and supported by the people who ran the company.

Acme's emphasis on individual attitudes and fair treatment continues today. When asked about race relations at Acme, one white executive noted, "I think part of working here is about antennae going out to people who aren't like I am. In fact, I was cautioning one of my department managers yesterday about the way he talked about blacks." Others noted that Acme has "zero tolerance" for racial jokes and bigoted language.

Ned Bowman spent a decade at Acme. Under his leadership and the vigilant support of the company's CEO and president (and their immediate successors), the culture changed. Although pockets of segregation and old attitudes remained, the company was fundamentally different. Racial integration was real, and an attitude of equal treatment and color blindness was dominant, all accomplished without changing the fabric of the company. In fact, several elements of the company's existing culture supported and helped these efforts. The company's production orientation meant that unit (and individual) performance was measured precisely, with objective and meaningful measures. Based on these established and publicly known measures, people of color were able to prove themselves outstanding as service representatives, operators, or first-line supervisors, a necessary condition for being promoted to higher positions in the company.

Moving Minorities into Positions of Responsibility

By the time Bowman left Acme in 1978, significant integration had been achieved in both the hourly and supervisory ranks. Management, however, and particularly upper-middle management and executive ranks, remained almost entirely white. Given Acme's promote-from-within orientation, this was not surprising. To reach the general managers position at Acme took an average sixteen to eighteen years. The test of the culture change that started under Bowman would be whether minorities in the first levels of management could make it to the highest levels.

During the 1980s, Acme's top leadership continued to actively pursue the practices that Bowman had put in place. The new CEO continued to support the assignment of high-potential but racially insensitive managers to special projects in communities of color. Senior managers and executives also pressed hard on the need to identify high-potential minorities.

Acme also began a process of low-key, but ongoing monitoring of its pool of minority managers. The aim was to ensure that people of color did not somehow get overlooked as the pyramid narrowed and that they received a pattern of assignments that would prepare them for general management. According to several HR executives, the key to achieving this was the way in which top management made it an issue in its ongoing discussions about the identification and development of talent within the organization. In the 1980s, group vice presidents began meeting with their division general managers at least twice a year to review the middle managers in their units. An explicit part of these discussions was the readiness of people of color and women to move up. While the affirmative action and HR functions supported these discussions, it was the line executives who were asked to take responsibility. A number of people underscored the role of the CEO in modeling this behavior and also in using his position as a bully pulpit to keep people thinking about diversity issues, frequently raising them at management retreats.

Many others below the CEO and president level took a personal stance to support the change. One division general manager described his own actions in the mid-1980s:

> When I went to that unit, there was only one minority reporting to me out of thirteen people. When I left there were four. I pulled the data on the workforce and showed it to my managers. I identified the departments in which we were lacking diversity. They said there was nobody qualified. I said,

"OK, until we get some people qualified we are not promoting anybody."
They suddenly found people.

By the mid-1980s, many senior executives were active mentors to many people of color. While these relationships were developed and shaped by the interests and personalities of the individuals involved, they were also strongly supported by the corporate leadership.

A unique element of the change process at Acme as compared to Gant and Advanced was the lack of significant mobilization by people of color as a group. There were never formal or informal support groups or advocacy efforts organized by minority groups. Instead, individuals relied on the formal system to respond to complaints. This would seem to fit the Acme orientation toward being a homogeneous culture. Mobilizing people of color as a group would have the effect of heightening differences and challenging the assumption of homogeneity.

Many felt that Acme's diversity efforts in the 1980s were also aided by larger changes in its business model. Through much of its early history, the corporate culture could be described as "hard nosed." The relationship between management and unionized employees was sometimes tense. Management development occurred mostly through on-the-job training. Acme had historically been a numbers-driven company that focused on volume, production, and revenue rather than on profit. By the early 1980s, however, competition in the industry led to a recognition that Acme's "boot camp" style of managing people was no longer effective in obtaining the high levels of commitment needed. The company began to emphasize people-management skills in its management training instead of rules and procedures. Acme's top executives were actively looking for managers whose behavior and management philosophy aligned with this new orientation. These efforts reinforced the emphasis on sensitivity to bias and racial stereotypes that Bowman had initiated.

Acme's top-down, color-blind, meritocratic approach yielded positive results. When we began our study, an African American was reporting to the chief operating officer with responsibility for half of the company's operations. One level down, one of the ten group vice presidents was a person of color and twelve of the company's ninety-four vice president–general managers were minorities. One quarter of Acme's total management force were people of color.

Summary of Acme's Approach

Table 7-2 summarizes the characteristics of Acme's assimilation strategy. In many respects, the evolution and implementation of Acme's diversity strategy is an example of an effective application of the assimilation model. For example, according to the assimilation model, race-relation problems stem from individuals, not the system. Interventions focus on changing attitudes and creating greater sensitivity. Prejudice is a behavior and therefore something that people can control and be held responsible for. The executives at Acme often talked about diversity in management as if it were a test of the degree of bias held by individual managers in the system. Their success at creating racial diversity legitimized the perceived virtues of the system as meritocratic and based on universal values. Similarly, the company's rhetoric also emphasized commonality among people. Ned Bowman

---

Table 7-2 Acme Industries: A Melting Pot

- Model

    Assimilationist

- Premises

    Racial differences are irrelevant

    Individual attitudes are the problem

    The goal is to be color blind

- Principal targets

    Individual attitudes and behavior

- Motivating rhetoric

    "All people are people" and deserve "fair and equal treatment"

    "It's not the color of your skin that matters, it's how green [the company's logo color] your blood is that counts."

- Core tactics

    Active sponsoring of minorities

    Strong mandate from the top

    Leadership models behavior

    Antibias training

    Benchmarking and monitoring

justified his early interventions—such as the speakers forum and the immersion program that assigned high-potential white managers to work in communities of color—as efforts designed to eliminate the perception that racial minorities were different. The organizational benefit, he reasoned, was the ability to treat everyone fairly in the workplace. The purpose of acknowledging race was to render it irrelevant in the service of eliminating discrimination.

In terms of impetus and initiative, the change process at Acme relied quite heavily on the top-down, centralized influence of the leadership. Employees throughout the company witnessed the top management's personal involvement in the change process. The use of power to make things happen is a vital element of this change process, as evidenced by white managers being compelled to work in minority communities.

The core tactics in the assimilation strategy revolve around changing individual attitudes. A critical activity is helping whites become more sensitive and less biased. Education programs focus on prejudice and helping people to "transcend race." This was the focus of both the community immersion program and the speakers forum that Bowman instituted. At Acme, the attitudes and behavior of white employees were not the only focus of change. Minorities were also expected to have a color-blind perspective. In part, this meant not focusing on race except as guided by corporate policy.

Another core tactic was a reliance on centralized corporate staff efforts to monitor the organization's progress. The data from these efforts were often used to identify areas where there were problems in hiring and retention and to identify people of color who might have been overlooked in the promotion process. At Acme, there was a vigilant review of management talent that included an explicit discussion of people of color. Although the responsibility for monitoring diversity rested unambiguously with division and group executives, the data made available through the corporate office made it possible.

What Acme's experience may suggest is that for the assimilation strategy to succeed, there needs to be a strong uniform culture and set of systems that support the exercise of top-down authority. An organization that has achieved significant results using a diversity strategy similar to Acme's is the U.S. Army. Like Acme, it is a uniform culture in which the leadership is expected to define the interests of the institution and is authorized to mandate action and sanctions for noncompliance.

◢ ADVANCED TECHNOLOGY: VALUING DIFFERENCES

Like Acme, Advanced Technology began its diversity efforts with a strong commitment to affirmative action hiring. By 1984, however, it had developed a diversity strategy that stressed differences as a source of individual and organizational enrichment. A former leader of the diversity effort described the corporation's journey:

> *It was an evolution. We were continually learning as we were doing. There was no grand plan [at the beginning] to go from just being in compliance to the kind of* valuing differences *orientation that was built up over the last twenty years. We were open to learning and the work of valuing differences evolved.*

The Pluralist Model

In an assimilation model, racial differences require attention for the purpose of rendering them irrelevant. In a pluralist model, differences are valued. Institutional, individual, and interpersonal factors that devalue differences are attacked. The rationale or motivating rhetoric of this approach emphasizes that differences are not inherently bad; that people are most effective when they feel valued for their common and individual characteristics; and that creating a culture in which differences are valued means engaging and exploring differences, not suppressing or eliminating them. According to a former leader of the diversity effort at Advanced, "Our approach asked employees to face up to their stereotypes and biases. Color blindness was the goal of the Civil Rights era and was rejected as an ideal. Productivity in our employees would be unlocked by managers being acutely aware of the diversity in their workforce."

Like the assimilation model, the pluralist model emphasizes individuals as the most important element of the problem and solution. The problem, however, is defined differently. Stereotypes lead not only to discriminatory behavior; they also prevent people from valuing differences. The prescription is to provide experiences that allow individuals to reframe their thinking about differences. For example, people must become comfortable discussing differences, whereas previously topics such as race, gender, and sexual orientation were taboo. Unlike the assimilation model in which distinctions of race are to be minimized, the task under the pluralist model is to eliminate the hierarchy of racial groups; white is not better than black, it is just different.

A core tactic of the pluralist model is to create opportunities for people to experience positive and open cross-race relations. This is important because, in the end, the pluralist model works only as a result of high-quality relationships forming across lines of difference. A premise of the pluralist model is that individuals need to create a positive integration of the salient characteristics that define them.

The valuing differences approach that emerged at Advanced Technology grew out of its early focus on affirmative action hiring and equal employment opportunity. The leaders of Advanced endorsed affirmative action in the mid-1960s as the "right thing" to do. The effort gained momentum in the early 1970s and produced significant results.

Opening the Company to Minorities

Two factors were critical to the success of Advanced's early affirmative action efforts. The first was the close relationship that developed between Chris Hornbeck, a white senior vice president of operations who oversaw the manufacturing and sales operations, and Jim Sawyer, an African American personnel manager who worked for him. With the former providing the authorization and symbolic leadership and the latter providing the strategy, they implemented an aggressive effort of recruiting and hiring people of color. Their early focus was on African Americans but soon expanded to include Hispanics and women. In addition to opening their non-exempt ranks to people of color, they focused on hiring professionals. These efforts resulted in many hires in a short period of time. Sales, finance, and manufacturing were the areas that most of these new recruits entered. Many came from other companies where they saw their opportunities limited because of their race. Sawyer, the African American personnel manager, described the period this way:

> *If it had not been for affirmative action, none of us old timers would be here. Advanced is a technology company and 15 percent of our management and professional population is people of color, [from] all over the United States. And to get that we put special programs in fifty-two colleges. We made deals with Stanford, MIT, Harvard, Berkeley, and Florida A&M to get the kind of minority talent we wanted. We used search firms to get the best from other companies.*

Sawyer commented on the success of these minorities:

> *If you trace them today, except for a few, they've all done very well here and at other companies. None of those folks would have gotten in without Advanced saying we are going to respond to affirmative action. They just would not have been hired. I can't think of a single African American executive at Advanced who didn't get help from such efforts.*

The second, equally important factor in the company's efforts was its location of major manufacturing facilities in two urban areas heavily populated by African Americans and Hispanics, and a third on the United States–Mexico border. The plants attracted not only skilled and unskilled blue-collar workers but also highly educated professionals of color from around the country. Not surprisingly, manufacturing was where most minority managers began their careers at Advanced. Five of the nine African Americans whose careers we studied at Advanced entered the firm through manufacturing. Three of the five would eventually become executives in other parts of the company. In many ways, manufacturing became an incubator of management talent for the company. It also became the organizational model for how to manage racial diversity.

By the late 1970s, some of Advanced's managers were ready to declare it an affirmative action success story. Based on the statistics, it was a much more diverse corporation than at the start of the process and more diverse than any of its competitors. While some areas had done better than others, no division of the company was without representation of people of color and, increasingly, African Americans, Hispanic Americans, and Asians Americans were populating middle management. It seemed to some that only the executive level remained to be penetrated.

From Counting the Numbers to Valuing Differences

In the late 1970s Advanced's products were in great demand because of their state-of-the-art technology. For its highly automated manufacturing facilities and their managers, this meant high levels of stress. It soon became obvious that the inner-city plants and the one located on the United States–Mexico border were underperforming. Many of the white senior managers and executives in the company accepted this situation as "the price of a social experiment." They reasoned that the "minority plants" could not perform up to the standards of the "normal" facilities where the employee population was mostly white.

Michael Pennings, the vice president who had taken over this group of plants in 1979, found this situation unacceptable. With the help of outside consultants and some internal staff, he came to see the problem as one of low expectations. His managers, with little experience working in interracial settings, expected and demanded less of these plants and their minority managers and employees. Changing this meant changing not only attitudes but also behavior and relationships.

To aid him in addressing this problem, he brought one of the external consultants, Deborah Jones, onto his staff full-time. Jones was an African American with a background in HR and organization development. Pennings and Jones formed a partnership to turn the situation around. The groundwork for Advanced's diversity strategy was developed out of their quest to change not only attitudes and behavior but also relationships between white managers and employees of color.

Dialogue Groups: Exploring Differences

The initial work began with an examination of the stereotypes held by white managers and their limiting effect on the performance of people of color and, ultimately, the organization. Through trial and error, minorities and whites were brought together into dialogue groups. Initially, the focus was on commonalties, stressing people's similarities. Eventually, they found that the power of this process came from the exploration of differences and, then, learning to value them. They soon established a process in which any group of employees in manufacturing could voluntarily form a dialogue group for the express purpose of exploring and learning about differences. The groups met on company property during working hours.

Three years after Pennings' decision to reverse the negative correlation between minority composition and plant performance, a coherent approach for managing differences had emerged. Its core logic was that in order for people to be most effective, they needed to feel empowered, which itself emerged from feeling valued. The link to diversity was that race was sometimes the basis on which people were made to feel devalued. According to this view, when managers feel uncomfortable working with members of another group or hold unexamined stereotypes about the group, they are no longer able to manage effectively. Thus, the focus of this strategy was on personal and interpersonal development. Leveraging the company's core value of "do the right thing," they argued that developing the capacity to value differences would both advance the goal of equal opportunity, and lead to a more effective workforce and a more profitable organization.

Dialogue groups became the heart of Advanced's diversity strategy and change process. Participation was voluntary. Dialogue groups were facilitated by trained personnel who were company employees. Eventually, other systems developed to support the work begun in dialogue groups: training programs to teach the basic skills necessary to be effective at dialogue and managing across differences, and educational events and modules to address identified common needs.

By 1983, the valuing differences philosophy and dialogue groups had spread throughout the worldwide operations of Advanced Technology. In a 1990 internal communication about dialogue groups, Deborah Jones said that "several hundred, perhaps a thousand" dialogues had happened across the company. Originally designed and sanctioned as an activity for heterogeneous groups, dialogue groups based on common identity characteristics also emerged. These allowed individuals who shared an identity to come together to explore its meaning and influence on their work. Eventually, a corporate office for diversity was established. One of its major roles was to consult and coach groups and individuals who wished to take action to advance diversity.

Networks of Understanding and Relationship

Over half of the participants in our study at Advanced, both people of color and whites, had been a member of at least one dialogue group. The personal learning they gained and, more important for minorities, the relationships they formed with colleagues and supervisors strengthened their personal networks. Many of these relationships achieved a level of closeness and authenticity that was uncommon in cross-race relationships.[6]

The relationships that developed were not only important to the social and emotional experience of minorities; they were also a fundamental part of doing business at Advanced. The company's culture was oriented to relationships. Many described it as a "network organization" in which relationships more than hierarchy or formal roles determined credibility and the ability to get things done.

Several of our participants told us that the African American dialogue groups they participated in helped them share ideas for coping with the problems of being minority managers. The groups also strengthened the informal African American network across the organization. Out of these discussions came formal initiatives to sponsor events and to advocate on issues with senior management.

The dialogue experience also moved people into action. In manufacturing, many executives became personally committed to diversity and considered it a business issue. Management opportunities beyond the minority plants began to open up for people of color. In other parts of the company, managers took action to bolster diversity in their units. Several white men told us that their experience in the groups made them more comfortable with and better mentors for the minorities and women who worked for them.

Leading from the Middle

In contrast to Acme, the effort at Advanced moved along with the quiet blessing, but not the visible participation, of its CEO. While

Chris Hornbeck, senior VP of operations, and Michael Pennings, VP of manufacturing, were quite visible, the overall participation of top-level executives was uneven. Advanced was an organization that allowed for local autonomy. A pivotal person in the diversity work at Advanced made a familiar comment: "Senior executives have allowed it to happen and have sometimes participated and dabbled in it. The leadership has not been as much top down as bottom up." The diversity strategy succeeded largely because of the personal investment of people in upper and lower levels of middle management, rather than top management.

In addition to relying on relationships, the Advanced culture expected ideas to percolate up and gain supporters through debate. Dialogue group participants showed what they valued through their expenditure of time. There were few edicts from top management about what to do. Hornbeck and Sawyer set goals and objectives to emphasize managers' responsibilities to practice affirmative action in hiring, but there were few formal sanctions for not achieving them. Instead, they spread the word about the dialogue groups, channeling resources to support the strategy, giving authorization for people to participate, and serving as role models.

Given the culture of Advanced, change—any change—needed to come from below, based on real commitment. Pennings and Jones came to believe strongly that people had to feel that change would directly benefit them and the organization.

Minorities as Leaders of Diversity

A key element of the change process at Advanced was the leadership provided by minorities themselves. We have already mentioned the partnerships of Jim Sawyer and Deborah Jones with white male executives. Sawyer and Jones also acted as mentor and coach to many people of color to help them understand how to leverage their skills and talents. Sawyer eventually became a senior VP reporting to the CEO and a member of the executive committee. Jones's success in manufacturing took her to a corporate-level job where she directed the institutionalization and diffusion of the diversity strategy.

Over time, other minority managers took active roles in moving Advanced's diversity efforts ahead, as well as in ensuring the development of people of color. In contrast to Acme, many executives of color were actively involved in promoting the valuing of differences, leveraging their networks to help other minorities, and serving as advocates with superiors on issues of race.

Attaining Diversity at the Executive Level

By 1986 minority representation in the ranks of middle management and senior management had increased significantly. Without a doubt, Advanced was the diversity leader in its industry. Advanced was now also the second-largest corporation in revenue and personnel in its technology sector. In the wake of its valuing differences strategy, Advanced's corporate office of affirmative action had gone into decline. The function and its personnel were not well respected and its role vis-à-vis diversity was unclear.

At the same time, many in the organization were becoming concerned about the ceiling that seemed to exist for minorities. The company had proven that in manufacturing, finance, sales, and, to a lesser degree, engineering, individuals of color could be developed and promoted to middle and upper-middle management. Beyond that, invisible barriers seemed to exist. Some began to wonder whether the focus on personal and interpersonal development had failed to address systematic or organizational-level issues that prevented minorities from reaching executive levels. Others felt that the grassroots approach had yet to influence the very top of the pyramid, where these decisions were made. This dissatisfaction spurred a realignment that tied the valuing differences strategy more closely to the affirmative action and EEO-monitoring functions as well as to corporate HR. Ultimately, all three groups reported to a common manager.

Almost all of the minority executives in our study reached the executive level at Advanced between 1986 and 1992. In no instance was selection the obvious result of a quota or "set aside" process, but rather of efforts to make senior executives aware that a talented pool of minority middle managers existed. That promotions occurred in this time frame suggests that the company had truly normalized its diversity efforts, for the company was going through its most daunting competitive challenges and significant downsizing during this period.

The Pluralist Model at Work

As the above description shows, the work at Advanced quickly moved beyond affirmative action and race to focus broadly on valuing differences of all kinds. Eventually, as one manager noted, "the philosophy supported the power of people's differences in race, gender, citizenship, and sexual orientation." Table 7-3 summarizes the salient features of Advanced Technology's pluralist approach.

The approach is a clear illustration of both the premises and motivating rhetoric of the pluralist model: Differences are not inherently

---

Table 7-3   Advanced Technology: Valuing Differences

- Model

  Pluralist

- Premises

  Differences matter

  Race is central to identity

  Being valued for who you are

    is critical to empowerment

    contributes to performance

- Principal targets

  Individual attitudes

  Relationships

- Motivating rhetoric

  "Do the right thing"

  "People are effective when valued for who they are"

  "People [and organizations] are more effective if they can engage their differences"

  "Our diversity effort is about empowering people"

- Core tactics

  Dialogue groups (vehicles for understanding differences/confronting stereotypes)

  Champions at the grassroots level

  Interventions at subunit level

  Development of networks

  Minority mobilization

bad, and people are most effective when they are understood and valued for their differences. Unlike the assimilationist model, we see a bottom-up as opposed to a top-down approach (and some of its inherent risks if the top does not become involved or buy into the process). The core tactic at Advanced was to get people engaged in discussing differences, understanding them, dealing with problems, and valuing essential differences. The main vehicle for doing this was the dialogue group.

At Advanced, dialogue groups allowed people to examine their stereotypes and biases while also experiencing cross-race interactions that challenged their views and alerted them to new possibilities. Individuals saw firsthand the reality of multiple perspectives as they shared interpretations of what was happening in the organization. Since the groups were ongoing, members could set the learning agenda for themselves. This meant discussions were more likely to focus on what was relevant to day-to-day reality rather than simply the generic issues that were addressed in short-term corporate diversity training programs.

The groups also gave people the opportunity to create personal relationships across racial lines. Discussions that occurred in these groups were often intense, but the product of successful engagement was trust and intimacy. In the manufacturing unit, white managers and managers of color were able to have discussions about the relationship among issues such as performance, expectations, and race—topics previously avoided and seldom acknowledged. Rather than being viewed as peripheral to the work, these issues became central to it.

Out of the experience with dialogue groups evolved a number of other practices designed to support their work. The recognition of differences and the notion of valuing differences created a springboard for homogeneous identity group work. This was consistent with the emphasis on personal growth and the validity of individuals acting from a sense of having multiple salient identities. The task for the individual was not to choose among these memberships, but to integrate them. Homogeneous dialogue groups, including white male groups, met to explore the relationship of racial identity to professional identity and role.

In a network culture such as Advanced's, it is easy to see the value of the relationships developed by aspiring minority managers with white superiors and peers as a result of the dialogue groups. They were vehicles for getting to know others deeply in one's own function as well as in other parts of the company. Similarly, the same-race dialogue groups (as well as the same-gender groups) enabled participants to gain help and often perspective in dealing with common problems.

What happens to EEO and affirmative action in the pluralist strategy? Advanced provided some interesting insight into this question. While we do not believe that EEO and affirmative action must go into decline under this strategy, they were certainly subordinate to it at Advanced. Our perspective is that affirmative action became a tool employed to guarantee the equality and fairness on which the valuing differences approach depends.[7]

◢ GANT ELECTRONICS: LEVELING THE PLAYING FIELD

The secret to getting ahead in corporate America is very simple. It's luck—opportunity and preparation meeting at the same time. Preparation and no opportunity equals bad luck. Opportunity and no preparation also equals bad luck.

We are not sure of the origin of this quote. Both of us have heard some variation of it over the years and found it to ring with common sense, if not universal truth. These words came to mind frequently as we examined the diversity strategy used at Gant Electronics. Gant's approach had two central elements. First was the concentrated self-help efforts of people of color to ensure their own development, and ability to exceed performance standards. Second was the process of negotiation and joint problem solving between minority groups and Gant's management to eliminate systematic barriers to equal opportunity and equitable treatment.

Gant's success in diversifying its management is evident in the results. In 1964, only 3 percent of Gant's total workforce was non-white. Ten years later, African Americans, Asian Americans, Hispanic Americans, and Native Americans comprised 15 percent of the workforce, which had quadrupled in total size. The representation of minorities among executives and managers increased from less than 1 percent to 7 percent in the same period. In total numbers, this meant an increase from a handful to over 400 minority executives and managers. By 1993, people of color occupied several of the most powerful positions in the company. Moreover, there were many talented young minority managers in the pipeline and ready to move up. One minority executive, Ben Richardson, was responsible for over half of the company's revenue stream and reported directly to the CEO as a member of the president's office.

The Intergroup Negotiation Model

When we examined the diversity strategy at Gant Electronics, it seemed a hybrid of sorts. On one hand, there was a significant degree of openness about race in the organization as consistent with the pluralist model. By the mid-1970s, for example, self-help groups were well established. A strong and obvious partnership existed between these groups and top management. Many of the company's most successful minority professionals and managers served on their steering committees. In these respects, Gant seemed to embrace the pluralistic model of Advanced.

Yet the ideology or rhetoric surrounding the efforts at Gant never emphasized the need to embrace differences. In addition to advocacy and monitoring, the self-help groups focused on helping their members fit into the Gant culture. A premium was placed on performance and understanding the "rules of the game," as one manager put it. There was also a significant reliance on bureaucratic systems to bring managerial behavior into alignment with diversity goals. In these respects the effort at Gant resembled Acme.

If Acme's focus was primarily centered on the individual and Advanced Technology's approach was centered on individuals and their relationships, then Gant's approach was centered on the organization as a system of structures and processes that shaped managerial behavior and the distribution of opportunity. Many of the leaders of the self-help movement focused on changing the system so as to undermine or moderate the effects of individual and institutional biases. Furthermore, the corporation's efforts were focused not so much on changing attitudes as on changing procedures to level the playing field.

On all sides, the rhetoric that supported the change process at Gant focused on improving or changing the system. Such an approach was consistent with Gant's overall culture, which incorporated many formalized processes, especially related to HR management.

Opening the Company to Minorities

Much like Acme, Gant's most senior executives were highly visible proponents of equal employment opportunity in the early days of affirmative action. An organization strong on systems and procedures, Gant's HR department was able to implement a program of affirmative hiring that affected almost every part of the company. Many of the professional hires went into the company's largest area, sales and marketing, which accounted for almost half of the company's employees; others entered manufacturing, engineering, and finance.

Gant had an early advantage in recruiting people of color, especially the well educated. The public commitment of its leaders to equal opportunity (described in Chapter 2) and the youthful feel of its culture made it seem more inviting to many young minorities than other companies. One interviewee described his choice to join: "I looked at IBM and some others, but Gant seemed more open. I didn't feel like I had to come here and totally forget who I was." More than two-thirds of the people of color hired during the 1960s and early 1970s were African Americans, and it was primarily their actions in the late 1970s that would help define Gant's diversity strategy and change process.

Once in the organization, many of these newcomers met with two forms of resistance. The more obvious was the inequity many experienced in assignments, compensation, and promotions; less obvious was the isolation. Even with the numbers rising fivefold between 1968 and 1978, they were often the only nonwhites in their work unit. This situation was exacerbated by their frequent exclusion from the informal social networks that facilitated access to information about the unwritten rules of the culture.

Creation of Self-Help Groups

The response of these young African Americans was to meet in groups for informal sessions to share their collective experiences and insights into the corporation. They also coached one another on the skills and techniques needed to exceed the standards and expectations set for them by management. This early focus on preparation and performance was based on the assumption that if they performed well enough they would eventually have to be recognized. With little or no overt coordination, these self-help groups sprang up in different regions across the country.

Despite these self-help initiatives, it became increasingly clear that pressure needed to be put on the system to address inequities in how African Americans were treated. In 1971, a group of black sales representatives filed a civil discrimination suit claiming discrimination in assignments, compensation, and promotions. The purpose of the suit was to get the attention of Gant's senior executives rather than to embarrass the company.

When word of the suit reached the CEO, an investigation followed. The claims of the suit were found to have merit and within days, remedies were applied. The claimants dropped their suit. From this experience, a relationship was born that would guide Gant's diversity strategy for the next two decades. One of the executives assigned to handle the situation was Gordon Kingsley, a corporate VP who later became Gant's CEO. In the process of this crisis, Kingsley developed a deep appreciation for Gant's African American self-help movement. He also began personal relationships with some of its leaders, several of whom had been parties to the suit.

Over the course of the next several years, a partnership developed between the leaders of the self-help movement and Gant's corporate executives and top managers. As partners, they jointly developed a process of negotiation and problem solving that led to many innovations designed to diminish biases in the system that unfairly advantaged or disadvantaged employees based on race. Kingsley was the glue that held it together. The trust between him and the African American managers involved in the self-help movement facilitated a level of openness and constructive conflict that would not otherwise have been possible.

Without officially recognizing or financing the self-help groups, Gant's senior executives instituted mechanisms to legitimize the participation of their leaders in developing ways to improve the company and its practices. Principal among these was the creation of advisory councils that called for employee participation. These councils provided an avenue for the leaders of self-help groups to bring their views and recommendations to bear on organizational decisions that affected their constituents.

Altering the System to Reduce Barriers

The minority self-help groups spurred change for all employees, regardless of race. For example, as a result of the advisory councils, Gant instituted job postings to promote open bidding for management opportunities. Prior to this, minorities often found themselves locked out of jobs because they did not hear about openings through the grapevine. Job postings, therefore, clearly aided African Americans but also created a more equitable system for all employees.

Other innovations included research to identify the common paths of preparation followed by senior managers. It was later negotiated that every candidate who met the general qualifications for a particular management position was guaranteed an interview. Knowledge about the prerequisite qualifications was also disseminated by the self-help groups. This enabled their members to effectively manage their careers and, at times, to demand consideration for opportunities. Similarly, managers were able to learn about viable job candidates that they were not aware of or otherwise may not have considered.

Dual Focus—Performance and Advocacy

By 1976, many of the local self-help groups had taken on a more formal structure with elected leadership and organized programs. No longer were they based first and foremost on friendship, but instead on the common goal of surviving and thriving as a person of color at Gant. One person described the groups as having waged the struggle for racial equality inside the corporation and the boardroom.

The groups continued to emphasize both performance and advocacy. For them, performance legitimated recommendations for change. Racism, the leaders preached, was not an excuse for poor performance. At times, this created tension. A company-approved history of

the self-help movement at Gant quoted one of the groups' early leaders on this subject:

> One of the things the rank and file didn't like about us was that we preached
> as much about you getting your act together and meeting performance tar-
> gets as we did about blacks having a right to an upper level job. The first
> thing we preached was that you have got to perform before we can start any
> kind of discussion about advancement.[8]

The other role these groups played was advocacy. Here, the partnership with management was critical. The leaders of the self-help
groups were conscious of the need to nurture this relationship. To
present their views to top management, they selected members whose
performance was far above standard, in order to establish credibility.
They focused their efforts on changing the way the system worked as
opposed to changing attitudes. The premise was that racial integration needed to be approached like any other business issue at Gant.
The leaders insisted on having data and analysis to support claims and
recommendations. They also demanded of their white executive partners that execution strategies be developed for meeting affirmative
action goals and promoting equal opportunity. Over time, their
approach proved successful both in creating change and in building a
lasting relationship with Gant's top management.

Most of the minorities in our study had participated in these self-
help groups. Several noted that they had been an important factor in
their own success. Others were more philosophical, using the imagery
of struggle and change to explain why it had been necessary for
minorities to come together in these formal groups. Many believed
that people of color could not succeed at Gant without this support
system performing its dual function of development and advocacy. A
senior African American executive, who also was one of Gant's top
officers, described the difference that the group had made for him and
others:

> The system is biased. Therefore only a few people get through, and they can
> only get through with help. I know I got help, and I know I couldn't have
> made it without help. I do not believe that one person could get through the

system without a lot of help, because the system is nothing more than a microcosm, whether it's Gant or AT&T—it's a microcosm of the U.S. The microcosm of the U.S. has racial biases, it has power-based biases, it has enough biases in there for a black person not to get through without having power bases.

People of color who think they can do it alone will ultimately hit a wall of prejudice. . . . In the end they will need help from us. When it happens, the person needs to be able to separate what is them from what's the system. We will tell you if we think you screwed up and we will help you make the system work.

Support from the Top and Initiatives from Below

There was both a bottom-up and a top-down aspect to the change process at Gant. Gordon Kingsley was fond of saying that the relationship with the self-help groups and their role in the advisory councils was the precursor to the broader programs of employee involvement that helped to turn the company around in the 1980s. Kingsley believed that many of the issues raised affected all employees, although with disproportionate consequences for minorities. Using this feedback, management was able to participate in improving the system for everyone. A political result of this strategy was that it put the squeeze on middle management. African Americans got a direct line to top management and the executives gained access to information from its rank and file and lower-level management employees.

Another critical variable in this strategy's success was the self-help groups' focus on their own performance—treating racism as a hurdle, but not as an excuse for poor performance. When people of color at Gant were afforded opportunity, they by and large delivered stellar performances. For example, between 1975 and 1983, the company's top performing sales divisions in the United States were headed by African Americans.

Corporate staff managers, especially in personnel, played key roles as the implementors and monitors of compliance with the new equal opportunity policies. In this respect, the process benefited from the fact that corporate staffs were both quite powerful and supportive of Gant's diversity agenda.

Change Takes Root

By 1982, the diversity strategy at Gant had taken hold. The evidence went beyond just the increased numbers of African Americans in upper management. The self-help model had also spread to other identity groups, such as women and Hispanic Americans. In almost every region of the company, self-help groups (by then called forums) were engaged in regular discussions with local management about the work of ensuring equal opportunity.

In the 1980s Gant developed a highly regarded affirmative action office based on the company's experience in the 1970s. This group worked to make sure that the HR systems addressed issues of equity, access, and participation. They also devised a sophisticated system of goals for creating a representative workforce that tied managers' compensation to achieving these objectives. Training efforts focused primarily on integrating diversity into regular training, consistent with the notion of changing the system and not creating separate or peripheral initiatives.

We found substantial evidence in our discussions with senior executives and managers at Gant, both minorities and whites, that diversity was indeed a core part of Gant's business paradigm. We heard a number of stories about senior executives proactively mentoring people of color and general managers who had explicitly set out to recruit a diverse management to run their business. One senior executive at Gant made the following observation:

> I think we do a fair job of identifying people who can move forward in their career. I think from top to bottom we believe that we are doing the right thing. It might get strained or dissipated as you go down the organization. I don't think our first level of management is devoted to diversity, but I do think the top of the company is. . . . I have only been here, as I said, for three-and-a-half years, but I have honestly not detected any resentment toward a balanced workforce concept among the senior managers.

Intergroup Negotiations at Gant

Table 7-4 summarizes the characteristics of Gant's diversity approach. The evolution and implementation of Gant's diversity strategy combined aspects of assimilation and pluralism, but is different in several important ways. Its two critical premises are (1) that racial biases are built into the system and to create a level playing field the system needs to be altered and (2) that mobilization is good for minorities and for the company if their efforts are focused on improving performance as well as advocacy. As the description of its history suggests, Gant evolved a number of tactics, the most visible of which was the self-help group.

Table 7-4   Gant Electronics: Leveling the Playing Field

- Model

  Intergroup negotiations

- Premises

  Biases are built into the system

  The system(s) can be changed

  Mobilization of minorities is good if focused on performance and advocacy

- Principal targets

  Total system

  Power relations

  Practices that unfairly advantage or disadvantage any group

- Motivating rhetoric

  "We need to change the system so that it works for all employees"

  "The most important thing for minorities to focus on is performance even in the face of bias"

  "Minorities' efforts at self-help benefit the company because they are better able to contribute"

  "Working with minorities to improve the system [level the playing field] is a form of employee involvement"

- Core tactics

  Self-help/advocacy groups

  Joint problem solving and negotiating

  Altering/changing unfair systems or practices

  Benchmarking and monitoring

  Top-down support of bottom-up initiatives

Formalized Negotiations. Perhaps the most critical tactic in Gant's strategy was the formalized negotiation between representatives of the self-help groups and members of management. Over time, these discussions developed the character of joint problem-solving sessions even when the parties disagreed on the optimal solution. Most often they negotiated a resolution.

Intergroup theorists note that for successful negotiation between groups to occur, the groups must be identifiable to one another, and the actual parties to the negotiations must be legitimate representatives.[9] It is also important that neither the group nor its representatives feel that the ultimate aim of the other group is to obliterate it. Gant's support of the self-help movement made it a viable and stable negotiating partner. The fact that Gant made changes in its system to create a more level playing field was matched by the self-help groups' emphasis on its members' performance. The delivery of excellent performance by people of color served to mute backlash and criticism that unqualified persons were being promoted simply because of race. Likewise, the company's good-faith efforts to implement changes in systems and procedures supported the self-help groups' internal emphasis on its members performing well even in the face of bias. Ultimately, opportunity did flow to many high-performing people of color, though not always without experiencing significant bias and inequity at various junctures in their careers.

Monitoring Diversity Efforts. In addition to the role of self-help groups, Gant developed other tactics that proved to be critical to the success of its diversity efforts. First was the development of centralized systems to monitor managers' compliance with affirmative action policies. The office of Equal Employment Opportunity and Affirmative Action grew stronger at Gant over the years, in contrast to Advanced. The office experimented with various systems to provide incentives for managers. For several years, manager compensation was tied to performance on affirmative action goals. By the late 1980s, a sophisticated system of goal setting and monitoring was in place that provided each division's executives a clear picture of how well they were doing at hiring, promoting, and retaining people of color, women, and white males. The approach was focused on creating a demographically diverse pool of talented and ready-to-advance employees.

Mainstreaming the Diversity Agenda. Second, the effort emphasized integrating the issues of diversity and race relations into the mainstream. An example of this was training and education to address issues of diversity. Very early on, the organization began including these issues in its required educational programs for all managers. The company also quickly ended its experimentation with sponsorship of courses aimed only at racial minorities in the organization. In these choices, Gant resembled Acme more than Advanced.

Leadership from the Top. Their third tactic relied heavily on executive support and follow-through. In this way, Gant is similar to Acme. There was, and continues to be, a top-down quality to the implementation and execution of the diversity strategy. Today, however, the emphasis is broadly accepted as a part of the company's culture and HR systems. We spoke with over fifty people at Gant, most of them white managers, and there was no question about the company's commitment to diversity or the expectation that managers should act to support its policies. One white male VP we interviewed was asked about his views of the company's efforts to create a diverse workforce. He responded,

> I think [diversity] is absolutely important to Gant. My personal beliefs have been influenced by two things. One is the company's encouragement and belief that you should do it. The other is my personal belief that everyone ought to be able to maximize and use their talents. I have always believed that you have to identify—or keep working until you have identified—candidates in every category of people who are qualified and give them a fair chance. Then you start working on the feeder system to make sure people grow.

This manager's thinking was aligned with the systems Gant had in place. Our observation of his work unit and efforts at hiring senior-level people of color was that his actions matched his rhetoric.

The critical role of leadership is related to the fact that Gant's change process was top-down. It depended greatly on the credibility that the leaders of the self-help movement and their white executive partners held with their constituencies. It also relied on the use of its corporate staffs to align managers' incentives with the company's diversity goals. In a parallel fashion, the self-help groups had a hierarchy that reinforced to its constituency the requirements for performance and "learning to play the game."

A COMPARISON OF THE THREE DIVERSITY STRATEGIES

At this point, the reader may be tempted to ask, Which of the three approaches is best? If we use either business performance or percentage of people of color in management and executive levels as a measure, then none of the three is clearly the best. All three companies were dominant leaders in their industries and all three had attained an integration of their executive ranks that is rare among corporations in the United States today. To be useful, the question has to address the approach's success more specifically in terms of distinct criteria such as the company's values, work styles, and leadership.

What is common to these three success stories is that the diversity approach used—including the premises, rhetoric, and especially core tactics—fits exceedingly well with the company's culture. For example, Acme's melting-pot approach fits its strong, uniform culture, meritocratic values, and top-down discipline, while Advanced Technology's pluralist approach fit its loosely coupled network structure, bottom-up style, and history of local initiatives.

We'll explore the relationship between company culture and diversity strategy more fully in Chapter 8, which begins with a review of the organizational ingredients that seemed to drive and sustain change. This brief preview simply indicates that all three approaches, when applied in the right context and with the appropriate organizational ingredients present, can be highly effective. In such cases, success in achieving racial and ethnic diversity is not random, but springs from focused and sustained efforts to create a conducive environment. As minorities put forth their own efforts to succeed individually, their organizations stepped in to minimize the drag that systematic or individual prejudice was imposing on their careers. The companies created the conditions that allowed preparation to meet opportunity.

8

Creating and Sustaining Change
The Common Enablers

W HAT ARE THE MOST SIGNIFICANT FACTORS in an organization's ability to sustain its diversity efforts over time and
achieve racial integration at all levels of the hierarchy? This is
perhaps the single most important question for organizations
committed to equal opportunity and diversity. Ours is not the
first study to take up this question. Others, most notably Ann
Morrison,[1] have benchmarked leading companies and found that
the involvement of executives and senior managers is a critical
driver. While our findings point to the importance of leadership,
like Morrison we found that the leadership's support and commitment is not enough. Nor does leadership take the same form

or style in all companies. The executives at Acme, Advanced, and Gant varied considerably in how visible and critical they were as drivers of the diversity effort in their companies.

We know of many companies where the CEO and other top executives were sincerely committed to diversity, but the desired results did not follow. Some of these companies now have *revolving doors* for talented people of color, recruiting the best and brightest among them, only to see them leave, frustrated or angered by their experience. Other companies are able to retain such individuals, but observe them plateaued in middle management. In these cases, the only executives of color are found in racialized jobs such as EEO, community relations, government affairs, or ethnic markets.

Some executives who want to see progress lament that diversity is not an integral part of the way their companies do business and think about management. Their organizations have not moved beyond numbers and issues of compliance. We asked why this may have happened and heard that, as the assault on affirmative action heated up during the 1980s, the company followed the government's lead or the leadership changed. Most recently, we are often told that the pressures of competition pushed diversity to the back burner.

Our three companies represent a stark contrast. Each had the same starting point in the 1960s as other companies. They too faced the competitive challenges in the 1980s. And yet not only were their results in diversifying the management ranks different, but so was their experience with diversity. Interviewees at each company described racial diversity—representation of people of color at all levels—"as part of the way we think about the organization." Even interviewees who were critical of their companies' efforts acknowledged that diversity was a core part of the company's self-image and philosophy. In the turbulent business climate of the 1990s, they warned about any potential loss of diversity. Their primary fear was the disappearance of a vital aspect of the company culture, and not simply the numbers of minorities declining or their companies' reputations being damaged.

In fact, for all the distinctiveness of the three diversity approaches we considered in Chapter 7—the "melting pot" at Acme, "valuing differences" at Advanced, and "leveling the playing field" at Gant—they all do share crucial features, specifically in terms of the processes that drove diversity. Our emphasis is on processes rather than programs—diversity policies and interventions—which have been the focus of other studies.[2]

We identified six common process elements that helped promote and sustain the diversity efforts at Acme Industries, Advanced Technology, and Gant Electronics.

1. Key executives and senior managers became involved in and committed to the inclusion of people of color in the organization.

2. At each company, a partnership emerged between change-oriented employees and white senior executives based on a shared commitment to equal opportunity. What began as vehicles for the design and implementation of the diversity strategy became crucibles for learning about differences as well as symbols of the possibility for change.

3. People of color were active participants in promoting change.

4. The companies' approaches to diversity supported not only the hiring and promotion of people of color, but also their development in core functions of the business.

5. During the 1980s, the companies revisited their diversity efforts with a special emphasis on ensuring opportunity at the executive level.

6. Racial diversity became an integral part of each company's basic assumptions about its workforce and institutional identity as a result of the evident alignment between the company's diversity strategy and its culture.

TOP MANAGEMENT SUPPORT

The importance of top management support cannot be overstated. Despite differences among the companies we studied, it was apparent at each. Top management's most obvious role was in making racial diversity part of their agenda and in authorizing action. As a result, other managers followed top management's lead and change agents felt supported in their efforts to promote diversity.

Legitimating Diversity

At Gant Electronics, for example, three successive CEOs publicly identified themselves with their organization's diversity efforts. In the wake of the urban race riots of the 1960s, the CEO committed the company to institute nondiscriminatory hiring and to help rebuild the urban communities in which Gant operated. This was immediately followed by intensive efforts to hire minorities into non-exempt and support staff roles. Even though inroads into the management and professional ranks were slower in coming, the CEO's leadership set the tone.

A decade later, the next CEO followed suit. African American professionals were about to file a class-action suit against Gant for unfair labor practices. The CEO stepped in, assessed the legitimacy of their claims, and negotiated a settlement, thereby setting a precedent for an ongoing partnership between the company's executives and minority employees, now including women, to monitor conditions in the company. This partnership directly influenced the employee-involvement effort that the CEO thinks helped to turn the company around in the mid-1980s.

At Advanced Technology, Chris Hornbeck, the senior vice president for operations, was singled out repeatedly in interviews as a white executive who supported diversity. Several of the diversity initiatives that moved Advanced beyond its original affirmative action hiring goals began in divisions reporting to him. On the other hand, Advanced's CEO simply allowed the changes to happen, thereby legitimating them though not taking an active part in the movement. His approach was characteristic of how things got done at Advanced, with its bottom-up culture. The CEO's practice was only to voice opposition or to exercise a veto when he questioned an idea's appropriateness to the Advanced philosophy. His behavior signaled that diversity was a legitimate endeavor for the company, but not one of his personal priorities.

Executive Mentoring

In addition to promoting or authorizing diversity practices, senior managers and executives also acted as mentors and sponsors to minorities. In each company, there was a cadre of three or four white senior managers and executives who had mentored several of our minority executives and middle managers. Many of these mentors had participated in the initial diversity efforts of the 1970s. Frequently our minority executives told us that these white executives had taken a risk to give them their big break, promoting them into new assignments with a higher level of responsibility. Not surprisingly, these white executives often managed the parts of the company that had demonstrated the most overall progress at becoming racially diverse.

These mentoring activities were important in several respects. First, they created opportunities for minorities. Sponsorship by these highly credible white senior managers helped their protégés get the high-visibility special assignments needed to boost their career trajectories beyond middle management where they might have plateaued without such sponsorship.

Second, the public symbolism of white executives' willingness to pursue diversity efforts and to mentor high-performing people of color signaled to white subordinates the seriousness and personal investment of the leadership in promoting diverse management. This, in turn, reduced the perceived risk that these subordinates might have associated with sponsoring minorities for high-visibility assignments.

Third, witnessing cross-race mentoring and sponsorship affected minorities' own perceptions and experiences. People of color commonly report feeling that while there may be much *discussion* of the value of diversity, there is little real *evidence*. They observe the apparent lack of personal involvement by managers and executives.[3] Signals such as cross-race mentoring alliances and the sponsorship of minority employees temper the doubt that may accompany an acute awareness of the many instances when contributions by people of color have been devalued or inhibited. The organization's employees of color can now believe that it is possible to develop alliances across racial lines and to be rewarded for their contributions. These white mentors then become sought after by potential minority protégés. Work by David Thomas on the formation of cross-race mentoring alliances suggests that protégés often seek mentors whose views about race correspond with their own. In some cases, they have been told by other minorities that the individual is open to mentoring minorities.[4]

Finally, the mentoring relationship can serve as a crucible for learning about race relations in the workplace. Thomas demonstrates that cross-race mentoring relationships can offer both parties the opportunity to learn about differences. And white mentors who openly discuss issues of race with their protégés are more successful in getting them promoted than those who do not.[5]

◢ PARTNERSHIPS FOR CHANGE

Clearly, top management support for change is important for diversity efforts, just as for any other major policy or strategic initiative. However, it is not sufficient to produce the unique level of racial diversity that was seen in the executive suites of Acme, Gant, and Advanced. A critical element is the emergence and maintenance of a *change partnership*—a relationship or set of relationships that involves stakeholders who collectively represent the interests of the corporation and its racial minorities, and who share a common goal of actively pursuing the racial diversification of the organization's management. Beyond their symbolic importance, these partnerships between powerful executives and people who became change agents helped to facilitate learning about racial dynamics in the organization and to implement the diversity strategy.

The change partners at Acme were among Ned Bowman, the CEO, and the president. The Gant partnership included the self-help groups and Gordon Kingsley, and was supported by key corporate managers, especially those responsible for HR. At Advanced, there were two significant partnerships: one between Jim Sawyer, an African American HR manager, and the white senior vice president for operations, and the other between white executive Michael Pennings and African American consultant Deborah Jones.

Consistently, one party in these partnerships symbolized and had responsibility for the broad interests of the organization. This party had a personal interest in protecting the organization from anything that might threaten its effective functioning. At all three companies, white male executives served this role. These individuals' credibility came not only from their formal positions but also from their track records, their reputations for integrity, and their tenure in the organization.

The other party in these partnerships represented and was personally invested in change. Most often this partner was a person of color. At Advanced it was the personnel manager, Jim Sawyer, and, later,

Deborah Jones. At Gant this party was a group, the leaders of the self-help movement. At Acme the partner was a white male, but one with connections to minority communities and the civil rights movement. In each case, these partners were credible because of their track records and their support from senior executives. Even more important, they had credibility with people of color in the organization. Often they acted as conduits of information and interpreters of management action to minorities. Frequently these persons were also central members of the informal networks that developed among minorities in the corporation.

Change didn't happen without resistance, both conscious and unconscious, overt and covert. These partnerships were critical to managing the tension and anxiety that developed as the organizations began directly to encounter the reality of diversity. Such partnerships also provided the mechanisms and context to solve problems and achieve organizational compromise.[6]

The parties in these partnerships adapted to organizational change by learning not only about race issues but also about other human relations concerns. Gordon Kingsley has said that his interaction with self-help groups helped him learn about both broader issues related to the management and deployment of the workforce at Gant and their disproportionate impact on employees of color. The importance of organizational learning is also reflected in the adaptive diversity strategies these companies pursued; for example, such learning led Deborah Jones and Michael Pennings at Advanced to launch dialogue groups as a corporate change tactic.

Finally, these relationships were all characterized by the ability to speak truthfully about difficult issues. People liked and trusted each other and were able to influence one another. These qualities help to explain both why the relationships may have been so successful and why they may be so hard to replicate.

◢ MINORITY ACTIVISM

In Chapter 6 we noted that many of our executives benefited from developmental relationships with other persons of color. These took the form of peer relationships—in which the parties worked to share information, coach, counsel, and support one another—and of mentorships between a junior person and a more senior person. While these relationships certainly possessed a personal element, they also served an organizational function by facilitating the active participation of minorities within the company, by creating opportunity, and by ensuring success for people of color as a group.

Self-help was a component of minority activism. At Advanced and Gant, the common characteristics of active self-help efforts by people of color included

- formal organizations, such as the minority forums that emerged in the early 1970s at Gant and in the late 1980s at Advanced;

- informal networks among employees of color; and

- the conscious and overt efforts of individual managers and executives of color to use their own power to facilitate diversity.

Formal Organizations

The dual commitment to help members succeed by means of high performance and to create opportunity through advocacy is at the core of formal support groups.[7] Focusing on performance and individual success helps people act with the recognition that racism is real but not completely determinative. They thus avoid fatalistic approaches to coping with the challenges race can present.

These groups helped people of color perform by teaching critical skills and passing along information to those with limited access to the informal social networks available to whites. They also served as a place to get a reality check on feedback received from whites whose motives and objectivity were not always trusted.[8]

In terms of advocacy, the groups formalized and crystallized the experiences of many individuals into distinct racial and ethnic patterns. The grievances of individuals were too often and too easily chalked up to explanations that diminished the significance of race, whereas grievances based on a pattern of experiences of many minorities got management's attention and action.

The advocacy role also provided protection to individuals. The leaders of these organizations, while running some risk of being labeled agitators, were less vulnerable and had more legitimacy when they spoke as representatives. Clearly some of the leaders of the self-help movement at Gant thought their jobs might at times be at risk. The reality, however, was that most went on to do quite well in their careers while at Gant and, in the case of some, when they moved to other organizations. Today, several of the original representatives are among the executives and upper-middle managers who participated in our study.

Advocacy also produced specific opportunities. Part of an advocacy role is reporting on how the system is doing. These groups pointed out the existence of glass ceilings and challenged the company to remove such artificial barriers. Often, following a period of agitation and advocacy on such issues, someone broke through the barrier.

Championing Diversity

The story of changing race relations in the American corporation during the 1960s and 1970s was, in essence, one of getting whites to exercise the moral authority and power to support equal opportunity. This was true at these three companies as elsewhere. However, by the 1980s people of color themselves increasingly began to occupy senior management and executive positions. They too had to make choices about how they would act to further the cause of racial integration. Some minorities decided that their personal success was contribution enough. There has long been a debate as to whether playing the role of racial advocate can damage the careers of managers and executives of color.[9]

In the context of our study, we discovered that several of our interviewees had made personal efforts to create opportunities for other people of color and, more generally, to demonstrate the benefits of diversity. For example, Jim Sawyer, who ultimately became a member of the corporation's executive committee, was described as having continually worked for the advancement of people of color, promoting several to the executive level. Other minority executives served as role models and mentors who lent their personal time and credibility to this goal.

◢ A DEVELOPMENTAL APPROACH

We have often heard from executives serious about achieving diversity, but new to such efforts, that there are no suitable internal minority candidates. The best talents have left or been steered into staff jobs early in their careers. We also hear of people of color whose stars once shone bright, but now have settled into a state of being "just as good as the average white guy." The implication is, "good enough to keep their job, but not to take a leading role within the corporation."

We didn't hear such complaints at these three companies. Gant, Advanced, and Acme were able to fill the pipelines in their key businesses and functions with high-performing minorities. Minority professionals were hired into core functions and not simply placed in non-essential jobs. Marketing, for example, was at the heart of Gant, and many of the professionals of color hired worked there. Operations was the heart of Acme, and it's where nearly all of the minority executives started. Advanced relied on its inner-city and border plants to attract people of color. One might argue that these sites were ghettos, but the work in the plants was pure manufacturing, engineering, or finance. The minorities we interviewed described these plants as exciting and challenging places to work, and were where many of the company's executives of color started their careers.

The results-oriented environments of these companies was another factor in minority development. This was true of the engineering and manufacturing environments at Advanced and Gant, just as it was for the operations and marketing areas of Acme and Gant. In the context of the efforts that were underway to ensure diversity, the organizations' ability to identify high-potential minority candidates was enhanced by having objective measures of their competence in core business functions and track records of measurable results. Similarly, it was perhaps easier for these individuals to establish and maintain personal goals for excellence in environments where at least some important elements of performance could be assessed objectively.

More generally, the three companies' diversity efforts benefited from their historical preference for promoting executives from within. Acme had a rigid system of advancing only internal candidates to upper management and executive positions. Gant and Advanced had implicit stances toward giving internal candidates preference at early management positions, but there was variation across departments. By and large, however, executive positions in all three organizations went to insiders. Managers early in their career could identify traceable paths to the executive suite. In particular, people of color could assess the pattern of assignments that might best prepare them for the executive level.

◢ A Focus on Diversity at the Top

Each organization in the mid- to late 1980s found it necessary to focus explicitly on minority representation at the executive level. Before this point, each company had promoted at least one person of color to an executive-level job, but it became obvious that for significant representation to occur, there needed to be a sharper focus and greater emphasis. This took several forms. At Acme, the CEO and group vice presidents asked their direct reports to identify and develop promising people of color and women. The HR staff also became more active in monitoring whether minority middle managers were receiving the developmental assignments needed to prepare them for executive jobs.

At Gant, the focus was on creating a demographically representative workforce at all levels. Succession planning processes at Gant explicitly began to take account of people of color in the pipeline. Several who later became executives were given special developmental assignments. Gant's affirmative action processes also set goals for minority representation at the highest levels of the company—goals that had largely been met by 1992.

At Advanced, the work involved two factors: (1) the creation of formalized minority networks to advocate with management and (2) the reinvigoration of the affirmative action monitoring function to feed data into the system about where people of color were getting stuck in the pipeline. Much of the focus was on managers. Jim Sawyer used his influence to create discussion on this issue at the top of the pyramid. People of color also took advantage of relationships made in dialogue groups to bring this issue to the attention of white executives with whom they were familiar.

One might ask, If the diversity efforts in these organizations were so successful, why was the added focus on minority development and advancement necessary? Our response is speculative, deriving as much from our clinical observations and research in other settings as from the interviews we conducted for this study. First, these organizations are not racial utopias; biases still exist within them. One widely shared bias is the unconscious tendency for people to attract and select people like themselves. Rosabeth Moss Kanter has called the organizational consequence of this bias "homosocial reproduction."[10] Therefore, just as it was important to focus on changing the numbers at the bottom of the pyramid and to create conditions conducive to full participation, the same was necessary fifteen years later at the top of these organizations.

Another reality is that the further up the organizational pyramid, the smaller the ratio of available openings to candidates. Related to this, the importance of these jobs makes the risk associated with failure more consequential than at lower levels of management. Decision makers under these conditions, who must sell their choice to a larger group of people, are likely to act conservatively, preferring candidates with whom they feel personally and professionally comfortable.[11]

We would argue, however, that the process of changing the general culture and mind-set around race is a critical precondition to being successful in advancing minorities to the executive level. Above all, having a truly diverse organization and a supportive culture helps ensure that there is a pipeline of qualified internal minority candidates. The very existence of such individuals puts pressure on the system to change, such that lack of representation at the executive level becomes a more obvious omission. Such efforts also help to diminish the affirmative action stigma that may be attached to making it into the executive ranks. Organizations that have created a pipeline filled with viable candidates are less likely to devalue the accomplishments of a person of color when there is an active effort to ensure that minorities have access to executive-level consideration.

◢ Alignment Between Company Culture and Diversity Strategy

The common enablers we've described so far in this chapter manifest themselves differently at each of our companies. These differences are easy to understand when viewed in light of the diversity strategies pursued at each firm. This observation underscores the final and, perhaps, most important common element in the approaches to diversity taken by Acme, Gant, and Advanced. In all three companies the motivating rhetoric and core tactics that constituted their diversity strategies were *aligned* with distinctive aspects of the organization's culture. Furthermore, the process used to implement the strategy exploited inherent strengths and weaknesses of the organization.

The notion of organizational alignment and its critical importance to strategy implementation and organizational effectiveness has been well documented.[12] The premise is that the elements of an organizational system should fit together in a manner that creates synergies and fosters an optimal degree of integration. Alignment in the context of diversity strategy requires that the language or rhetoric used to motivate action should build on corporate values that are universally acceptable within the organization.

Why is a motivating rhetoric critical? Business organizations do not exist as social enterprises dedicated to the betterment of racial inequality. In order for an initiative that requires long-term commitment to succeed, it must be viewed as consistent with—if not also enhancing—the organization. Creating this perception is not only a matter of actions but also of framing those actions for others so as to link the initiative to meaningful outcomes. These can be of two types: outcomes linked positively to task performance, and outcomes that justify or enhance members' investment in core or shared beliefs about the organization. For example, at Acme, diversity was framed as if it were a test of whether the corporation was a true meritocracy. Later, as the culture began to focus on effective people management, diversity was linked to progress on that dimension.

Success at diversifying management in these companies required action. Each company used many different tactics, most importantly the ones we described in Chapter 7 that were applied across the organization and considered by the organization members to be at the heart of the diversity strategy. Such core tactics supported rhetoric consistent with the premises on which the diversity effort was said to be based. And they leveraged aspects of the culture, especially norms related to task performance, to influence progress on diversity goals.

This took the form of exploiting weaknesses or unmet needs as well as supporting valued aspects of the performance culture of the company. Diversity effort leaders used already legitimate structures, systems, and modes of behavior to gain acceptance of racial diversity as a goal and its adoption as a basic assumption of the corporation. At the same time they worked to alter aspects of the culture or system that negatively impacted minorities' access to opportunity.

Alignment at Gant

Gant Electronics was a well-established, sixty-year-old company in 1970. New technologies patented in the 1950s had spurred tremendous growth in the 1960s. So in some respects it was a young company, but it had a long history and a supply of seasoned managers.

With its products well received in the marketplace and patent protection providing it a virtual monopoly, Gant's main concern was increasing the sales volume of its high-margin product and trying to meet manufacturing demand. Marketing was clearly the dominant functional group in the organization. Most of the company's corporate leadership came from this area. Many employees felt that a stint in marketing was a prerequisite for entering the executive ranks.

Gant's marketing image set the tone and external perception of the company. Following the style of its "super salesman" president, its sales force was aggressive and professional. Sales representatives were well educated, polished, and articulate. A college degree was a prerequisite. Since competition was not fierce, they focused on selling the client on the "best" products appropriate to their needs. This often translated into the most expensive.

With its success, Gant developed an inward focus and invulnerable attitude toward the marketplace. One interviewee described it this way: "It was like we owned the world. Our whole attitude toward the marketplace was one of arrogance. We did not treat our customers very well. We were the only game in town." This description of the company was echoed by several interviewees who reflected on this early period. They admitted that during the 1970s, this attitude was not considered arrogance; it was viewed as a justified sense of superiority over its competitors. After all, Gant hired the best people and made the best products. It also treated its people well, providing things such as professional development opportunities and promotional opportunity.

Gant's fast pace and youthful culture belied its bureaucracy. To manage its growth over the years, the company had become hierarchical and oriented toward formal systems. Corporate staffs had substantial power, and, unlike Advanced, most change was initiated at the top. A source at Gant went so far as to describe the culture of the 1970s as a "staff-driven organization," referring to the power held by those in the central bureaucracy.

Market dominance facilitated by patent protection had also created an inward focus. Turf wars were legendary. Disagreements between design and manufacturing often had to be resolved at the vice-presidential level at corporate headquarters. Coordination between marketing and manufacturing posed continual problems. Managers felt the need to maintain their power bases. One executive described his decision not to relocate and take a major promotion in the North American Sales Organization's corporate headquarters in Detroit: "They asked me to come to Detroit, but I refused. I knew they would crush me. I did not have a base of power there. In those days, if you were too far from your network, it was not good." Coalitions were important and formed and dissolved as interests changed.

Gant also took pride in being a results-oriented organization. Production quotas were set on the basis of prior performance and internally generated demands for revenue growth. Goals were set for individuals at each level of the hierarchy. These individual goals fostered little sense of interdependence or cooperation among individuals or units and bred a very competitive culture. One interviewee, reflecting on the period, noted: "It was results, results, and results. That was it. It did not matter how you got there. As long as you got results, you just kept moving up. In fact, it didn't matter if you stepped over a few people or killed a few along the way."

The intergroup negotiation diversity strategy that emerged at Gant was easily accommodated in Gant's corporate culture. The self-help groups emphasized individual performance. In a culture that valued professionalism and polish, the visibility of these high-performing minorities was important. By 1970, Gant had in place a system of performance goals and metrics that made it relatively straightforward for individuals to prove their abilities. The performance of members of the self-help groups also legitimated the support the groups received from the corporation. At Gant, self-help groups met on their own time, which was viewed as indicating personal commitment to "going the extra mile to be the best."

Self-help groups evolved naturally in the political climate of Gant, with its turf wars and attention to power bases, and constituted a point of leverage. Corporate leaders were accustomed to negotiating turf battles with business unit leaders and understood the need to manage constituencies and power bases. The lawsuit brought to management's attention the power of a previously undefined constituency, one whose interest now had to be addressed, either through collaboration and negotiation or means of dismissal. Some in the corporate leadership initially resisted the idea of working with the self-help group leaders. They argued that the group represented a union-like threat that should be resisted. However, once the decision was made to collaborate, the corporate staffs knew how to use their negotiating skills to work with the self-help groups' concerns.

The timing of the self-help groups' emergence was critical. In the 1970s, executives at Gant were becoming aware that the corporate culture needed to change. Many knew that the high level of politically motivated behavior was hurting the company, despite the value traditionally placed on individual performance. It was also clear that the New York–based executives were out of touch with the daily realities of the company, with its sales and manufacturing in Detroit. The alliance with the self-help groups gave the executives another line of communication outside the normal bureaucratic channels.

The drive of the self-help groups to become fully enfranchised and their focus on performance represented a potential model for organizational improvement and cultural change. Here was a group calling for the removal of barriers to performance, but not a dismantling of the core values of professionalism and goal-driven achievement. Gordon Kingsley noted many years after the beginning of his relationship with the self-help group leaders that it was the precursor of employee involvement at Gant, a step that had been credited with turning the company around in the late 1980s.

Alignment at Advanced

Robert Testa came to Advanced Technology in 1970 and, a decade later, was one of its chief technologists. He described the culture he found on his arrival:

> *The culture was terrific. The value system here was based on the founders' concepts of "do the right thing." Everybody had to understand that doing the right thing meant doing it on a multitude of dimensions, for co-workers, subordinates, the company, and the customer. Wherever you could help, you made sure that people had some idea of what direction to go in. There was enough freedom to discover new things.*

In many ways, Advanced was the precursor to the high-tech ventures populating Silicon Valley. Its culture valued technical knowledge; engineers and scientists held the reins of power; ideas and creativity were all important. Advanced attracted many top-flight people from companies that had long stopped being technological leaders.

For employees, there was another side to Advanced's culture. Several of our interviewees described having difficult transitions into the company Coming from larger, more established firms, they underestimated the extent to which Advanced was loosely organized. Authority did not always follow responsibility, and roles were unclear.

> *It was difficult getting acclimated. The kinds of systems you would have thought were in place simply were not. A lot of it was because the company was growing so fast. All of this added to the complexity. It also afforded ... a lot of creativity, a lot of growth and opportunity. Risks were acceptable.*
>
> —MINORITY EXECUTIVE

> *Complete randomness of management is the only way I can put it. I went into my first meeting and there were 100 people in the room trying to define the future product content in a high-end product. The product manager was standing in the front wearing a helmet and holding a baseball bat. It was a wild environment.*
>
> —WHITE EXECUTIVE

So, if Advanced was this open, creative place on the edge of chaos, what held it together? Our data provide a clear answer: *relationships*. The importance of relationships and networks echoed through every interview we held at Advanced, with whites and minorities. Relationships were the glue that held the organization together. Academics who have studied the organization describe it as a "network organization." In other words, it was a place in which hierarchy and formal roles were not determinants of interaction patterns, nor did formal authority guarantee the ability to get things done. Instead, the key was how one was connected in a web of social relationships and interdependencies.

The most fundamental relationship in this network culture was the tie between each employee and the company itself. This bond, in the form of a social contract, obliged employees to "do the right thing" in exchange for the broad latitude and empowerment the company gave them. The phrase itself—*do the right thing*—was coined by the company's founder and has remained a touchstone for individual and group behavior and decisions at Advanced. Achieving diversity became clearly identified as "the right thing" for all Advanced employees to do.

Another critical element in Advanced's diversity strategy was its grassroots nature. Just as this bottom-up style was an integral aspect of the corporate culture, many felt that it was also an important element of the diversity strategy. The pluralist, valuing-differences strategy first emerged in the company's manufacturing operations and attracted support from other parts of the company as it proved successful. This pathway was important in the engineering-led culture of Advanced, where ideas needed to be supported by hard evidence or buttressed by experience. People could see the results of the inner-city plants' improved performance. The rhetoric of empowerment matched the company's emphasis on creativity and individual initiative.

The dialogue groups that developed at Advanced produced outcomes that were characterized in terms of the company's core values. Dialogue groups promoted self-development in the form of individual learning about biases and more effective ways of engaging others who were different. Dialogue groups also helped build relationships that would help people get things done in the future. Corporate management evidently saw direct benefits in terms of organizational improvements, for they legitimated the dialogue groups by encouraging them to meet during work hours despite typically hectic and full schedules.

Perhaps the most important aspect of Advanced's strategy was its focus on transforming relationships. Moving people of color into executive-level roles would ultimately depend on the quality of relationships that formed across race.

Alignment at Acme

Acme's ability to become racially diverse at all levels was in several respects a test of the culture's values. Many saw Acme as a pure meritocracy, especially at the lower- and middle-management levels. A common refrain among Acme employees and management is that people's origins do not matter: "People are differentiated by what they do, not where they come from." Acme had already proven this with working-class white males, many of whom had been immigrants or first-generation Americans in the company's early years. The integration of racial minorities was positioned as an extension of the company's firmly entrenched melting pot strategy. The assimilation strategy that emerged at Acme fit with the company's preference for promoting from within, its development of firm-specific skills, its ownership by employees, and its military-like environment.

Interestingly, the change partnership at Acme did not include a person of color. Instead, it was Acme's CEO, president, and Ned Bowman, all three of whom were white males. Bowman, however, was a bridge between the as-of-yet unfamiliar and untapped communities of people of color and the white-dominated hierarchy. He understood both the organization's culture and the life experiences of people of color, especially African Americans, and could serve as a guide for Acme's management. Bowman was able to successfully open Acme's culture by convincing its leadership that racial integration was an extension of Acme's core values. Focusing first and foremost on top management was consistent with Acme's culture, as was Bowman's community service program for managers with high potential but unacceptable racist attitudes. The goal of these efforts was not to change the system, but rather to change individual attitudes and behaviors.

While Acme's nondiscrimination and equal opportunity policies were clear, its monitoring of racial minority advancement and development was less visible in the 1980s to the broader employee population. Unlike Gant and Advanced where minority managers and executives spoke directly about the impact of their companies' diversity efforts on their careers, Acme interviewees almost never discussed it. This too fit with Acme's assimilation model and the normative stance that race should not matter.

At Acme, minority networks did not play the part they did at Advanced or Gant. Throughout the 1960s, 1970s, and 1980s, there were no organized self-help groups at Acme. People of color served as role models and mentors, but apparently no minority networks were established to assist in development and advancement. Individual minority executives at Acme acted to ensure equity within the organization, as did white executives, but they did this as part of their job, not as minority advocates. Instead, a common sentiment that emerged in our interviews at Acme was one in which race was not expected to be a primary source of identity at work. Both minorities and whites described themselves as being color blind:

> In my upbringing within Acme, I worked as an individual and aligned myself with individuals. But I have not aligned myself with any particular racial group.
>
> —HISPANIC AMERICAN EXECUTIVE

> I tell them [other African Americans], I'm not your brother. I don't talk slang. It eliminates favoritism. I've had more problems from blacks [than whites]. When I went to Florida some thought, "Oh we got a brother coming down here, he's gonna take care of the brothers." I said, "I'm here to take care of every Acme employee. I don't have any brothers here."
>
> —AFRICAN AMERICAN EXECUTIVE

The difference in behavior at Acme and the other two companies may not depend strictly on differences in racial attitudes or levels of racial consciousness. Instead, these distinctions seem to emerge from the specific approaches to diversity taken. At Acme, racial differences were deemed to be task irrelevant, so diversity efforts focused on homogenizing identity and creating a true melting pot. In this way, the behavior of minority employees was clearly aligned with the culture and diversity strategy of the organization. Acme's approach resembles the pattern reported by Charles Moskos and John Butler in their study of the U.S. Army.[13] They observed that African American officers were less likely than civilians to see the need to openly engage in discussions of race in the workplace. Such seeming lack of racial-group awareness or self-promotion occurred in the context of the Army's very proactive efforts to eliminate bias and racial harassment and, like Acme, to create a true meritocracy.

Indeed, the success of Acme's strategy may have depended on minorities assuming a stance about race that complemented that of the Acme culture and its assimilation strategy for achieving diversity. Common responses to questions about race were as follows: "I never felt anything about being black at Acme"; "I can honestly say that no one I worked for was ever a racist"; and "I don't think race ever held me back."

Note that these statements are focused on the corporation. In other parts of their interviews, minority managers and executives sometimes mentioned feeling pressure to perform better than their white peers or to be a role model, and lamented that people sometimes saw them as a "minority VP," instead of just an "Acme VP." Yet somehow, these pressures were not viewed as products of the Acme system, but more the unavoidable realities of individual prejudice—the stuff people brought to work with them. The good news was that the system did not let such prejudices infect its processes or belief systems and, ultimately, the opportunities available to people of color.

A final point: We noticed that in several interviews when minorities shared experiences of encountering prejudice, they did so after the tape was turned off. One interpretation might be that they would only share this information off the record because they distrusted the confidentiality of the interview process, though this is unlikely because they shared many personal confidences on tape. Furthermore, there is no reason to believe that they would be less trusting than interviewees at Advanced and Gant. A more plausible explanation is that comments that might acknowledge race as a factor in the work experience violates the psychological contract between minorities who feel they have prospered in the system and the company that has worked so hard to ensure that they could.

◢ A FRAMEWORK FOR MINORITY EXECUTIVE DEVELOPMENT AND ADVANCEMENT

In this chapter and Chapter 7 we have detailed both the distinguishing and common features of the diversity efforts at each of the companies. Our findings call attention to the importance of processes and enabling conditions rather than specific policies or programs, such as mentoring, targeted development, and recruitment initiatives. Much of what we describe about the role of leadership, the importance of partnerships, and the necessity of alignment between corporate culture and change resonates with other studies of organizational transformation and renewal.[14] Our work, however, grounds these common aspects of change in the specifics of achieving racial diversity in management. Central to this change process is the company's diversity strategy. It is at the core of creating an environment that enables people of color to reap the benefits of their development at each successive stage of career.

At any given point in their careers, minority individuals must be in possession of the attitudes, intellect, and skills needed to expand on the foundation of competence, credibility, and confidence. Their ability to do so requires access to opportunity and development at each career stage. *Opportunity*, here, means assignments that place individuals in a position to perform and advance further.[15] *Development* is the personal growth and expansion of human and social capital that individuals gain from engaging in the opportunity, which includes enhanced relationships as well as skills and knowledge.

Racial barriers can limit minority access to the opportunity and development needed to advance at a particular stage of career. It is possible, for example, for a company to reduce race-related barriers to opportunity and development in Stage 1 or Stage 2, but then discover that in later stages minority access to opportunity is blocked or development is hindered. A major aspect of an effective diversity strategy is ensuring that opportunity and development are as available to minorities as to whites. Doing this requires focusing on diversity issues explicitly and making the culture of the organization more tolerant and inclusive. Without these actions, discrete programs to target minorities will not succeed because they will not be able to overcome the invisible barriers to minority advancement.

Cultures that truly support minority advancement also enable individual action. Managers in such cultures are more likely to act as sponsors of minorities or to take personal responsibility for the diversity climate in their organizations. Minority individuals begin to assert their own desires for mobility and to work at ensuring access for others.

Our work suggests that producing minority executives cannot depend on programs, but rather on processes that enable individuals to apply themselves to the work of ensuring minority access to both development and opportunity. The role of corporate leaders in making this happen is the subject of our next chapter.

IV

THE LESSONS

9

Corporate Leadership for Minority Advancement

WHAT CAN GENERAL MANAGERS, HR executives, and others wishing to promote racial diversity in their organizations do to achieve it? This is a question that increasing numbers of executives in corporate America are struggling to answer. The fact that many of them are not satisfied with the status quo makes us optimistic about the possibility of more companies being able to join Acme, Advanced, and Gant as institutions where race is not an insurmountable obstacle to reaching the highest levels of corporations.

Despite facing economic and social conditions very different from those of the 1960s and 1970s, many firms find themselves in a position not unlike the one faced by our three companies in the mid- to late 1970s: they have proven themselves able to recruit and hire talented people of color into entry-level professional and managerial jobs, but are unable to ensure their development and advancement into positions at the upper ranks of core business units. It is to these corporations and their leaders that the findings of this study are perhaps most applicable and to whom we wish to speak directly here.

Knowledge about specific processes for assessing an organization's current environment for diversity already exists. Applied behavioral scientists such as Clayton Alderfer, Taylor Cox, and Roosevelt Thomas have written extensively on these issues elsewhere.[1] Similarly, research by individuals such as Ann Morrison identifies the array of practical programs and tactics available to corporations to aid them in achieving their diversity goals.[2] Much of the work can provide guidance at both the HR policy and at the tactical intervention level. In contrast, the focus of this chapter is on the implications for general managers and senior level executives in shaping and driving such efforts. Corporate initiatives must begin where the company is today.

What follows in this chapter is an articulation of seven lessons that can provide guidance to the current diversity efforts of companies. This discussion assumes that a desired result of these efforts is to enable the company to become more effective in developing and advancing people of color to its upper-middle and executive levels. These lessons are organized around the three themes at the heart of our study:

1. Creating an enabling organizational context

2. Ensuring that opportunity exists

3. Ensuring that development takes place

We end the chapter with a discussion of several questions raised by our study concerning the two tournaments described in Chapter 3 and their implications for minority careers.

◢ CREATING AN ENABLING ORGANIZATION

One of the clearest findings from our study is that the type of diversity strategy is less important in producing minority executives than is creating a strategy that is aligned with the culture. Three ingredients are critical to developing this capacity to create alignment: leadership at the top, the ability to build successful partnerships, and changing and maintaining corporate culture.

Lesson #1: Corporate leaders must become personally involved in diversity initiatives.

The support and commitment of key members of the corporations' executive leadership is critical to the success of diversity efforts. As is the case with any major change, they play a key role in legitimating the process. This is conveyed by both their official actions and the symbolism of their behavior. The leader must behave in ways that communicate that the diversity effort is congruent with the organization's core values and goals. This goes well beyond attaching one's name to proclamations about the importance of diversity. Executives must become personally involved and articulate the ways in which the diversity strategy is related to the company's vision, mission, business imperatives, or values. In each of our three companies, there were corporate executives who personally engaged in the diversity effort. In addition to acting as champions of the change process, they mentored and sponsored minority managers. They were also involved as co-facilitators and initiators of the diversity work with others. Their behavior created tangible results (e.g., significant opportunities for the minorities they sponsored) and provided role modeling for those who were responsible for the implementation of the diversity effort.

Lesson #2: Corporate leaders should build partnerships to ensure the long-term success of diversity efforts.

Ultimately the ownership and the leadership of change must be shared. The chances of leading a successful change are enhanced by the existence of a partnership like the ones we described in Chapter 8. They provide a place where the tensions that result from changing the organization can be constructively contained and where learning from the experience of attempting change can take place. Within this setting, the elements of the organization that resist or support change can be identified, worked with, and exploited.

Many companies that are having difficulty implementing diversity goals lack such an alliance. The result is that diversity efforts become the sole responsibility of HR departments, out of the hands of top leaders who are in the most powerful positions to make things happen. Even more problematic is when these efforts move forward with little or no participation of minorities.

Although the partnerships that developed in our three companies occurred in the 1960s, 1970s, and 1980s, similar successful partnerships are emerging in U.S. companies today. One such example is the partnership that developed at the Core States Bank in the 1990s, when then-CEO Terry Larsen formed a critical alliance with Yvette Hyatter-Adams, who ultimately became a senior vice president and corporate officer. Hyatter-Adams had initial responsibility for the diversity effort. Working closely, the two realized that diversity needed to be linked with the other major changes unfolding at the bank. This was accomplished by consolidating the reengineering, diversity, and culture change efforts of the company under one umbrella run by Hyatter-Adams. It was obvious that in a time of major change at the company, the diversity effort could not be put on hold as other significant changes were rolled out. As a result, they avoided the trap that has imperiled other companies' diversity efforts: When the corporate focus shifted to efficiency, quality, and cost reduction, the diversity effort was lost. This gives rise to the belief that diversity is a "fair weather" issue that is not critical or integral to the business goals of the company.

Over time, Larsen's own understanding of diversity evolved. Starting with a vision that focused on a color-blind approach, he came to articulate a vision in which diversity was connected to individual and organizational performance. His learning and that of his leadership team were direct results of the partnership with Hyatter-Adams and the larger group of managers and employees who came to share their commitment to diversity.

The most powerful effect of such partnerships is that they encourage the formation of other, similar partnerships in two ways. First, they show results. At Gant, for example, top management's practice of meeting with representatives of self-help groups to identify issues and explore solutions spread to lower-level units. The further down the hierarchy the practice went, the more effective the organization's diversity efforts became as a whole. Not only was the structure mirrored but so were the personal alliances and relationships that developed at lower levels. The result was deeper levels of exchange, trust, and problem solving. The involved parties became more effective in their individual as well as collective efforts to support Gant's diversity initiatives.

Second, such partnerships model a type of collaboration seldom observed. People find them enticing and potentially enriching. The dialogue groups used at Advanced produced many such alliances. People who worked in the same unit began to unite their efforts to address performance problems. They worked at educating one another on differences of race and gender. Others joined because they saw potential benefits for themselves and their units.

A question frequently asked is, What does a firm do that has an initiative underway but no partnerships of this type? Simply put, it has to build them. The key to doing so is to create opportunities for those who are already committed to the process to strengthen their bonds. Remember that such partnerships are often more than just a two-person relationship. Partnerships can also involve groups, such as the self-help groups at Gant or a group of executives or managers. Clayton Alderfer and his colleagues built a partnership for change at "XYZ" Corporation that had at its core a race relations advisory team. Over a period of years this group, which was composed of minority and white managers, guided extensive intervention efforts with impressive results.[3] Critical to the evolution of their partnership was the participation of high-level executives and the direct involvement of the Black Managers Association, both of them groups that could build legitimacy and support for the effort.

Partnerships can also be facilitated by the person chosen to be responsible for diversity efforts. When Gant sent Gordon Kingsley to investigate the validity of discrimination claims and authorized him not only to protect the company but also to deal fairly with the complainants, this opened the possibility that a partnership could be formed. Corporations should give thought to who they make responsible for the diversity effort and how they authorize them. Routinely corporations place their most senior minority managers (there usually is not a minority executive available) in charge of it. A more effective choice might be to create an integrated leadership team, engendering the motivation for a cross-race partnership.

A final note on the creation of partnerships. The impetus for diversity efforts often originates from the grass roots. People who have experienced firsthand the challenges and tensions of being a minority usually are the ones most motivated to mobilize such change efforts. As was the case with the Gant self-help groups, it is critical to treat these efforts as opportunities to partner, rather than as threats. Maximizing the potential for partnership means treating the concerns of groups such as these as opportunities for growth and development. It is important not to assume that the motives of such individuals are antithetical to corporate interest.

Lesson #3: Corporate leaders must understand that creating alignment implies both maintaining and changing the corporate culture.

We believe that engagement by the leadership and the existence of partnerships are the key elements in creating the capacity for learning that makes the diversity strategy work. We must be clear that their existence does not guarantee success or make the task easy. Alignment does not mean unchallenged support of the status quo. Given the current state of most corporations, diversity efforts by definition will imply change and, in some cases, the altering of deeply held, but unexamined aspects of managing people and their careers.

Changing a culture while trying to reinforce critical elements of it is not easy. Yet according to James Collins and Jerry Porras, authors of *Built to Last*, a study of visionary companies, that is exactly what great companies do. Accomplishing this requires being aware of the corporation's core ideology and requirements for effective task performance, as well as finding a way of framing and enacting diversity initiatives so that they are experienced as enhancing the organization.

A vital aspect in creating alignment is the framing of the diversity effort and its role in the organization. In many respects, success is dependent on creating a rhetoric for diversity that motivates, based on its consonance with core values and its contribution to effective performance. We saw in Chapter 7 that each of the three companies framed its diversity effort so that it supported performance goals and was congruent with universal elements of its core ideologies—the value statements that form the basis of institutional identity. Thus, their diversity initiatives were positioned as enhancements and tests of the organization's ability to be its best.

An important implication of this focus on alignment is that the staff who are supporting diversity initiatives need to be change agents. They need change-management skills as well as the positional power and frame of reference to integrate the organization's diversity efforts with its mission and core business practices. An example is Ned Bowman, who was hired with a mandate to change Acme and was subsequently made head of HR. Deborah Jones at Advanced was brought in as a consultant and, after extensive work in the organization, hired into a position with direct access to the senior executives in manufacturing.

Finally, once alignment is achieved, it needs to be maintained by constant adjustment, learning, and monitoring. It is critical that organizations consider not only their internal corporate environments but also the external environment from which they draw employees. Take, for example, the question of what model or type of diversity strategy to choose. In some instances, organizations with homogenizing cultures such as Acme's may discover that their "color-blind" strategy is becoming less viable because of larger societal trends toward pluralism and people's desires for greater integration of personal and professional identities.

By 1990, all three of the companies found themselves needing to reexamine their diversity efforts to make sure they were in alignment with the company's business realities. Today, we live in a fast-paced, changing corporate world. This makes the need for ongoing, vigilant learning critical.

ENSURING OPPORTUNITY

There are many potential motivations for wanting to ensure racial diversity at all levels of a corporation. Similarly, there are many starting points in trying to accomplish this. Some focus initially on recruitment or hiring, while others begin with attitudes and awareness. The small number of minorities at senior levels of U.S. companies suggests that many of these efforts have stopped short of creating the kinds of opportunities needed for minorities to make it to these levels. Having a diversity effort is not sufficient for achieving this. A theme in the experience of each of our companies is that top management needs to focus on ensuring that qualified minorities have access to opportunities to develop and prove themselves.

Lesson #4: Corporate leaders should monitor the distribution of and pathways to opportunity.

The first step in the monitoring process is to understand the organizational opportunity structure. Gant Electronics was the corporation that demonstrated the smallest difference between minority and white executives' Stage 1 rate of promotion. We believe this is because early on Gant began a process of examining the opportunity structure that led to benchmarking upper-middle management positions. This information was used by Gant's self-help groups to educate their members and by the corporation to monitor the distribution of opportunity across demographic groups. Acme took a similar set of actions somewhat later and with equally effective results.

An organization's ability to ensure opportunity can be enhanced by creating a systematic understanding of the performance requirements, social norms, and signals that govern upward mobility. Where, for example, one clearly finds a tournament model at work, as was the case for whites at Acme, it is important to understand its impact on the organization. A consequence of the tournament model is not only the built-in disadvantage it gives racial minorities but also the premature ceilings it may set for some talented whites, whose full potential is never developed because their early career did not signal that they were "executive material."

Here are some essential questions that organizations might ask: What is the model of mobility in this organization? Does a tournament exist? If so, what rules govern it? Are there different implied norms or rules governing the distribution of rewards to minorities as compared to whites? If so, why? In addition to these kinds of questions, organizations can also identify the dominant pathways to their critical executive jobs and the developmental experiences that correspond with them. The answers to these questions can be used to create more effective career development systems and to provide talented minorities with information that they can use in making career deci-

sions. Such information can also be used in determining what practices need to be changed or better understood.

*Lesson #5: Corporate leaders must spotlight the threshold between
upper-middle management and executive level positions.*

Reaching the executive level cannot happen if opportunity is not
provided in Stage 3, the upper-middle management phase, for individuals to prepare, audition, and prove themselves qualified to succeed to
the executive level. Many companies now have glass ceilings for minorities because these opportunities are never made available to them and
thus they are unable to break through to the executive level. Acme,
Advanced, and Gant each found it necessary to spotlight the threshold between upper-middle management and the executive level and to
allow qualified minorities to be tested in these threshold jobs.

For our three companies, this spotlighting began in the 1980s. A
more recent example of spotlighting is Pacific Gas and Electric Company, the San Francisco–based utility company. In the early 1990s the
company's CEO took a look at his workforce and saw significant
racial and gender diversity at lower and middle management levels
but not in key line positions and not in the critical region general
manager jobs.[4] The traditional path to these general management
positions was through engineering and power distribution. Traditionally, women and minorities had not come up through these areas, but
many had reached significant levels of responsibility in the customer
service and regulatory areas. Not content to wait a generation to create a pipeline to the region general manager job, he took some of the
best minority talent from the non-engineering areas and tested them
in this position. He rationalized that at that level, the key skill was
management and not engineering. One of the consequences was that
they infused the region operations with customer service and regulatory perspectives that were previously missing. This move paid off; in
addition to providing demographic and functional diversity, these
minorities headed regions that became among the best performing in
the company. The CEO's actions had also challenged and disproved an
assumption about what it took to be effective in this critical threshold
role. Left unexamined, the unstated requirement that candidates

come from engineering or power distribution would have continued to put artificial ceilings on people's careers.

A persistent theme emerges from all of these cases: When executives have involved themselves in the diversity effort, organizational initiatives to remove the glass ceiling have been both easier and more effective. At Acme, several senior executives had been heavily involved in mentoring promising minorities for several years, so that when the CEO began to focus on finding qualified minorities for executive-level jobs, personal knowledge of talented minorities and their abilities was already available. This facilitated achieving the goal of diversity at the top. Certainly, not all corporate executives and senior managers had been involved. All that was needed, however, was a critical mass of Acme executives with firsthand knowledge combined with the CEO's support.

◢ ENSURING THAT DEVELOPMENT TAKES PLACE

Development needs to accompany opportunity. We make this point explicit because it is possible to provide opportunity that does not contribute to development.[5] Affirmative action policy, goals and timetables, and judicial consent decrees can produce opportunity, but they cannot legislate that development be an outcome of it. The result is a lack of adequate preparation for subsequent opportunities leading ultimately to failure. One of the distinguishing characteristics of the minorities who made it to executive levels was the strength of their developmental experiences compared to minorities who plateaued. This stood out at every stage, but was particularly critical in Stages 1 and 2. Where people of color are involved, a high-visibility failure can also damage the prospects for other minorities. We believe that because of the obstacles that race can present for minorities, steps need to be taken to ensure that development accompanies opportunity.

Lesson #6: Corporate leaders need to facilitate the formation of developmental relationships.

An obvious factor in the advancement of the minority executives in our study (and the plateaued minority managers as well) was their acquisition of key mentors and sponsors. These were people who took an active interest and involvement in supporting and enhancing their careers. Early in their careers this support took the form of direct coaching, counseling, and providing opportunities for greater challenge and growth. To our knowledge these relationships developed organically and naturally. They were not formalized. Certainly, at their core both parties were willing to engage with one another.

Interviews with both minority managers and executives made it clear that they benefited greatly from these developmental relationships. The mentors and sponsors we interviewed reported that they too had benefited by virtue of their protégés doing high-quality work for them. They also benefited by gaining different perspectives on their organization and, in many cases, race relations. Some of these became strong relationships that had all the characteristics of fully developed mentor–protégé relationships—close personal bonds that provide both career and psychosocial support.[6]

Organizations cannot legislate that two individuals should form the intimate bonds of a mentor–protégé relationship, nor is it healthy to ask someone to sponsor people for opportunities or promotions that they feel are undeserving. Companies can, however, take steps to improve the availability of developmental relationships for people of color by identifying potential mentors and ensuring that promising minorities are given assignments that put them in close contact with strong developers of managerial talent. A major factor in the formation of developmental relationships is close contact with seniors on important tasks.

Organizations should also give careful thought to job placement and design. Great performance in a routine, noncritical job is not likely to increase the willingness of others to mentor. Kathy Kram's research on mentoring identifies several job factors that hinder the formation of developmental relationships. These include: (1) reward systems that do not emphasize HR development objectives; (2) work designed so as to minimize opportunities for interaction between individuals with complementary relationship needs; and (3) performance management systems that do not provide forums and specific tools for coaching and counseling.[7]

In early career and at major career transitions, such as entering a company or changing the level of management responsibility, the relationship with one's direct manager is key. Our research confirms that the immediate supervisor is the most likely source of mentoring and sponsorship. A significant difference between minority executives and plateaued minority managers is instructive: Executives formed their first developmental relationship within the first two years of career, while plateaued managers, on average, did not do this until their fifth year.

Efforts to increase the awareness of potential mentors about their role as developers can aid this process. Many managers, especially younger ones and those promoted on the basis of being good individual producers, do not approach the management task from a developmental perspective. They do not understand how to work with subordinates, especially minorities, to ensure that performance in their current jobs prepares them for future opportunity. Our own experience and the findings of other studies suggest that this can be changed by educating managers about the developmental role and giving them skills to mentor effectively. This educational process must also include increasing their awareness about the complexities of cross-race mentoring.[8]

It is also important to create incentives for sponsoring minorities and to reduce the perceived risks. Individuals become active in the development of others for a host of reasons, some intrinsic and some extrinsic. When organizations make clear that creating a diverse workforce is a high priority and provide incentives to achieve it, they are likely to influence the willingness of people to provide at least instrumental career support for minorities. This also increases the likelihood that a deeper connection might be built. Remember Nydia Padilla at Acme. Her mentor was committed to diversity and affirmative action, and their relationship became a close mentor–protégé alliance.

Acme, Advanced, and Gant took distinct approaches to encouraging the emergence of developmental relationships, but in each company it was clear that diversity was desirable and that these relationships were pivotal. Their importance was reinforced by the behavior of key corporate leaders as well as by corporate practices such as making diversity a topic of discussion at staff meetings and executive conferences. All of these ongoing actions were incentives for identifying and developing minority talent. These messages also reduced the perceived risk of sponsorship. Sponsoring individuals for opportunity requires that the sponsor spend his or her credits in the system. If one perceives that it costs more to make an opportunity available for a person of color than a white, they may be less likely to act as a sponsor. If they do make an effort, it is likely to be only after the person of color has remained in the position longer than comparable whites. The greater length of time allows the sense of risk to be dispelled and gives the sponsor irrefutable evidence with which to deflect detractors.

Organizations should ensure that other kinds of developmental relationships are also available. For example, some mentoring functions such as coaching and counseling can be performed by peers. The peer-based self-help groups at Gant and the cross-level groups at Advanced are both excellent examples. These groups can be critical to helping a person achieve a high level of performance. Such early career support can also help the individual later gain sponsors who are impressed with the individual's performance. Clarence Williams is an example; he received significant support from self-help groups and peers early in his career, which helped him take advantage of the opportunities his boss provided.

Corporations often find it easiest to facilitate the formation of developmental relationships in early career. Managers of new hires are often more aware of their coaching role and of the developmental impact they can have. Professionals in the early career stage are also more receptive to developmental support and less critical of its quality.[9] The greater challenge is in enabling such relationships to form in Stages 2 and 3.

Educating executives about the dynamics of cross-race mentoring relationships can help them more effectively create them and coach others to do so.[10] Part of this education process is to alert executives that supporting minorities for high-visibility promotions can feel riskier than supporting whites. Often white sponsors of minorities don't have the same level of personal knowledge about minority protégés as they have in same-race relationships. As a consequence, responses to objections or questions about a minority protégé lack the same depth of personal connection. Whether or not minorities gain an important opportunity then becomes contingent on people's ability to accept the objective record of the minority manager's performance and live with a greater sense of risk. This is more likely to happen when executives understand that this is a common consequence of racial minorities being dependent solely on white sponsorship to achieve executive jobs.

Lesson #7: Corporate leaders must directly address attitudes that create low expectations for minority performance.

There is a fair amount of research establishing the link between a superior's expectations and an individual's ability to perform.[11] We saw at Advanced how lower expectations of minorities translated into lower performance expectations for plants located in minority areas and run by minority managers. What followed was substandard performance and a willingness, on the part of white managers, to accept this as the cost of "social responsibility." It took a white leader with the courage to challenge his managers to question this situation and to change it. The turnaround also required him and his direct reports to take responsibility for their own complicity in this scenario.

When managers possess low expectations of racial minorities, they will be poor bosses and even poorer mentors. Instead of giving straight feedback, the minority individuals are "counseled" into nonessential jobs or leave out of frustration. In more performance-based, up-or-out cultures, the minorities will likely exhibit higher rates of attrition and leave earlier than expected. Over time, as the attitude of racial inferiority goes unchecked, minorities become less likely to be hired at all. Where lower expectations are accepted, they often become self-fulfilling prophecies to the detriment of both the minority individual and the company.

◢ Some Remaining Questions

Should corporations actively promote a two-tournament model of managerial mobility based on racial differences?

This question has emerged in numerous discussions with colleagues and executives who have previewed the findings of Chapter 3. Minorities reach the executive level despite a moderate or slow takeoff in Stage 1. While velocity of movement appears critical in predict-ing white advancement, quality of experience is the critical element for minorities. The solid foundation built in Stage 1 helps to propel their movement in Stages 2 and 3. These findings make sense in light of the challenges of prejudice, social discomfort, and the risk avoid-ance that racial difference engenders. These obstacles can be over-come, but doing so requires time, extra time. But more important, it requires high-quality developmental experiences and relationships.

Against the daunting challenges presented by these racial barriers in early career, there is a strong temptation not only to accept the two-tournament model as an empirical reality but also to make it pol-icy by either tacitly accepting that minorities cannot be fast-tracked in early career or formally creating two separate career tourna-ments—one for minorities and one for whites. The underlying premise of this conclusion is that all minorities will move more slowly during Stage 1 because of the racial barriers described in Chapter 1, so why not take it as a given and plan accordingly? Take the added time in Stage 1 to ensure that high-potential minorities are overprepared to meet the social, technical, and racial challenges when they reach Stage 2, as did the minority executives in our study. The obstacles to minor-ity advancement are not likely to disappear anytime soon.

We believe that such a conclusion would be a mistake. While organizations may want to question promotion systems that behave too much like the tournament model, institutionalizing two separate tournaments is not the answer. There are a number of negative conse-quences of creating systems in which there are different normative expectations for racial minorities than whites. First, it unfairly insti-tutionalizes the "tax" of added time that minorities have to pay as a result of existing racial barriers. The result is that a higher standard is set for their participation in the main competition for executive jobs. Indeed, this appears to have been the case for the minority executives in our study, though there was never a formal policy.

Second, such a policy would likely result in a number of high-per-forming and ambitious minorities leaving in Stage 1. Our retrospective examination of minority executive development and advancement precludes our ability to know how many persons of color with execu-tive potential left during Stage 1, before their careers could begin the upward climb. In some respects the minority executives we studied may have lived with a de facto two-tournament model because of the times. They knew that they were part of a changing racial reality in corporations. This may have strengthened their resolve to stick it out. Moving at a rate comparable to *most* of their colleagues may have been sufficient to keep them motivated. They may also have been more naïve about the dynamics of managerial careers than high-potential people of color would be today, especially those with MBAs or other graduate degrees, whose skill sets are in demand.

Today, we know that people of color, like whites, are likely to be more savvy and more ambitious in their expectations for reaching the top of the corporate ladder. They also may be more sensitive and suspicious about the possibility of race-based inequities limiting their early career prospects. The likely result is that the best will leave prematurely where a two-tournament model is institutionalized. We imagine this dynamic is already at work in many companies. We frequently encounter executives who are surprised that their best minority talents leave "just as good things were about to happen." Corporations are much better off working to ensure opportunity and development and to eliminate race-related barriers than investing in formalizing or legitimating a two-tournament model.

Another liability of the two-tournament model is its contribution to white backlash. Our research suggests that the minority executives we studied were, by and large, stellar performers in the first stage of their managerial careers. They could have justifiably been placed on the fast track. Instead they moved at rates similar to white managers who eventually plateaued. Imagine for a moment how, in today's climate of resistance to affirmative action, seemingly sudden accelerations of a few minorities' careers affects whites who perceive that they are equal to them. The reaction of these "average" whites is likely captured by the following sentiment: "The only ones being promoted around here are minorities." They are not likely to remember that a small number of fast-trackers was earlier sorted from the larger group and that they were all white. Nor is it the case that most of the corporate executives and senior managers they would complain to would point out this fact. Left unchecked, such attitudes build resentments and, given the critical role of middle managers in organizations, can ultimately undermine diversity efforts and race relations.

Consider too that minorities are likely to hold a very different view. To them these opportunities to move on the fast track seem well earned and overdue. They then confront white resentment with unsympathetic responses. In today's environment, we imagine that some minorities may react with an intolerance and sense of entitlement misinterpreted as arrogance. The result may be backlash that erodes their relations with colleagues and retards further progress.

Our conclusion concerning the undesirability of formalizing a two-tournament approach may seem inconsistent with advice we give to minorities in the next chapter, where we recommend that they not value fast movement more than quality of the experience in choosing between opportunities. If a company is working to eliminate racial barriers and inequities of opportunities, individuals can make the choice about what they need to develop to meet their goals. Minority individuals cannot yet expect that their ability to advance will be without the negative influence of race. They must make informed choices that ensure their ability to build the requisite levels of competence, credibility, and confidence at each career stage.

Is a single-tournament model governed by fast early movement the only alternative to the two-tournament system?

We are not advocating that the only path for corporations is to keep a tournament system of fast tracking while eliminating the race effect. Many would argue that the pattern of development exhibited by minority executives in this study is superior to a fast-track start. It avoids the potential downfalls that can derail talented managers who move too fast, too early. Corporations may want to consider how to make such a pattern of development more widely acceptable. Perhaps what is needed is a range of different paths and patterns of movement, uncorrelated with race, that could bring people to the executive suite. Producing this outcome, however, would require effectively integrating the principles of opportunity, development, and diversity into the fabric of the organization's management practices and human resource systems.

Should organizations select individuals based on background characteristics?

We believe it is important that minorities meet the same criteria for entry as whites. However, we caution against extrapolating from our observations in Chapter 4 that it is better to hire people from two-parent households. While this was the case for most of our minority and white executives, there were also successful executives who did not fit this profile. Similarly, one should not assume that coming from a background that included no exposure to a majority white setting precludes one from succeeding in the mainstream. The key was that individuals experienced success in a multiracial environment. We believe that in an enabling environment, a person of color could experience such success during their early career in the corporation. This assumes, of course, that they come with the requisite academic training and that the corporation is working to create an environment conducive to all employees.

◢ CONCLUSION

Our hope is that this book and, in particular, this chapter provide some anchors and guidelines for pursuing diversity efforts in which one of the principal goals is the development and advancement of minority executives. Perhaps the essential take-away is that creating and producing minority executives is about a relationship between the individual and the organization. The job of the corporate leader is to ensure that an enabling environment is created that supports opportunity and development.

In none of the companies we studied was much effort, if any, spent in trying to "fix" the minorities. To the extent that there were developmental activities designed exclusively for minorities, minorities initiated them. Rather, corporate leaders and their partners focused on fixing themselves and their companies. Their efforts went to making sure that their senior managers and executives possessed the will and ability to identify and develop minorities at all levels.

In the next and final chapter, we speak to the other central group for whom this study has implications: people of color currently working in corporate America. Our belief is that where corporate leaders are acting in concert with the lessons of this chapter and minorities are making choices consistent with the next, positive and powerful results will occur.

10

Lessons for the Next Generation of Minority Executives

THE AVERAGE AGE OF the twenty minority executives we studied at Acme Industries, Gant Electronics, and Advanced Technology is fifty-four years. In less than fifteen years, the youngest will be eligible to retire with thirty years of corporate service. This group came of age in times different than those that young minority professionals now live in. Yet their experiences offer some timeless lessons for any person of color attempting to navigate his or her career in the mainstream of predominantly white corporations in the United States, especially if they are playing in the tournament for executive jobs.

This is not a how-to book. There are not six easy steps. The development and advancement of minorities to the executive suite is a matter of opportunity and preparation meeting at the same time. There are no guarantees. Yet we hope that by now it is clear that the making of minority executives is less random, mysterious, and paradoxical than many imagine. Creating the necessary levels of preparation and opportunity is dependent not on programs but on processes, at both the individual and organizational level.

The most salient findings of our study suggest that reaching the executive level is a function of the individual's ability to build a foundation of competence, credibility, and confidence by the end of the early career. This foundation is based on formative preprofessional and Career Stage 1 experiences. Once this foundation is in place, it is critical that the individual continue to build on and reinforce each of its elements. The organizational context can enhance or diminish one's ability to mobilize these resources in response to the generic challenges of career advancement and the specific challenges related to race. Where the environment is unsupportive of diversity, through benign neglect or overt hostility, it is possible that no amount of individual effort can overcome the barriers.

What are the key take-aways for the person of color who now ponders the implications of this book?[1] Presented here are seven lessons we believe to be the most important and relevant to the findings of this study. Taken together they form a perspective we believe will be useful to people of color at various phases of career. Within each lesson we discuss the specific implications for action and perspectives necessary to meet the challenges of being a racial minority at crucial stages of career.

We encourage nonminority readers to heed these lessons as well. Two potential benefits can come from doing so. First, those in a position to assist minorities, as mentors, bosses, counselors, and teachers, will likely find these lessons helpful in their efforts. Second, the lessons themselves, while grounded in our focus on minority executives' career experiences, are relevant to an even broader audience, so that there may be personal value in what follows. In addition, knowing what is articulated here can add to existing knowledge of what is particular to people of color and what is more universally applicable.

◢ EARLY CAREER

Racial minorities in predominantly white corporations face a number of challenges throughout their careers, but they are perhaps most vulnerable in the early career period. Failure to develop essential levels of competence, credibility, and confidence in Stage 1 can jeopardize future advancement. Indeed, many of the plateaued minority managers in our study found themselves limited because they had not built an adequate foundation in their early career. Drawing on the experience of our study participants, we see three critical lessons for managing one's career in this period.

Lesson #1: Choose work and an organization that suit your personality.

Successful people take advantage of the resources at their disposal, including their own innate personality. Work that fits your strengths, interests, and motivation will increase the odds that you will be able to persist in the face of challenge and disappointment. Remember Ben Richardson; he loved selling, was a top salesman, and was still passed over five times for the sales manager job. Yet he continued to be number one because he loved sales. Clarence Williams, who had shown a talent for things mechanical since childhood, wanted to be a top-notch design engineer. His motivation and desire to be a great design engineer allowed him to persist in building his competence and reputation, even as he watched his peers pass him by as they were promoted into management. Why were they able to persist? In no small measure, it was because they drew intrinsic value from their work. They certainly were not being motivated by fast early promotions. It was their intrinsic love of the work that made it easier for them to get up, confront the challenges, and stay in the game.

It is important to choose an organization that suits your personality. John Kotter noted in his study of general managers that in their early careers these executives "joined a firm (or industry) that closely fit with their interests and values."[2] It is no accident that seventeen of the twenty executives in our main study and twelve of the fourteen minority executives in the follow-up study rose through the ranks of their companies, starting at the bottom of the professional or managerial ladder. Another point of empirical observation is that most of the minority executives who currently appear to be future candidates for the CEO position at a *Fortune 500* company have spent the majority of their careers at a single firm. There are exceptions, but almost none fit the profile of the highly mobile manager who ascends by moving between lots of companies.

In today's more fluid labor market, choosing a firm that suits you does not necessarily mean assuming lifetime employment. Even if you do change firms, it is still important to build your human capital in the early career so that external options are created. We are simply suggesting that you not choose an organization that is a poor fit, even if the job content is intrinsically interesting and motivating.

It is far easier to hear this advice than to act on it. Other criteria, such as compensation or location, can lead one to overlook organizational fit when choosing a job. Individuals may lack the skills to put the advice into action. For example, we have watched thousands of our students choose jobs as they approached graduation. A common attitude students take is, "Pay now, enjoy later." This begins when a person takes a job at an ill-fitting company assuming that the short-term pain will produce long-term gain. The motivations are most often company prestige—resume value—and compensation. The problem is that when you hate the work or the firm is a poor fit, you will probably not perform at your best and leave prematurely. The final result is that you will not take full advantage of the opportunity.

Everyone is capable of making unwise career choices. However, racial minorities pay a higher price for them. Because of biases, their failures are more likely to lead others to doubt their ability to perform. Feeling like a misfit or being unmotivated by the work will rapidly pull one into a negative performance spiral.

People of color should also remember that the existence of prejudice means that reputation matters even more for you than it does for your white counterparts. Research indicates that negative information about an individual's performance hurts minorities in the reward allocation process more than it does whites.[3] Working at one organization for a while then leaving is acceptable as long as you do not let your credibility be undermined.

Well-developed self-assessment skills are what enable people to choose a job that is a good organizational fit. To make a choice that is congruent with who you are, you need to understand yourself on multiple levels: What motivates me? What matters most to me? What are the characteristics of my ideal organization? Most important, you need to be able to learn continually from your experiences in order to create and exploit opportunities as they arise. This is crucial because what is a good fit today may not be later. People usually have some awareness that change is necessary, but seldom take action until some existential crisis forces action. Several of our interviewees described such moments of personal learning and self-assessment. At times, they were able to take the necessary action to create better alignment between their actions and goals. In two instances, people passed up promotions or took a demotion to create a better fit. Some, though not all, took self-assessment classes or training that helped them develop or deepen their self-awareness and self-assessment skills. Many books and courses exist today that can help one develop these skills.[4]

Lesson #2: Choose high-quality experiences over fast advancement.

As the findings of Chapter 5 illustrated, a quality experience is one that positions you to build competence, credibility, and confidence. Establishing this foundation is most often the result of a pattern of assignments that allows you to grow and facilitates the formation of developmental relationships with superiors and peers.

The velocity of upward movement is relevant, but not the most important factor. On average, most of the minority executives we studied moved slower than white executives, but faster than most minorities who plateaued. Therefore, in early career a moderate pace is not bad, as long as it is accompanied by opportunities to develop critical human and social capital.

This does not mean that minorities should forgo fast movement when it is offered. Getting on the fast track is a great accomplishment, but without a solid foundation, one may be excessively vulnerable to race-based obstacles, such as racist managers, worker resistance, and exclusion from the informal networks available to support young white managers.

Lesson #3: Build a network of developmental relationships.

People make some of their most difficult transitions at the beginning of their careers, including entering and becoming acclimated to the organization and job. The pressures of this period can make it hard to see beyond the immediate demands of the task. Help from others is the best inoculation from the pitfalls of early career. Thriving in one's career is a result of being able to get the career and psychosocial support that mentors, sponsors, and special peers can provide.

Again, this advice is easier said than done. How does one find a mentor or transform a decent supervisory relationship into a developmental one? This is a million dollar question. If someone could devise a technique that guaranteed the ability to acquire mentors or sponsors, people would be willing to pay. We do not pretend to have such a technique, and we actually think that technique is less important than perspective. Creating relationships depends on one's interpersonal skills and the receptivity of the other party. The perspective that we advocate is one that focuses on development.

Most often—and incorrectly—discussions of developmental relationships center on the idea that mentoring and sponsorship are the keys to opportunity. Young people move into a corporation and instantly look to the senior vice president to mentor them, often overlooking more likely candidates such as their boss or, in professional service firms, more senior peers. We recommend that in early career you think about creating relationships that will help you develop your foundation and discover, create, and exploit opportunities as they come.

Certainly, a mentor's power in the organization matters. A mentor who wishes the best for you but has credibility problems of his or her own is less desirable than one who does not have such problems, all else being equal. Still, such an individual is not ineffective. People of color frequently find valuable developmental support in the form of advice, feedback, friendship, and information-sharing from people who might not be on the fast track or senior, but who understand the corporation. In many cases, these developers are people of color who have learned from their own experiences and are passing it on. Such assistance can help you gain sure footing and excel at getting results. This then attracts other supporters.

Recall Emma Simms, the executive at Gant. Her early mentor was an African American male senior research engineer. He facilitated her acculturation and shared his network with her, helping her to apply her full talent to performing well. Her confidence built to the point that on one occasion she felt comfortable enough to challenge the views of an executive, who was impressed with her though he continued to disagree. In time, he became a primary mentor. Emma clearly gave credit to this powerful, white male executive for the extraordinary opportunities afforded her. She was also unambiguous that the support of the African American senior research engineer in her early career was critical to getting her career off to a strong start.

This story calls attention to another pattern that may be worth conscientious replication. Minority executives were more likely than minority managers to have had another person of color as part of their support system during Stage 1 or Stage 2, either in the form of individual mentors or bosses or as a result of their participation in support groups such as the self-help groups formed at Gant. Other research supports the conclusion that racial diversity in the networks of minorities corresponds with greater opportunity.[5] We urge people of color to build diverse networks of support and to start that process early in the career.

Finally, think in terms of developing a portfolio of relationships that support your development, not simply a single mentor.[6] Do not fall victim to what has been dubbed the "sidekick effect"—close attachment to an early mentor that inhibits the formation of other contacts.[7] Such overdependency can leave you vulnerable if the mentor exits the organization or the relationship ends. Periodic assessment of your network of relationships and the benefits it provides in light of current needs and goals can be helpful in avoiding this.[8]

We want to emphasize the importance of peer relationships in the portfolio. Most discussion of mentoring support points attention upward. However, peer relations have been shown to be a vital source of support.[9] In today's dynamic marketplace there is always the potential that a peer today is a boss tomorrow. We observed this frequently in our study. Remember Clarence Williams's experience. His former peers were strong supporters when they became his bosses. It is also consistent with the faster rate of promotion to middle management of white executives. Good relations with peers can help open doors for development and opportunity.

Some behaviors can help increase the likelihood of developmental relationships forming. First, proximity matters. Familiarity breeds fondness and connection. Working together in the same physical location facilitates the formation of relationships simply because of habitual contact. The most frequent mentor in early career is one's manager.[10] Proximity is one reason for this, but so too is the interdependence involved in this liaison. When individuals work on projects of mutual importance, and especially nonroutine ones, the possibilities for a relationship are enhanced. Three implications for action flow from these observations. One is to seriously consider your first manager as a potential developer, not just a boss. Therefore, if you are faced with a choice about who to work for, consider the possibility of a relationship forming that transcends the scripted boss-subordinate roles. Sometimes you can identify potential managers' reputations by asking, Who has been a good developer of people in the past? Who has mentored a diverse group of protégés? We found that several names appeared frequently as mentors or sponsors of our minority study participants. This may not be coincidence.

Second, look for opportunities to work with people you think might make good mentors or developmental partners. Some of our executives met their mentors while working on task forces or special assignments. Sometimes our interviewees later discovered that a person they met through these broadening experiences was assessing them as they worked on an ad hoc project or committee.

Third, because racial difference often limits the likelihood of strong chemistry in the early stages of a relationship, do not rely on it as a basis for initiating or forming a relationship.[11] Instead, rely on your good performance and reputation to move the relationships beyond the superficial. Also, help the relationship grow by being open about your own experiences of the work and the ways in which you are trying to learn. A frequent comment about our minority executives was that they were open to learning and followed up on feedback.

◢ LESSONS FOR ALL TIMES

The remainder of this chapter details learnings that are relevant throughout a career.

Lesson #4: The organization matters.

Every major corporation in America has hired people of color who possessed raw ambition, intelligence, and interpersonal acumen equivalent to the minority executives we studied. Yet relatively few companies have produced minorities from their own ranks who have made it into their executive level. In systems terms, the problem is not with the input—that is, the people—but instead with the internal systems designed to create desirable outputs. The reasons for this are numerous, but can be captured in two categories of firm-level explanations.

First, there is a widely shared set of unchallenged biases that have the effect of setting low targets for minority advancement. Where such biases exist, the internal system is consistent with the expected outcomes. In these corporations the glass ceiling metaphor does not apply because the expectations for minority advancement are so low. Few nonwhites even make it to upper-middle management jobs, the equivalent of the plateaued managers we studied. The executive level, in these companies, is inconceivable. Instead of a glass ceiling, these companies have "squishy floors" and "revolving doors." Minorities can never gain a firm enough footing in the organization to even test whether they can penetrate the top. As a result, the best of them leave. A sign of this corporate malaise is when the highest ranking people of color were all hired in from other firms. In other words, they were "developed" elsewhere.

The second category of explanations applies to corporations in which there is some genuine intent to diversify the workforce. Lower expectations for minorities as compared to whites is less an issue here than is a lack of alignment between the organization's diversity strategy and its culture and values. Often its diversity strategy is comprised of a patchwork of disconnected programs and compliance efforts. Typically there is a history of fits and starts. Momentum builds, great plans are made, and then they fizzle. Later, an incident rekindles the flame and a new round of diversity efforts begin.

In these corporations, there is often a glass ceiling. Minorities make it to threshold positions in middle or upper-middle management, but seem to get stuck. For people of color the pattern often involves being stuck in staff roles that were initially given as broadening assignments, but become dead ends. An indication of this pattern is that despite an organization's good overall numbers and the demonstrated ability of minorities to reach into middle management jobs, they are not able to ascend further. These companies are usually pursuing diversity as a goal, but are using a strategy that consists of many discrete programs that are neither coordinated nor aligned with the company's culture. Leadership of diversity efforts is usually lacking or inconsistent. Senior managers are not involved and those responsible for the programs behave as bureaucrats not change agents. So what are the implications of this for people of color just starting out?

Be Selective. Choose the corporation wisely. Today, there is no glory in being a "first" at the lower level of an organization. Look closely at the composition and distribution of people of color throughout the hierarchy. Avoid companies that fit the profile of the "squishy floors" and "revolving doors." One of the hardest parts of teaching talented MBAs has been watching students of color enter the same organizations time and time again only to see them have similarly debilitating experiences. Oftentimes this negative experience is fundamentally destructive. Individuals leave less confident in themselves, deskilled to some degree, and with damaged reputations and relationships. They retreat to lower aspirations.

Looking at today's corporate landscape, the necessary choice for many people will be companies with glass ceilings. The Acme, Gant, and Advanced's of corporate America are few and far between. You will need to enter the organization with your eyes wide open to the existence of a ceiling and attuned to what is being done about it. The good news is that today many are serious about removing barriers. But there are also many that are not.

This advice is clearly relevant for those just beginning their careers. It is, however, no less important for individuals making career choices at later stages. In today's business environment there is a strong likelihood that most individuals will change organizations at least one or two times after the age of thirty. We are familiar with a number of individuals who changed organizations after developing good technical skills, track records, and reputations, only to land in a racially inhospitable environment. In some cases the symptoms were obvious: no people of color in the executive ranks; a few in high-level support jobs with small staffs; and a history of hiring people of color from other companies into middle management jobs, none of whom were able to reach significantly higher levels of management.

You might wonder, if the symptoms were so obvious, why did these individuals choose to join? In some instances, it was objectively the best choice they had for achieving their personal goals. In other instances they failed to get the data that might have tipped them off to the potential problems. Talking about race in interviews can seem awkward and it is not uncommon to go through a series of job interviews at one company and never talk to a person of color.

A few were blinded by overconfidence, sometimes coupled with racial naïveté. These individuals had done well up to this point in their careers at firms that had a more enabling environment. Not fully understanding the importance of the organization, they assumed it did not matter. As a result, they were unprepared for the subtle effects that a less open and enabling environment would have. In some cases the damage was irreparable. In others, the individual's progress was retarded, but he or she recovered and learned a valuable lesson.

We need to be clear that our message is not that one should avoid risk in choosing a company, nor are we suggesting that race should be the overriding factor. We do believe that it should be taken into account and given weight equal to other significant dimensions, and that individuals should avoid companies that clearly have poor records on diversity.

Support Diversity Change Efforts. We frequently hear from people of color that they are tired of assuming additional responsibility for this issue. Certainly, we understand and think some degree of skepticism is healthy. You should avoid being boxed into corners that place you in the role of "race-relations troubleshooter"—the minority manager who gets all the "trouble minority employees"—while white managers are let off the hook for effectively developing and supervising them. This negative kind of effort needs to be distinguished, however, from a coordinated effort to create an enabling environment.

A central theme from our interviews at these three companies was that minority participation in diversity efforts was critical, though not without risk. This participation took multiple forms, both informal and formal. The evidence suggests that it influenced the success of both the companies and the individuals who made it to the executive level. How you support these efforts is up to you. What matters is that you do. It is also vital that your efforts be aligned with those of your organization. Your efforts should promote and leverage ongoing efforts that support your organization's stated business goals.

Lesson #5: Take charge of your own career.

Throughout most of our executives' careers, the model corporate employee was one who fit the description of William F. Whyte's "organization man."

> *The fundamental premise of the new model executive . . . is, simply, that the goals of the individual and the goals of the organization will work out to be one and the same. The young men have no cynicism about the "system" and very little skepticism. . . . They have an implicit faith that the Organization will be as interested in making use of their best qualities as they are themselves, and thus with equanimity they can entrust the resolution of their destiny to the Organization. . . . The average young man cherishes the idea that his relationship with the Organization is for keeps.*[12]

This, by and large, was not true for our minority participants, including those who made it to the executive level. They could not fully depend on the system to work for them as it did for whites. Our findings in Chapter 3 regarding the patterns of movement and rules of the two-tournament system are the best evidence of this. The playing field was not level and, while more level today, continues to favor whites.

The minority executives we studied benefited from the fact that they were not passive about their careers. They were characterized by an openness to feedback, an orientation toward learning, the ability to set personal goals, and an internal definition of success. Self-assessment tools and processes are particularly useful in early career, though they are clearly relevant in all stages. Clarence Williams, for example, had a five-year planning cycle that kept him focused on his goals and provided an internal clock that signaled time for reassessment.

Another critical element in taking charge of your career is creating developmental partners out of key people in your network. These partners are individuals who help you manage your career. They provide support and opportunity, but also "tough love"—critical assessment at important times. This can be invaluable in Stage 3 when the criteria for the executive level are ambiguous and require major developmental leaps. The higher one is in the organizational hierarchy, the harder it is to create such interpersonal connections. It is preferable to create these partnerships with people who know your context in the organization, though it is not always possible. Seek them from the outside if necessary. The key is that you have these partnerships.

A final note on managing your career is to remember that high-quality performance is critical at every step. While old adages such as, "Organizations are political, and connections count"; "Good work unseen is seldom rewarded"; and "Who you know sometimes counts more than what you know" are still true, corporate America is less and less forgiving of underperformance, especially where minority managers are concerned. Remember that your performance, and others' evaluation of it, is dynamic, not static. Commitment to excellence means *ongoing* mastery of the technical and social requirements of the work.

Lesson #6: Race matters, but it alone does not determine your fate.

So far in this chapter we have discussed the lessons of minority executives' experience with race in the background. Much of this advice is valuable to everyone, though it is especially important for people of color. In this section, we want to address race itself. More precisely: How should minorities orient themselves toward race as a factor in their work lives?

The most important feature of an effective perspective on race is that while it does matter, it does not determine your fate. This is how most of the executives in our study approached the issue of race: Despite the existence of extra challenges and scrutiny, they never took it to be a determining factor. This did not mean being naïve or denying that race was sometimes at the root of problems. It meant treating problems as solvable. Sometimes this meant moving out of a bad situation so as not to get derailed. Often it meant improving performance and developing strategies to overcome obstacles. Putting good strategies for career advancement in place can make one less vulnerable to racial obstacles and better able to cope with them when they do emerge. Even taking into account the potential benefits of their companies' emphasis on diversity, programs like affirmative action did not guarantee our executives success or freedom from race-related challenges.

Here are some additional implications derived from our observations and discussions with minority executives and managers and with the people who worked with them.

Be Conscious about Race, but Not Self-Conscious. Many of our minority executives and some managers talked frankly about the influence of race on themselves and their organizations. These individuals seemed to be racially conscious. On the other hand, race did not make them self-conscious. Most seemed comfortable with themselves as people as well as with their identities as minority executives or managers. Because each was unique, there was no single minority style. Most found a way to bring much of who they were to their work. In a few cases, their feelings of conspicuousness as minorities made them self-conscious and even doubtful. Overcoming this required a process of personal development. Several people noted that this process was helped by developing connections with other people of color, individually and through the self-help groups at Gant and the dialogue groups at Advanced. What we are describing is the notion of an *integrated self*—the successful union of racial and professional identity.

There are a number of theories about the development of racial identity.[13] While each identifies developmental stages and emphasizes dynamics differently, all have one thing in common: The final stage of development is one that allows for a healthy integration of one's racial self-definition with the other aspects of identity. To reach this point an individual goes through a number of transformations in thinking about the role of race in one's life. Most of these studies suggest that people begin with a passive acceptance of racial norms and values in which European American culture is considered superior to minority cultures. Moving out of that stage requires the emergence of a racial awareness, but going further means integrating one's race with other important aspects of identity. To pass through that threshold one needs to be in a work environment that is not so rife with racism that responding to it is a daily, oppressive requirement. Integration also requires the capacity and opportunity for personal growth and reflection. Social supports can aid this process.

We did not set out to test these theories in this study. Yet our observations from discussions with minority executives suggested that many of them—especially the most successful—have integrated race into a larger sense of who they are. They were comfortable as people of color in their organizations. Those who had been executives for some time also seemed comfortable with the demands of exercising great power and authority over the lives of others. It was clear that they had achieved an integrated identity by how they described their behavior and the critical race-related incidents they encountered.

The implication of these observations is that you will benefit by working to create a healthy integration of your racial and professional identity. You can facilitate this process by creating integrated support systems and finding ways early in your career to break out of constricting behavioral norms that leave you feeling self-conscious, inauthentic, and ultimately resentful.

Wesley Jackson, an African American manager at Gant, believed that African Americans seldom, if ever, were authentic in the presence of whites. "We don't tend to be as aggressive in the white world as we are in the black world. This carries over to business. It's a subtle thing, but it's there. I know I separate who I am at work and who I am at home. I separate out all the personality stuff from the work."

Jackson's comments were confirmed by some of the people we interviewed about him. Several described him as nice and competent, but hard to really get to know. Perhaps this sense of distance increased the reluctance or discomfort that bosses and potential sponsors felt when they were deciding whether to support him for assignments that might have put him in line for an executive job, especially since he was one of the minority managers whose early career had many of the same qualities as the minority executives, except that he had no strong mentors until he reached middle management.

Another distinguishing feature of Jackson's career was that he did not participate in networking with other people of color. He described his most central mentoring relationship with a white male executive as his boss's "project to create a black vice president." They never got to know each other personally. Yet when being interviewed for this study by an African American male, he was animated, funny, reflective, likable, and warm. Mind you, he took a while to warm up, as if he were deciding whether to reveal his full self.

Ella Bell has coined the term "bi-cultural stress" to describe the tensions created by the demand of moving between two cultures.[14] It is particularly acute when those cultures seem incongruent or in conflict. Reconciling these tensions is a matter of creating an integrated sense of self so that you are not internally torn by external, and especially racist, tensions. Being a racial minority in a particular job may seem to others like a contradiction, but it does not have to be experienced that way by the incumbent. With greater internal integration, one's bicultural background can translate into a set of skills that enhance one's ability to thrive in the corporation. Remember, for instance, how Ben Richardson developed the ability to use his bicultural skills to gain confidence from his professional experiences in both the African American community and predominantly white institutions.[15]

Commit and Recommit to Excellent Performance. When minority executives, and some minority managers, described how they dealt with the challenges of race, they consistently returned to the issue of performance. It is probably not an accident that most of them spent Stages 1 and 2 in jobs where performance could be measured objectively, through production quotas, sales revenue, product launches, or on-time delivery. Many described themselves as competitive, which aided their ability to be performance oriented.

An internal commitment to excellence means setting personal standards that allow you to gauge your success. A good rule of thumb is that when you feel unable to do your best because of a lack of motivation, it is time to move on. We firmly believe that the inability to sustain a commitment to excellence is tantamount to self-sabotage for people of color.

Be Consistent. One thing we noticed about minority executives is that they went about solving race-related problems in much the same way as they solved other problems. Earl Randolph, an executive in the follow-up study, told us that he always approached career disappointments by asking himself and others "what he could have done differently." Later in the interview, he said there had been times when he felt race had limited his opportunities. Asked how he coped with this, he replied, "I asked myself what I could have done differently to achieve my goals. That's what I always do. Same thing, same thing." With this reasoning, Randolph refused to give any single factor in his life control over his fate, whether it was a skill deficiency or race.

Too frequently when issues of race emerge, individuals are paralyzed or address the issue in ways that are foreign to them. For example, one who is direct on most issues can become hesitant when they think race is becoming a negative factor. A mental exercise for remedying this is to pretend that the same problem exists, but imagine that you don't think race is the issue. How would you address it? Ask yourself what the difference is between that response and how you would behave when you believe that race is the source of the problem. Now try to figure how you would *act* according to the race-neutral solution, but hold constant the fact that race *is* part of the problem. Is there a way to treat race as one of a few alternative hypotheses that can be tested?

Here is an example of this mental exercise. Amy Chen worked for a large telecommunications company. She had a good developmental relationship with a previous boss who was succeeded by a twenty-eight-year-old white male manager. It was not long before the two clashed. Chen felt that he was a micromanager who talked down to her and used phrases that seemed tinged with stereotyped assumptions. On more than one occasion, he asked where she was born and seemed surprised when she said Chicago. He also made assumptions about her background, for example, that she came to marketing from the technology side. He insisted on overseeing her client contacts. Chen, an Asian American, was the only woman of color in the group. Well-trained and educated in predominantly white elite universities, she found him the epitome of white male entitlement and arrogance.

After turning to her support network for advice, Chen decided that rather than conclude her new boss was racist—in which case the situation was hopeless—there was an alternative hypothesis. Perhaps the new manager was insecure because of the pressure of being young and in charge of a seasoned group of professionals. She engaged him on this basis, assuming he could be open if he was made to feel she was considerate of his interest. Almost immediately, this produced change in their relationship, and they were able to become more open with one another.

After a while their relationship improved, and she did talk to him about aspects of style and language that she did not appreciate. He took her criticism well and whether his attitude changed or not, his behavior did. Chen was not derailed by the situation and was promoted to her next assignment. Reflecting on this, she realized that she is action oriented, but when race came on the table, paralysis set in. With the combination of inaction and bad interaction, resentment built and the manager confirmed her worse fears. Luckily, she had a developmental network that helped her work through these feelings and take positive action.[16]

Neither Earl Randolph nor Amy Chen abandoned their hypothesis that race might be influencing the situation. But they treated it as only one factor affecting the situation and discovered a way not to let it paralyze them. Sometimes race blinds us to the complexity of a situation. In Chen's case, the boss may have been prejudiced and insecure, but both hypotheses needed to be taken into account to reach a successful resolution.

Lesson #7: Make sure it is worth the price.

In this section, we go beyond the findings presented earlier and share our observations and feelings about the personal demands of journeying to the executive suite. Looking at the twenty minority executives and thirteen white executives we studied in the three companies and the fourteen minority executives in the follow-up study, two things stand out. One, the great majority seemed content with the career success they had attained. In an almost humorous way, some of our minority executives said they were surprised at it, and happy. Two, their achievements came with a price.

At Gant and Advanced, most of the executives were on their second marriages. None blamed the divorces on the corporation. Instead, they placed it on themselves and their relationships. For some, work served as a refuge from troubled relationships. Regardless of the reasons for the dissolutions of their marriages, it is clear that they paid a price: long hours at the office, incomplete or non-existent home lives, frequent moves.

The most frequently mentioned work-related impact was time away from their children. Some of the women were single parents. All struggled to strike some sort of balance between work and family life. Even now that they made it to the executive level, there is little sign of the pressure letting up. A few even seemed guilty for taking the time to participate in this study, especially once they began to enjoy the reflection process. It was time away from work.

In the end, many are called but few are chosen to lead corporations. Getting on that path means sacrifice. Understand that there is a price to be paid. When we last talked to Ben Richardson, he told us that he had to decide what he wanted for himself next. He realized that many people within and outside Gant had ambitions for him. At the time, he was as close as an African American had been to the top job at a *Fortune 500* company. Richardson also realized that it would be yet another stretch with a new set of sacrifices.[17]

Minority executives also face the additional scrutiny and demands that race imposes. The language that surrounds promotions of minorities sometimes hints that their elevation is a publicity stunt. Then there are the expectations of other people of color, made even more complicated by the recognition that the struggle for equality has benefited too few. Some experience this life as a high-wire act, only without a safety net below. In 1997, the *Wall Street Journal* told the story of an African American female who became a powerful executive at Duquesne Power and Light Company. She showed herself to be a results-oriented and loyal executive, who brought many changes to a company deeply in need of them. But she also paid a price, especially in not having adequate personal support. When her mentor, the CEO, left and she became a target of investigation for falsifying her credentials, her explanations were not accepted. Isolated, she committed suicide. This case is certainly extreme, but there is ample evidence that the stress of reaching for the top and the demands of being there can be overwhelming.[18] Here again we see the need for heightened self-awareness and maintenance of relationships in and outside the corporation that keep the ramification of these choices within one's awareness.

Emma Simms is one who has made her choices very consciously and carefully. She is the mother of a young child and an executive with a bright future at Gant. Simms has sought to design an executive life that would not sacrifice home for work. This goal is dependent on the support she gets from a working spouse. She is aware that most of her male counterparts are divorced at least once. She makes her needs and boundaries clear, but sacrifice she does. Her life has room for only two primary activities, work at Gant and home. Much of the rest of what she would like to do falls to the wayside.

There were others who consciously balanced work and family, but they were rare among all races. Anyone else getting on this path to play in the main tournament needs to do what Simms did. Ask yourself if it is worth it and under what terms. This is especially important because, even without race as a factor, the odds of making it are always slim. Factor race in and they get slimmer.

The essence of these lessons is that minorities' careers are not just at the mercy of their organizations. This is particularly true in the early career period when one's psychological and skill foundation is being built. People of color must be prepared to take advantage of opportunity when it arises.

◢ A MODEL FOR DEVELOPMENT IN THE TWENTY-FIRST CENTURY

Each month it seems there is a new article or book pointing out the changing nature of careers and the new social contract between individuals and organizations. Observers warn that it is the person and not the organization who controls the individual's career. No longer is vertical mobility up the hierarchy the only definition of good opportunity. We are told to build relationships, the more diverse the better. Most important, career theorists tell us to continually enhance our skill set and to stay technically current. Be prepared to sell yourself and prove your worth at any moment. With mergers and acquisitions likely to happen in any industry, you no longer need to change jobs to find yourself working for a new employer (to whom your previous successes matter much less than what you can do today).

What would a person's career look like if they managed it in response to these new realities? Assume too that this person would want to identify with his or her work, excel at it, and be personally invested in the employing organization.[19] One viable answer is that it would look a lot like the careers of these minority executives, as represented in the lessons articulated above.

After reading a draft of this book, a colleague concluded that it seemed as if plateaued minority managers tried to "play the white man's [career] game," while the "minority executives were playing their own game." Queried further, we discovered that the "white man's game" he referred to was the traditional career orientation in which one focuses on velocity of movement over quality of experience and where good opportunity always comes with a promotion. In this traditional model, career choices are governed less by intrinsic love of the work and internal standards of excellence than by the desire to ratchet up the hierarchy. Minority executives we studied took a different path, for reasons no doubt related to their personalities, the barriers they faced, and the people who supported them. Even their networks of relations seemed to reflect who they were, as much as what was needed to succeed. Thus, in careers that started long before this advice was given, these individuals were living it.

Returning to our colleague's observation, it may be that the "white man's game" he referred to is no longer a good game for anyone to play. We hope that many, if not all, of these lessons resonate with people of all races reading this book.

Appendix A
Research Design and Methods

T HE INTRODUCTION TO *Breaking Through* describes in detail the goals, design, and methods of the study, including the criteria used for selecting the three companies and participants. It also describes the dimensions along which the individual cases were paired as well as the definitions we have used in operationalizing executive level and plateaued middle management jobs. In many respects, the introductory chapter provides much of what is typically included in a methodological appendix. Rather than repeat that discussion, this appendix will expand on it and provide a more detailed discussion of the design choices we have made.

◢ The Research Design

As described in the Introduction, the research design consists of a comparative study of the career experiences of fifty-four minority and white executives and plateaued middle managers in three large U.S. corporations. As an exploratory study, the research had two basic aims: (1) to illuminate the career experiences and career trajectories of successful minority executives (particularly as compared to those of similar whites who succeeded to the executive level in the same company and similar minorities who did not); and (2) to identify the effects of corporate context (in terms of policies, practices, corporate leadership, and culture) on the development and advancement of minority executives and managers.

With these aims in mind, the research was designed to be comparative at the individual level (in terms of career experiences and career configurations), at the organizational level (in terms of corporate contexts and their effects), and at the institutional level (in terms of differences and similarities among corporate contexts and the effects of these differences and similarities on the corporate diversity strategies that emerged). In terms of Yin's typology of case study research, the design can be described as an embedded, multicase, comparative study with three levels of analysis.[1]

At the organizational level of analysis, we attempted to identify the salient dimensions of how each company influenced minority development and advancement on a company-by-company basis. At the institutional level, we did a comparative analysis of the histories, practices, policies, and corporate leadership initiatives of the three companies and of their effects on the emergence of each company's unique diversity strategy. The comparative analysis was also used to identify commonalities in their approaches over time that might have had a bearing on the success of their change efforts. At the individual career level of analysis, comparisons were initially conducted by company, using extreme-case comparisons, paired-comparisons, and cross-level comparisons by identity groups. Once we were able to replicate the within-company patterns in all three companies, we conducted comparative analyses across companies by level attained (plateaued manager versus executive), identity group membership (minority versus white), and career stage (Career Stages 1, 2, and 3).

Figure A-1 *Study Design and Levels of Comparative Analysis*

Acme Industries	Gant Electronics	Advanced Technology	Institutional Level/Cross-Company Comparisons
			Organizational Level
5 Minority Executives 5 White Executives 5 Plateaued Minority Managers 5 Plateaued White Managers	6 Minority Executives 4 White Executives 4 Plateaued Minority Managers 3 Plateaued White Managers	9 Minority Executives 4 White Executives 4 Plateaued Minority Managers	Individual and Racial Group Level
20 Career Cases	*17 Career Cases*	*17 Career Cases*	*Total: 54 Cases*

The decision to use an embedded comparative case study approach was motivated by several factors. The first was our desire to understand the effects of corporate and temporal context on the careers and advancement of minorities.[2] The approach was also consistent with the theory-generating and exploratory goals of the research (as compared to hypotheses testing), as well as with the types of questions we were asking—that is, "how" and "why" questions about a contemporary phenomenon that is still relatively rare and only partially understood.[3] As described by Yin and others, these are the classic conditions under which a comparative field-based case study is appropriate.[4]

Five sources of data were used in this study. Semi-structured interviews were conducted with each of the fifty-four focal managers and executives and with three people in their "role sets" (a current superior, a current subordinate, and a peer or past superior who had known them over the course of their career). Open-ended interviews were also conducted with corporate officers, human resource personnel, and other corporate informants in each of the three companies. In addition, personnel records were used in constructing individual career biographies and in validating certain of the interview data. Archival records of all executives and upper-middle managers at Acme were also used to validate the basic career trajectory patterns that we found among the focal people's careers. Finally, published and unpublished documents were gathered on each of the three companies' diversity efforts over the preceding thirty years.

EVOLUTION OF THE RESEARCH DESIGN

The initial design called for studying four cases of people of color who met our criteria for executive in each of the three companies and to pair each of these executives with a matched white executive and a matched plateaued minority manager in the same company. Two subsequent decisions were made that modified the initial design.

The first modification was the decision to oversample minority executives in our first two company sites (Advanced Technology and Gant Electronics). Our initial effort at identifying target companies that might have as many as four minority executives who met our criteria left us convinced that such people were rare and that they comprised a very small segment of the target population. As a result, we decided to take opportunistic advantage of the relatively large number of minority exec-utives that existed in the first two companies we studied. As described in the Introduction, we felt that oversampling minority executives was appropriate because they were the group of theoretical interest and were greatly underrepresented in both the target pool and the popula-tion as a whole.[5] Thus, seven of the twenty minority executives we studied at Advanced Technology and Gant Electronics were not paired with white executive or plateaued minority manager counterparts. As a result, these seven cases were not used in the paired comparison analy-ses reported in Chapters 5 and 6. By the time we started work at our last research site (Acme Industries), we stopped oversampling the minority executive group. Instead, we decided to increase the number of cases for each cell at Acme from four to five in order to get a larger number of paired comparisons in our last company site.

The second modification we made to the original design occurred as a result of initial patterns of differences that appeared in our first site (Advanced Technology). Our initial comparisons of the career paths of minority executives and their plateaued minority manager counterparts suggested that their career trajectories seemed quite dif-ferent in terms of assignment patterns and in their frequency of job changes. It was not clear, however, whether these differences were salient only to minorities or were more broadly characteristic of dif-ferences that could be found between executives and plateaued man-agers in general, regardless of race. As a result, we decided to study white plateaued managers as well as plateaued minority mangers in the remaining two companies (Gant Electronics and Acme Indus-tries). These data are used in the analyses reported in Chapter 3 which compare the career trajectories and rates of progress by career stage of the four groups. The results of both of these modifications to the orig-inal design are reflected in the final design.

◢ DATA COLLECTION

Interviews

Interviews were conducted with the 54 focal executives and man-agers, 158 people in their role sets, and an additional 28 corporate-level personnel, as described above. All of the focal and role set interviews were conducted by a multiracial, multigender research team that included the two authors (an African American male and a white Hispanic American male) and two research associates (an African American female and a white female). The decision to have a multiracial and multigender research team is based on the belief that the validity of both the data gathered and its interpretation would be enhanced if it were collected by a team that was itself diverse and representative of different racial, ethnic, gender, and cultural perspectives. This premise is a basic tenet of both Intergroup Theory and the clinical orientation that follows from its perspective.[6]

Focal Interviews

Interviews with the fifty-four focal people consisted of two different interviews separated by an overnight break. While we planned each interview to last two hours, all of the focal interviews were extended, in each instance at the focal person's initiative.

The focal interviews had four purposes: (1) to collect the information needed to build detailed personal histories and career biographies; (2) to explore specific issues that were salient to their experience of their careers (e.g., race, developmental relationships, key assignments, critical career incidents); (3) to gain an understanding of the effects of corporate context on their career and development; and (4) to enable the focal people to describe their careers from their own personal perspective; in other words, to allow them to "tell their own story" in their own words and in their own way.

For this reason, the main purpose of the first interview was for the focal person to describe their upbringing, education, and career in chronological order as *they* experienced it. No questions were asked by the interviewer about either race or the effects of company context unless the interviewee raised them. Our interest was to discover how individuals framed these issues as they told their own "stories."

The second interview was designed to enable the interviewer to ask specific questions about race, mentors, what the focal people thought were the "high" and "low" points of their careers, management style, and perceptions of their strengths and weaknesses. (Please see Exhibit A-1 for the protocols used for the focal person interviews.)

Procedure. Each team member interviewed both whites and minorities, men and women. The two senior researchers interviewed all but six of the focal people. The two research associates conducted the remainder. The researchers conducted the two interviews with each focal person on a one-on-one basis, which took from six to fifteen hours. The majority of the interviews were conducted in the focal persons' offices, although for site and scheduling reasons, two were conducted via telephone.

At the end of the second interview, the interviewer asked each focal person to list four or five people, of whom at least one was a boss (someone who had been the focal person's boss for at least a year within the last three years), one a peer or a former boss who had known the focal person over his or her career, and one a subordinate whom the focal person believed could give a balanced perspective of their managerial style, strengths and weaknesses, and, for the peer or former superior, a perspective on their career and development as a manager.

Role Set Interviews

From the list of names provided by the focal person at the end of the second interview, we selected three people for role set interviews. Focal people were asked to speak to the role set people they had nominated in their interview about participating in the study. The role set people were then contacted by the researchers via telephone to set up an interview. If the role set person had not been informed of the study by their respective focal person, the study was explained to them over the phone by one of the researchers. This phone call was followed up with a letter confirming the date and time of the interview.

The 158 role set interviews were designed to last approximately one hour. Their purpose was to get additional perspectives on the focal person's strengths, weaknesses, management style, and, at a broader level, the development of the person's career and the extent to which the focal person's race and gender influenced his or her behavior. In most cases, the interviews took approximately an hour. (Please see Exhibit A-2 for the protocols used in the role set interviews.)

The entire group of role set people consisted of the following: (1) 53 male supervisors (four African Americans, 49 whites) and one white female supervisor; (2) 43 male peers (four African Americans, one Native American, and 38 whites) and three female peers (one African American and two whites); and (3) 42 male subordinates (one Asian American, one Hispanic American, four African Americans, 36 whites) and 16 female subordinates (one African American and 15 whites). Participation was voluntary.

The two research associates were responsible for carrying out all but twelve of the role set interviews (these were done by the two senior members of the team). Role set people were interviewed for approximately one hour on an individual basis. Similar to the focal interviews, the majority of the role set interviews were conducted in their offices. However, for site and scheduling reasons, some of these interviews were conducted via telephone. The interviewer reviewed the same information given to the focal people (e.g., general purpose of the study; see Exhibit A-2) at the beginning of the role set interview. The interviewer then asked the role set person several questions (see Exhibit A-2 for interview questions).

Transcription of Interviews

Focal and role set interviews were taped and detailed notes were taken. All but one person agreed to a tape recording. In that instance the interviewer (one of the senior researchers) took detailed notes, which were amplified immediately after the interview and then typed. The tapes of the interviews were transcribed by a professional transcription company. In instances of tape recorder failure or poor quality reception, the notes were typed and used in lieu of the tape transcript.

Corporate Interviews

In addition to the focal and role set interviews, twenty-eight interviews were conducted with corporate officers, HR professionals, and others who were, or had previously been, in key succession planning, affirmative action, or diversity management positions. The purpose of these interviews was to develop an in-depth understanding of the three organizations—their histories, cultures, orientations toward executive development, and approaches to promoting racial diversity in management. Those interviewed included people currently or formerly in charge of human resources, succession planning, training, executive development, compliance, personnel systems, corporate staff administration, employee relations, affirmative action, and diversity. They also included three people at the chief operating officer level and the chief executive officer of one of the three companies. In addition, several line officers who had been identified as having played key roles in their firm's diversity initiatives and two former consultants were interviewed.

Records, Archival Data, and Other Documents

As described in the Introduction, extensive use was also made of four types of archival information. The first was personnel records of all fifty-four individual cases; these served as a check on the recollections reported by individuals of their career progression and on the nature of particular moves and assignments. A second type of data was the promotion records for all 554 Acme managers who were at the upper-middle management and executive levels of the company. These data were used for the event history analyses presented in Chapter 3 and described in Appendix B. The third type of archival data were internal documents and memoranda that were relevant to understanding each company's approach to diversity and its orientation to management and executive development. Finally, the fourth type of archival data included published materials on the three companies, their cultures, and most important, their diversity efforts.

DATA ANALYSIS

Career Experiences and Trajectories

The first step in the analysis of both the career experiences and career configurations of the fifty-four focal cases was the construction of a career chronology for each individual. The career chronology consisted of a chronological history of critical events in the individual's pre-professional, educational, work, and personal lives with a specific (or, in some instances, approximate) date affixed to each event. The career chronologies became the basis for each individual's career biography and for the analyses of the fifty-four careers. The chronology was based on a coded reading of transcriptions of the interviews with the focal person and his or her role set people, which were then checked against the individual's corporate personnel records. Where a discrepancy existed between dates and titles, the entry in the personnel record was used. Surprisingly, such discrepancies were rare and, typically, minor.

Coding Categories. The transcripts were coded using fifty-five event code categories. (Please see Exhibit A-3 for the event code categories.) The coding categories were initially identified by the two senior researchers and one of the research associates based on complete readings of the focal and role set interviews of eight focal people from each company. The actual coding of all fifty-four cases was done by three research associates (two white females and one African American female).

Using the initial coding scheme, two pretest coders separately coded one case (i.e., one focal person and his or her respective role set). Based on this initial coding, some revisions to the initial coding scheme were made. Agreement among coders was high (.84). The pretest coders then coded four new cases using the revised coding scheme. Coder agreement was improved (.87) with differences occurring mainly in cases where one coder categorized an event as involving more categories than another. For example, an event such as "first supervisory experience" was sometimes also described by the focal person as being an "eye-opening experience." The focal person might also describe it as resulting in the onset, or beginning, of a relationship with a mentor. Such examples of an assignment or change being coded in multiple categories was not uncommon.

Extreme Case Comparisons

As described earlier, "extreme case" comparisons were made within each company of highly successful minority and white executives with early- or long-plateaued minority and white managers. These "stress" comparisons were the basis for identifying several gross patterns of differences between minority executives and plateaued minority managers and their white counterparts.

As a result of the extreme case comparisons, a series of more complete comparative analyses were then conducted by company for career trajectories, assignment patterns (i.e., laterals, function changes, etc.), and developmental experiences and relationships. It was during this stage of the data analysis that we developed the career stages used in subsequent analyses in which the stages were related to the attainment of benchmark managerial jobs rather than age.

The gross patterns found in the extreme case comparisons were treated as hypotheses and tested using the coded data from the full set of fifty-four career chronologies. Initially, we compared group means within companies. Given that our sample size precluded the reliable use of regression techniques, we conducted paired comparison means tests on a subset of the sample. During the selection process, we chose each white executive, minority plateaued manager, and white plateaued manager so as to be matched with a minority executive. The basis for the match was company tenure, functional background, and education. This procedure offered a more conservative test of differences in group means while controlling for factors that might influence individual experiences independent of race and managerial status.

Career Trajectories. The development of the career stages enabled us to do the company career trajectory analyses presented in Chapter 3 and led to a testing of these patterns (which were replicated in all three companies) by doing an event history analysis of the total sample of upper-middle managers and executives at Acme to see if we could find the same pattern. The results of both of these analyses are reported in Chapter 3 and Appendix B.

Finally, after replicating the paired-comparison findings in the three companies we did a cross-company analysis by stage, race, and level that, along with the paired comparisons, is the basis for the findings described in Chapters 5 and 6.

Corporate Context

The analyses and comparisons of the corporate contexts are reported in Chapters 2, 7, and 8. Chapter 2 provides a descriptive history of the diversity efforts in each of the three companies over three decades in terms of the larger social, political, and economic contexts of these periods. These descriptions as well as the comparative analyses presented in Chapters 7 and 8 were based on readings of published and unpublished documents, interviews with key informants (as described above), and readings of the focal and role set interviews.

Exhibit A-1   Protocol for Focal Interviews

FOCAL INTERVIEW #1 GUIDE
(SEMI-STRUCTURED/OPEN ENDED)

Introduction

1. A. *Purpose of the Study.* To examine the development of middle and executive level managers in *Fortune 500* companies.

   Focus. To understand the factors that influence managerial development and effectiveness, and how these dynamics differ among managers with different backgrounds.

   Approach to the Research. To examine the career experiences of several managers in-depth through interviews (with a focal person and his/her former mentors, subordinates, and superiors or peers) and the creation of career biographies.

   B. *Use of Information.* Several copies of the results of our research at _____ will be given to management. _____ also will receive a larger report comparing findings across the participating companies.

   Confidentiality of Responses. Our agreement with _____ is that no copies of transcripts or interview notes will be given to the company. At no time will you, or _____, be identified by name in research reports of published documents.

   C. *Request for Taping.*

Rapport Building

2. Please state for me your name and title. Would you tell me what your job responsibilities are now? Include:

   - Span of control (How many people report directly to you?)
   - Upward reporting relationship (To whom do you report?)
   - Tenure in job (How long have you been in this position?)

3. Before we start to talk about your career, I'd like to hear a little about your background.

   A. Where did you grow up?

B. Tell me about your parents and your childhood. (Probe about education background and early career goals.)

C. Is there anything significant about your background that you think is critical to understanding you as a manager and your career choices?

D. Tell me about your job before _____. (From college or military to _____.) How long were you in each position?

Core Questions

4. Now I'd like to focus on the series of jobs and career moves that you've had at _____. I'd like to start at the beginning and have you bring me up to the present.

   A. How did you first come to work at _____? Why did you choose to come here?

   B. What was your first impression of the company?

   C. What was your first job, second, third, etc.? For each job find out:

      • Title and duties

      • Geographic location

      • How and what precipitated the change

      • Any major shifts in functional area

      • Significant learnings associated with each move

      • Number of years in each position

   D. Examining the different jobs, or perhaps periods, in your career, are there any points that are particularly significant for understanding your development as a manager or personally?

      • Example: first job or personal crisis

      • Probe: for why, and when it occurred

   E. Have any individuals been significant in your development as a manager?

      • Who was the person?

      • When did the relationship occur?

      • How were they important?

5. Were there any failures that were significant?

6. How would people who work for you describe your style?

7. How would you describe your management style?

8. What would you say are your strengths? Why?

9. What would you say are your weaknesses? Why?

10. What have been the major transitions that have occurred in your career? (personally or career-wise)

    • Probe: for context

11. What have been the most significant developmental events?

    • Probe: What makes this/these incident(s) major?

(Ask interviewee for a resume or CV.)

FOCAL INTERVIEW #2 GUIDE

1. I'd like to start by asking if since our last discussion you have had any reflections on the conversation?

2. What have been the highest (and lowest) moments of your career?

3. **For Minority Executives Only:** You have achieved a level of success that is rare among minority supervisors. Would you agree?

    • To what do you attribute this?

    • Are there ways in which you think your experiences at _____ have been different from most minority supervisors?

4. Has your race, ethnicity, or gender been a part of shaping your managerial style, approach, or philosophy?

5. Has pursuing an executive career impacted your family life? How would you describe the relative priorities that you set for work and family life?

6. I want to spend a few moments talking about the current job transition. How would you describe the approach you are taking to assume this role?

    • Do you have moments when you feel unsure or doubtful about your actions or decisions? How do you deal with this?

    • Earlier you had mentors; do you have people who now serve in that capacity?

7. What does it take to be successful at _____?

   - _____ has been described as a very relationship-oriented company in which networks are important. How would you describe the ways in which you use your networks?

8. What challenges remain for you in your career?

9. I'd like to get the names of four or five people that I could interview to get additional perspectives regarding your career and management style. Preferably, one of these should be a boss from within the last three years.

Wrap-up and Conclusions

Exhibit A-2   Role Set Interview Guide

Introduction

1. A. *Purpose of the Study.* To examine the development of middle and executive level managers in *Fortune 500* companies.

   Focus. To understand the factors that influence managerial development and effectiveness, and how these dynamics differ among managers with different backgrounds.

   Approach to the Research. To examine the career experiences of several managers in depth through interviews (with a focal person and his/her former mentors, subordinates, and superiors or peers) and the creation of career biographies.

   B. *Use of Information.* Several copies of the results of our research at _____ will be given to _____ management. _____ also will receive a larger report comparing findings across the participating companies.

   Confidentiality of Responses. Our agreement with _____ is that no copies of transcripts or interview notes will be given to the company. At no time will you, or _____ be identified by name in research reports of published documents.

   C. *Request for Taping.*

Rapport Building

2. Would you take a moment to tell me how long you have known _____ and in what capacity?

   - How did the two of you meet?
   - What was _____ doing at the time?
   - What were you doing?
   - Probe: Get specifics. For example: If interviewing a subordinate, did you meet _____ before being hired or were you hired after meeting _____.

3. What was your initial impression of _____?

Core Questions

In the case of former supervisors and subordinates ask the following questions. (Compare perceptions today to those in the beginning of their relationship. Obtain clear and accurate summaries.)

4. A. How would you describe _____ as a supervisor?

   - What is it like to work for him/her?
   - What adjectives best describe the kind of climate he/she creates in his/her work group?
   - What is the best (and worst) thing about working for him/her?

or

   B. How would you describe _____ as a subordinate?

   - Describe his/her relationship with peers.
   - Were there any particular things that you tried to develop in him/her or encourage him/her to do?

5. What would you say are (were) his/her major strengths (as a manager, if it applies)?

   - Probe for an illustration of each point. Ask for examples of words used to describe strengths.
   - Get a critical incident for each phrase or word that describes the person.

6. What are (were) _____'s weaknesses?
   - Probe for an illustration of each point. Ask for examples of words used to describe weaknesses.
   - Get a critical incident for each phrase or word that describes the person.

7. Based on what you know about _____, how would you describe his/her managerial style?
   - Is this style fairly common at _____?
   - Are there any aspects of _____'s style you think are unique?

8. How effective do you think _____ is as a manager? Why?
   - How do _____'s weaknesses impact his/her style and effectiveness?

9. Do you think there are any ways in which _____'s race and gender influence his/her style or way of interacting with others?
   - Have you ever talked with _____ about his/her experience of being [racioethnic group and gender, e.g., Mexican American man] in the company?

10. How has _____ changed in the time that you have known him/her?

11. Do you feel as though you have at some point played a role in _____'s development? If so, how?

12. Is there any way that you have benefited from your association with _____?

13. **For Executives Only**: What factors account for _____'s success at _____? (Success means level of career attainment)

Conclusions

14. Is there anything that we have not discussed that would be helpful for me to hear?

15. Do you have any comments or feedback for me about the interview or the project?

Exhibit A-3   The Fifty-five Event Code Categories

PREPROFESSIONAL

1   Childhood
2   Military

EDUCATION

1   High School Degree
2   Bachelor's Degree
3   Master's Degree (non–MBA)
4   MBA
5   Doctorate
6   Other Degree
7   Executive Education
8   Training Course

PERSONAL

1   Births
2   Deaths
3   Divorce
4   Marriage
5   Retiring
6   Information About Spouse

(ONSET AND ENDING OF) RELATIONSHIPS

1   Significant Boss
2   Coach
3   Mentor
4   Sponsor
5   Subordinate

WORK

1   Career Change
2   Demotion
3   Department Change
4   Exit Company

5   Exposure to Flawed Boss
6   Fired Subordinate
7   First Supervisory Experience
8   Function Change
9   Innovative Idea
10   Laid Off
11   Lateral Job Change
12   Line/Staff Change
13   Mistake/Failure
14   Minority Manager
15   Project/Task Force Assignment
16   Promotion
17   Setback
18   Start-up Assignment
19   Stretch Assignment
20   Subordinate Performance Problem
21   Turnaround/Fix-It Job
22   Entered Company
23   Significant Exposure to Other Departments
24   Exposure to Senior Management from a Junior Level
25   Location Change
26   Big Career Decision (Choice Point)
27   Big Success
28   Eye-opening Experience
29   Additional Responsibility

OUTSIDE EVENTS

1   Major Organizational Changes
2   Industry Changes
3   Economic Change

IDENTITY GROUP/RACE-RELATED EVENT

REFERENCE TO CORPORATE INITIATIVES, POLICIES, OR ACTIONS RELATED TO DEVELOPMENT OR DIVERSITY

Appendix B
Event History Analysis

IN THIS APPENDIX, we present a statistical examination of a hypothesis we formulated in Chapter 3. Specifically, we use event history analysis to look at the different effect that time spent in the first managerial position (supervisor) has on the probabilities that white and minority managers gain promotion from division operations manager to vice president and general manager (VPGM). While this is a key element in our argument that the rules regarding promotions differ for white and minority managers, this analysis does *not* represent an examination of all promotion patterns in the managerial hierarchy. Rather, we are looking only at how those managers who reach the division operations manager level differ from one another.

◢ 1. DATABASE

We constructed a database from the personnel records of the line operations of Acme. The records we obtained were created in 1995 and consisted of the employment histories of all those who were holding a division operations manager or VPGM position at that time (621 individuals over the two levels). However, the records of managers who became division operations manager from outside the operations groups or the company (67 managers or 11 percent of the population) did not have comparable information on their employment histories and therefore had to be eliminated from the analysis. This left a sample of 554 managers, of whom 74 had been promoted to VPGM.

The managerial hierarchy at Acme consists of four levels: supervisor, unit manager, division manager, and VPGM. Within our data set, there are no records of demotions. In addition, since we only have records for individuals holding a division operations manager or VPGM position at the end of 1995, we have no employment histories of individuals who became division operations manager and then left the company. Therefore, we look at advancement as a process with only two possible outcomes at any given time: promotion to VPGM or continued service as division operations manager.

◢ 2. COMPARISON OF GROUPS

As a way of exploring the data, we compared the mean time to and within each level of the managerial hierarchy for four groups: (1) white managers who had been promoted to VPGM, (2) minority managers who had been promoted to VPGM, (3) white managers who remained at the division operations manager level, and (4) minority managers who remained at the division operations manager level (Table B-1). We ran t-tests to test the significance of differences between the mean time in months for each group at each level. By examining differences in these means, we hoped to discover career

Table B-1 *Mean Months to Position*

	Total Sample	1 White VPGMs	2 White Division Operations Managers	3 Minority VPGMs	4 Minority Division Operations Managers	Statistically Significant Differences between Groups*
Time to Supervisor	44.7 *31.3*	34.8 *25.0*	45.3 *30.9*	40.4 *30.9*	49.9 *35.7*	1-2, 1-3, 1-4, 2-4
Time as Supervisor	47.2 *29.4*	31.4 *18.2*	48.1 *30.2*	51.0 *29.7*	54.3 *28.8*	1-2, 1-3, 1-4
Total Time to Unit Manager	91.9 *40.2*	66.2 *33.1*	93.4 *38.9*	91.4 *43.8*	104.2 *43.0*	1-2, 1-4, 2-4
Time as Unit Manager	77.2 *47.7*	63.1 *35.7*	79.1 *50.1*	61.2 *40.9*	81.1 *42.9*	1-2, 1-4
Total time to Division Operations Manager	169.2 *54.6*	129.3 *46.8*	172.6 *53.5*	152.5 *48.9*	185.3 *52.2*	1-2, 1-4, 2-4
Time as Division Operations Manager	76.8 *53.5*	114.2 *55.0*	71.6 *49.4*	98.2 *50.6*	70.5 *59.8*	1-2, 1-4
Total Time to VPGM	—	243.4 *55.7*	—	250.7 *48.1*	—	(none)
N	554	63	395	11	85	

Note: The standard deviation is reported below each mean in italics.
* Statistical significance is reported at the $p < .10$ level.

patterns that distinguish those individuals who rose to VPGM from those who have stayed at the division operations manager level.

In comparing white and minority managers who had been promoted to VPGM, white managers spent significantly less time as supervisor than did minority VPGMs, about the same time as unit manager, and more time as division operations managers (though this last difference is not statistically significant). The difference between levels evened out over the course of the career—the total time it took for white and minority managers to reach the top level is not significantly different. Indeed, if one subtracts the mean time it took each group to become a supervisor from the total time to VPGM (to come up with a figure for the mean time in the managerial hierarchy), minority and white managers differ by less than two months over 17.5 years.

In comparing those managers who advanced to VPGM with those who remain at division operations manager, we see different patterns within the white and minority groups. White managers who attained the VPGM level spent significantly less time as supervisor and as unit manager than did white managers who remained at the division operations manager level. However, the time minority VPGMs spent in any level is not statistically different from the time those minority managers who were not promoted spent in the same level. (While the differences in some of these means are quite large, the small number of minority managers in the sample limits statistical power.) This suggests that while rapid advancement in early positions may be important to those white managers who are promoted to VPGM, it is not as important for minority managers.

However, further examination of Table B-1 shows some of the limitations of comparing mean times in position. At the time the records were created, the mean time that both white and minority division operations managers had spent in their position is less than the mean time that those who advanced to the VPGM level spent as division operations manager. This strongly suggests that a number of those who were division operations managers at the end of our observation period will some day become a VPGM. Comparing means does not take into account that our observations have taken place at a point of time in the midst of unfolding career lines. To truly test our hypothesis, we need to control for the way time in the division operations manager level influences promotion.

In addition, we are interested in controlling for other characteristics that might somehow effect the link between first managerial position and the probability of advancing to the VPGM level. As Table B-2 demonstrates, the four groups differ in terms of education and in terms of the era in which they were hired.

◢ 3. EVENT HISTORY ANALYSIS

Fortunately, social scientists have devised a method (called event history analysis) to help untangle some of these influences. There are many different forms of event history analysis, but they share the characteristic that individuals in the sample are conceptualized as being at risk for the occurrence of an event. The probability or the rate at which the event occurs at any given moment in time is treated as the dependent variable.[1] In this study, from the moment an individual becomes a division operations manager, they are "at risk" for the "event" of gaining a promotion to VPGM.

Event history analysis allows us to compare individuals who have not experienced the event with those who have without bias that comes from the records being taken at an arbitrary point in time in a dynamic process (such as the unfolding of a career). If an individual has not experienced the event at the end of the observation period, their record is considered "censored" and the information that they have not experienced the event to that time is included in the analysis. In our analysis, all those individuals who remained at the division

Table B-2   Distribution of Control Variables

	Total Sample	White VPGMs	White Division Operations Managers	Minority VPGMs	Minority Division Operations Managers
Hired after 1974	50.7%	14.3%	57.2%	18.2%	51.8%
Has college degree	28.3%	27.0%	28.0%	36.4%	25.9%
N	554	63	395	11	85

operations manager level at the time of the observation are considered censored.

In terms of event history analysis, our working hypothesis is that each month spent as supervisor will decrease the likelihood or the rate that a white division operations manager will be promoted to VPGM (as Rosenbaum suggested in his tournament mobility model[2]). However, we expect that for minority division operations managers, time as supervisor will increase the likelihood of gaining promotion to VPGM.

In order to test this hypothesis, we conducted two forms of event history analysis: the Cox proportional hazards model and the discrete-time logit model. As noted below, the two forms differ somewhat in their specifications of time and risk. However, the independent variables are operationalized in the same manner.

Three independent variables bear directly on our hypothesis. The dummy variable MINORITY is coded '1' if the respondent is a minority group member. The variable FSTMAN represents the number of months each individual spent as a supervisor. The variable INTFST represents the interaction between being a minority group member and time spent in the supervisor's position (MINORITY*FSTMAN). If our hypothesis is correct, FSTMAN should be significantly negative (each month decreases the likelihood of the event—promotion to VPGM—occurring for managers), while INTFST should be positive (indicating that the reverse is true for minority division operations managers). In addition, the absolute value for the INTFST must be greater than the absolute value of FSTMAN. (For minority managers, the probability of gaining a promotion from the division operations manager's level as a function of time spent as supervisor is derived by adding the parameters of FSTMAN and INTFST and a constant for the overall effect of being a minority).

We also included two control variables. COLDEG is a dummy variable coded '1' if the respondent has a college degree and represents a control for educational credentials. COHORT is a dummy variable coded '1' if the respondent was hired after 1974 and represents a control for the effects of being hired in different eras. We constructed this variable to account for generational differences in the company start dates and as a proxy for age differences. We would have liked to have controlled for age, but this variable in the Acme database was corrupted and not available in our analysis.

Cox Proportional Hazards Model

The Cox proportional hazards model is perhaps the most widely used semi-parametric form of event history analysis. It is semi-parametric in that we do not have to assume a specific form for the distribution of event times over the risk set. The general form of a Cox model is:

$$r(t) = h(t) \exp(A(t)\beta)$$

Where the transition rate $r(t)$ is the product of an unspecified baseline hazard rate $h(t)$ and a vector of covariates $A(t)$ and their associated regression parameters β. To specify β, the model estimates a partial likelihood function, which eliminates the unknown baseline hazard function and accounts for censored observations.[3]

Equations 5, 6, and 7 of Table B-3 show the results of the analysis. As expected, FSTMAN is negative and INTFST is significantly positive, supporting our hypothesis. While neither COLDEG nor COHORT are significant or had any substantial influence on the variables of concern, it is interesting to note that MINORITY becomes significantly negative when entered into the equations with the variables for time in the first managerial position. This suggests that the effect of time in the first managerial position suppresses the negative effect that being a minority has on gaining a promotion. (Also note that there are no parameter estimates for the INTERCEPT term or time. This is because these are contained in $h(t)$, the unspecified baseline hazard rate.)

The Cox model is called a proportional model because it assumes that the influence of the covariates does not vary from one time period in the risk set to the next. In other words, it assumes that the effect of being white on promotion chances is the same during the first month of being a division operations manager as it is in the 100th month. To test the proportionality assumption, we constructed a time-varying, interaction variable between the log of time in the set and MINORITY and the log of time in the set and FSTMAN and entered each, separately, into equation 6 (analysis not shown). Neither test variable proved significant, showing that the proportionality assumption holds.[4]

The partial likelihood function used to estimate the parameters also assumes that there are few or no ties in terms of times to censoring or

Table B-3 *Parameter Estimates from Event History Analysis*

	Discrete-Time, Logit Model				Cox Proportional Hazards Model		
	1	2	3	4	5	6	7
INTERCEPT	-5.9336***	-5.5046***	-2.4951***	-5.3451***			
	0.4932	0.5444	0.3627	0.5514			
DURA	0.4279***	0.4156***	a	0.4150***			
	0.0961	0.0958		0.0957			
DURA2	-0.0136***	-0.0133***		-0.0132***			
	0.00381	0.00444		0.00443			
MINORITY	-0.2168	-0.1520	-1.1213*	-1.1376*	-1.1322*	-.1614	-1.1244*
	0.3346	0.3368	0.6502	0.6518	.6625	.3291	.6607
COLDEG	-0.1073	-0.1232	-0.0994	-0.1149		-.1060	-.1052
	0.2631	0.2633	0.2636	0.2636		.2593	.2596
FSTMAN		-0.0095*	-0.0154**	-0.0148**	-0.0117*		-0.0115*
		0.00572	0.00678	0.00679	.0068		.0068
INTFST			0.0236*	0.0235*	0.0242*		0.0231*
			0.0121	0.0122	.024		.024
COHORT	-0.6283*	-0.5849*	-0.6053	-0.5574		-.1481	-.0849
	0.3492	0.3511	0.3482	0.3517		.3510	.3534
Log-likelihood	757.8	674.0	664.6	670.7	696.7	700.9	696.4
D.F.	5	6	13	7	3	3	5
N	4,210	4,210	4,210	4,210	554	554	554

Note: Standard errors are printed below each parameter estimate.
[a] Time in risk set modeled as series of nine dummy variables representing two-year segments.
*** $p < .01$. ** $p < .05$. * $p < .10$

promotion. Unfortunately, while duration times were reported in the smallest unit available (months), 69 percent of the duration times involving 89 percent of the individuals were ties. The SAS PHREG procedure makes certain assumptions for handling ties that allows for estimation of the parameters, but there is no agreement about the acceptable percentage of ties that can be included in an analysis without creating unstable results. Therefore, we decided to conduct a discrete-time analysis to see if we could confirm our results using a slightly different model where the number of ties does not affect the outcome.

Discrete-Time Logit Model

Rather than estimate the rate of transitions, a discrete-time logit model estimates the odds that a person will be promoted at any given time. The general form of the model is:

$$\log(P(t)/(1-P(t)) = \alpha + \Sigma \beta x_k$$

Where $\log(P(t)/1-P(t))$ represents the log-odds of making a transition at any given time, α represents the intercept term, x is a vector of covariates, and β is a vector of parameters for those covariates.[5]

Unlike the Cox model, the discrete-time logistic model looks at each specified time period in the risk set separately. For our purposes, we defined a year as the length of time for each observation and transformed the data set so that each respondent had one observation for each year as division operations manager (i.e., a person who spent ten years as division operations manager generates ten observations). In our data set, there were 4,210 observations for the 554 respondents.

In the discrete-time model, the influence of time in the risk set must be explicitly modeled. At first we created dummy variables for each two-year period as division operations manager (see Equation 3, Table B-3). However, an analysis including time as two continuous variables—DURA (the number of years the individual had been in the risk set at the time of the observation) and DURA2 (the number of years squared)—proved to be more parsimonious. (From Table B-3, we see that the increase in likelihood between Equation 3 and 4 is only 6.1 for 6 D.F.) Interestingly, the parameters estimated for these two variables create a log-logistic curve where transition probabilities start low and rise until thirteen years in the risk set and then decline with each increasing year at risk. This type of inverted u-shaped distribution of probabilities is consistent with other studies of promotion rates.[6]

As evidenced by Equation 4 from Table B-3, the hypothesis holds within the discrete-time model. For white managers, each additional month of being a supervisor decreases the probability of gaining the VPGM position. This relationship, which is consistent with Rosenbaum's tournament hypothesis, is not true for minorities. The benefits of a fast early start do not accrue to them. In fact, as we show below, the opposite is true. For minority managers, the probabilities of being promoted from division operations manager to the VPGM executive position actually rise with time at the supervisory level. We also tested quadratic terms for both time in supervisory position and the interaction, but these terms did not prove significant (and are not shown here).

▰ 4. Interpreting the Results

In order to better interpret the results in Equation 4, we have transformed the logit parameters into odds and added the interaction terms to get the overall effect of time in a supervisory position on gaining a promotion from division operations manager to VPGM. The odds of white managers gaining a promotion to VPGM as a function of time in the supervisor's position (all other things being equal) is:

$$\text{Odds} = \exp(\beta_1 MONTHS)$$

Where $\beta_1 = -0.0148$ (from Equation 4 in Table B-3) and $MONTHS =$ the number of months as a supervisor. The odds of minority managers gaining a promotion to VPGM as a function of time in the supervisor's position (all other things being equal) is:

$$\text{Odds} = \exp((\beta_1 + \beta_2)MONTHS + \beta_3)$$

Where $\beta_1 = -0.0148$, $\beta_2 = 0.0235$, $\beta_3 = -1.1376$ (from Equation 4 in Table B-3) and $MONTHS =$ the number of months as a supervisor. The results of these transformations are graphed in Figure B-1.[7]

It is important to reemphasize that Figure B-1 does not show the odds of gaining promotion to the VPGM's position from the supervisor's position. *Minority supervisors should not think that their odds of becoming a VPGM increase with every day in the position.* Our analysis was of individuals who had already risen to the division operations manager's position. If gaining a promotion to the unit manager's level from supervisor follows the same distribution of event times as that of gaining promotion to VPGM from division operations manager, supervisors who do not get promoted within a certain length of time run an increasing risk of not getting promoted at all. What our analysis shows is that once having reached the division operations manager level, the time minority managers spent as supervisors will (all other things being equal) actually increase their chances of gaining promotion.

While results from the two different event history models give us some confidence in our hypothesis, there are a number of factors that limit the generalizability of our findings. First, the data records were

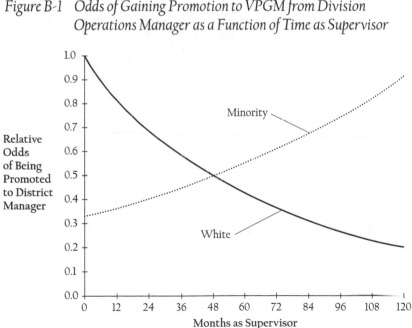

Figure B-1   Odds of Gaining Promotion to VPGM from Division Operations Manager as a Function of Time as Supervisor

collected retrospectively and therefore we do not have information on people who retired or quit the company after becoming division operations manager or VPGM. If white managers who spent a long time as supervisor actually did gain promotion to VPGM but then retired at much higher rates than most VPGMs, this retrospective bias could affect the hypothesis. (Conversely, a similar bias could occur if minority managers who spent a short time as supervisor actually gained promotion to VPGM but then left to seek other opportunities.)

Finally, it is important to point out that this analysis is of one company at one particular stretch in history. These might have been unusual times for Acme, or Acme might have unusual promotion practices relative to other companies.

◢ Notes

INTRODUCTION

1. There are numerous survey studies that establish this reality of racial difference and divide. For a compelling analysis of these data see Andrew Hacker, *Two Nations*; Bobo and Hutchings, "Perceptions of Racial Group Competition"; Bobo and Kluegal, "Opposition to Race-Targeting"; and the *Public Opinion Quarterly*'s special issue on race (vol. 6, no. 1, 1997).

2. According to recent statistics from the U.S. Department of Labor's Glass Ceiling Commission, the proportion of African American men and women holding the title of vice president was 1% in 1982 and 2.3% in 1992. During the same period, the percentage of Hispanics rose from 1.3% to 2.0%, and the percentage of Asian top managers rose from 0.4% to 1.8%. U.S. Department of Labor, *Report on the Glass Ceiling Initiative*, 14.

3. Collins, *Black Corporate Executives*, 42–43.

4. Cox and Nkomo reviewed all of the articles published in the twenty leading organizational behavior and human resource management journals between 1964 and 1989 to assess the extent to which research on race was included. They found that of 11,804 published articles only 201 addressed issues of race and, of those, 17 addressed

issues of leadership and/or management development. Cox and Nkomo, "Invisible Men and Women," 422–423.

5. One such study is Bell and Nkomo's monograph "Barriers to Workplace Advancement," prepared for the U.S. Department of Labor's Glass Ceiling Commission, which focuses on the experience of African American managers, both men and women.

6. Fernandez has written a number of books that make use of thousands of survey responses from minority and white management and nonmanagement employees. See, for example, Fernandez, *Survival in the Corporate Fishbowl*. Other examples include Alderfer, et al., "Diagnosing Race Relations"; Greenhaus, Parasuraman, and Wormley, "Effects of Race"; Kossek and Zonia, "Assessing Diversity Climate"; and Morrison, *New Leaders*.

7. See, for example, Thomas, "Impact of Race"; Denton, "Bonding and Supportive Relationships"; and Hayes, "It's Not What You Know, It's Who You Know."

8. See, for example, Morrison, White, and Velsor, *Breaking the Glass Ceiling*—a study of executive women.

9. In *Rage of a Privileged Class*, Ellis Cose poignantly describes the pervasive encounters with racism experienced in the workplace by middle-class African Americans. Bari-Ellen Roberts describes her experience as one of a handful of African American middle managers at the Texaco Corporation in *Roberts vs. Texaco*. Roberts was the lead plaintiff in a class action racial discrimination suit brought against Texaco. When this case was settled out of court, the value of the settlement was the largest amount that had ever been won in a suit of this kind, $176.1 million. Roberts and White, *Roberts vs. Texaco*, 276.

10. Collins, *Black Corporate Executives*, 42–43; Work, *Race, Economics, and Corporate America*, 91; and Work, "Management Blacks," 28–30.

11. The purpose of our exploratory study was to generate a grounded theoretical understanding of individual and organizational characteristics and processes that produce minority executives. We selected our study participants based on the dependent variable we were attempting to explain. When we interviewed them we were not blind to their race or level of career attainment. Sampling on the dependent variable is normally not advised in social science research. The exception to this is exploratory research designed to develop theory about a phenomenon not yet well understood. See March and March, "Performance Sampling in Social Matches," 450–452, for cautions about this sampling method, and Glaser and Strauss, *Discovery of Grounded Theory*, 45–77 and

161–183, for discussion of theoretical sampling in qualitative research. See also March and Sutton, "Organizational Performance."

12. Harrington and Boardman's study of people born into poor, uneducated families who have achieved high levels of career success is an example of a recent careers study in which the group of primary interest is overrepresented in the study population. Like our research design, they conducted a field study with intensive interviews. Harrington and Boardman, *Paths to Success*, 31.

13. Acme and Gant each had one minority female executive who met our criteria. The minority female manager at Advanced was included for two reasons. First, on a number of dimensions she was the best minority manager match available for several executives. Second, when we started at Advanced, we had not secured access to the other sites. With no knowledge of the gender composition of the other sites' minority executive population, we ran the risk of having an all-male study population. Alternatively we could include females in the plateaued managers group. Therefore, we included the female manager to find out if it was essential to match on gender.

14. Plateaued white managers were not included in the study population at our first site, Advanced Technology. We chose to oversample the minority executive population because it was very diverse. This group included African American, Asian American, and Hispanic American executives. Our choice to exclude white managers at Advanced was justified by the fact that white managers were not a primary comparison group for minority executives, unlike white executives and minority managers.

15. We are aware of two major undertakings to address this dearth of research. Ella Bell and Stella Nkomo have conducted a multiyear study of African American and white female managers, the findings of which were published in *Our Separate Ways*. Catalyst, a research and advocacy institute that works with business to promote women, is also engaged in a large-scale study of women of color in the corporate world. See Catalyst, *Women of Color in Corporate Management: Dynamics of Career Advancement*, and Catalyst, *Women of Color in Corporate Management: A Statistical Picture*.

16. We do not report separate analyses of these informant interviews in this book, but they were used to construct the career biographies of each focal study participant. Separate analyses of these data are reported in Thomas, Hammond, and Phillips, "Perceptions of Minority and White Executives and Managers."

17. An advantage of this typology is that it creates a qualitative control for the different levels of responsibility that result from differences in company norms and functional disciplines. More normative age or career development models such as those posed by Levinson et al. in *Seasons of a Man's Life* or Schein in *Career Dynamics* would make this difficult given our small sample. Statistical controls would be problematic or inappropriate given the size of the sample and qualitative nature of the data.

1: MINORITY SUCCESS IN THE CORPORATE MAINSTREAM

1. The names of all study participants and companies have been disguised.
2. More extensive reviews of the literature pertaining to barriers to minority advancement are Bell and Nkomo, *Barriers to Workplace Advancement*, 78–123; Pettigrew and Martin, "Shaping the Organizational Context"; and Braddock and McPartland, "Minorities Continue." Each organizes their review differently, but supports the conclusions we draw here.
3. Morrison found that prejudice (racism) was the most often mentioned barrier to minority advancement (Morrison, *New Leaders*, 34–39). Feagin and Sikes also identify racist attitudes, manifest in subtle forms of treatment discrimination, as major barriers to African Americans' full enfranchisement in the workplace (Feagin and Sikes, *Living with Racism*, 135–222).
4. See Bell and Nkomo, *Barriers to Workplace Advancement*, 37–68, and Fernandez, *Racism and Sexism*, 1–179, for a detailed discussion of the organizational-level manifestations of prejudice.
5. Many scholars have found that members of lower-status culture groups lacked the "natural" basis for authority and had to struggle with establishing legitimacy (Cox, *Cultural Diversity*, 190; Nilson, "Components of Social Standing"; and Wiley and Eskilson, "Interaction of Sex and Power Base"). Eden has shown that members of minority groups underachieve at work because they are expected to do poorly by supervisors (Eden, "Industrialization as a Self-fulfilling Prophecy"). In his study of cross-cultural teams, Webber found that persons from minority culture typically responded to their work rejection by either becoming passive, violating group norms, or withdrawing. This included behavior that would negatively impact the minority person's own reputation, such as coming late to meetings or not being prepared (Webber, "Majority and Minority Perceptions").

6. Recent research even suggests that whites and men experience heightened psychological discomfort as their work groups fill up with minorities and women. Tsui, Egan, and O'Reilly, "Being Different," 572.
7. D. Thomas, "Mentoring and Irrationality," 286–287; D. Thomas, "Impact of Race," 488–489.
8. Ragins, "Diversified Mentoring Relationships," 497–498.
9. In his work on cross-racial mentoring, David Thomas found that white mentors often felt frustrated by their inability to sell their white colleagues on an African American protégé. Thomas's work also showed that white mentors who could talk openly with their black protégés about race and race relations made it easier for the pair to think together about how to overcome obstacles created or exacerbated by race. Open discussion helped protégés maintain their motivation or confidence when opportunities were slow to materialize and were less likely to doubt whether the mentor was doing all he or she could. D. Thomas, "Strategies for Managing Racial Differences."
10. Kotter, *General Managers*, 46–47.
11. See Greenhaus, Parasuraman, and Wormley, "Effects of Race," 74–79; Tsui and O'Reilly, "Beyond Simple Demographic Effects," 417–421.
12. Alderfer and Tucker, *Measuring Managerial Potential*; Alderfer, "Changing Race Relations Embedded in Organizations"; Alderfer et al., "Race Relations Advisory Group."
13. McCall, Lombardo, and Morrison, *Lessons of Experience*, 15–65; McCall and Lombardo, *Off the Track*, 9.
14. D. Thomas, "Impact of Race"; D. Thomas, "Racial Dynamics."
15. Steele and Aronson, "Stereotype Threat," 798, 808; Steele, "Threat in the Air," 618.

2: DOING DIVERSITY

1. See Collins, *Black Corporate Executives*, 42–43; and Work, *Race, Economics, and Corporate America*, 91.
2. No figures were available for Asian Americans. Calvert, *Equal Employment Opportunity*, 22.
3. U.S. National Advisory Commission, *Report on Civil Disorders*, 203.
4. Amott and Matthaei, *Race, Gender and Work*, 82–85; Griswold de Castillo and de León, *North to Aztlán*, 125–147; Hammersback, Jensen, and Gutierrez, *War of Words*; Mooney and Majka, *Farmers' and Farm Workers' Movements*, 180–183; and Rosales, *Chicano!*, 112–247.
5. Amott and Matthaei, *Race, Gender and Work*, 277; Korrol, *From Colonia to Community*, 221–234; and Sanchez, "Young Lords."

6. Wei, *Asian America Movement*; Amott and Matthaei, *Race, Gender and Work*, 212–213; Lifshey, "Yellow Power Genesis."

7. U.S. Bureau of the Census, *Statistical Abstract of the United States 1996*, 552; U.S. Bureau of the Census, "Average Annual Growth Rates of Gross National Product (Percent): 1909 to 1970."

8. Scott, *Kent State/May4*, 1.

9. "Thomas W. Jones Talks about Race in America," *Journal Graphic Transcripts*, 18 May 1995. Transcript #1380-3.

10. U.S. Bureau of the Census, "Percent of Persons 25 Years Old and Over Who Have Completed High School or College."

11. See Zweigenhaft and Domhoff, *Blacks in the White Establishment*.

12. In his autobiography, Reggie Lewis, the late CEO of Beatrice Food International, tells the story of how his performance in a Harvard Law School–sponsored summer program for minority students secured his admission there (Lewis and Walker, *Why Should White Guys Have All the Fun?*, 47–55).

13. Leonard, "Employment and Occupational Advance"; Heckman and Wolpin, "Contract Compliance Program," 544–64; Goldstein and Smith, "Estimated Impact of the Anti-discrimination Program."

14. Collins, *Black Corporate Executives*, 146–147.

15. Ibid., 99–118.

16. Holloway, *The Bakke Decision*; U.S. Commission on Civil Rights, *Toward an Understanding of Bakke*; Dreyfuss and Lawrence, *The Bakke Case*; *Bakke v. Regents of the University of California*, 438 U.S. 265 (1978).

17. Gallup Organization, *Votes by Groups in Presidential Elections*.

18. Lynch, *Diversity Machine*, 13, 30–32; Belz, *Equality Transformed*.

19. Amaker, *Civil Rights and the Reagan Administration*, 124–129.

20. The Reagan Administration also proposed that back-pay awards no longer be awarded in class-action suits, except to identifiable victims of discrimination. Though the EEOC commented that this violated current case law, it took this proposal as its cue, and only less effective suits on behalf of individuals were pursued. Parikh, *Politics of Preference*, 128–129; Amaker, *Civil Rights and the Reagan Administration*, 119–128; Bergmann, *In Defense of Affirmative Action*, 170.

21. By the late 1970s there were several movies and books about Wall Street that were box office hits and best sellers. Among these were the films *Working Girl* and *Wall Street* and books by Tom Wolfe, *The Bonfire of the Vanities*, and Bryan Burrough, *Barbarians at the Gate*.

22. Bastian and Taylor, *Young Black Male Victims*; Lichtblau, "Attacks, Bias Against Gays"; "National City Crime Growth Down," *San Diego Union-Tribune*, 9 March 1988, B-5.

23. Fernandez, *Survival in the Corporate Fishbowl*, 234–235.
24. Murray, *Losing Ground*; Lynch, *Diversity Machine*; W. A. Beer, "Whose Straw Man?"; W. A. Beer, "Resolute Ignorance."
25. See Sowell, *Civil Rights, Rhetoric or Reality?*; Adelman et al., "Where We Succeeded"; C. Thomas, "Why Black Americans"; Loury, "Beyond Civil Rights"; Steele, *Content of Our Character*.
26. Collins, *Black Corporate Executives*, 125–127.
27. U.S. Department of Labor, *Report on the Glass Ceiling Initiative*.
28. This quote comes from the January 31, 1994, issue of *Business Week* (Friedman and DiTomaso, "Myths About Diversity," 55–57). Friedman and DiTomaso point out that this statistic and its implications were greatly distorted. In fact, from 1991 to 2005, the percentage of non-Hispanic white males in the labor force will only decrease from 41 percent to 38 percent.
29. See, for example, R. Thomas, "From Affirmative Action to Affirming Diversity."
30. U.S. Department of Labor, *Report on the Glass Ceiling Initiative*.

3: THE CAREER TOURNAMENT AND ITS RULES

1. The most extensive description of this theory can be found in Rosenbaum, *Career Mobility in a Corporate Hierarchy*. The empirical test of his theory was based on managerial promotion data collected in a large industrial firm. Readers may also want to see Sheridan et al., "Career Tournaments," and Bruderl, Diekmann, and Preisendorfer, "Patterns of Intraorganizational Mobility," for empirical tests and theoretical extensions of Rosenbaum's theory.
2. Given the clinical approach to this study, we determined to do this after identifying the same promotion pattern differences within each company. Appendix B discusses the statistical methodology for these analyses.
3. The sample is composed of five sets of matched individuals from each of the study groups: minority executives, minority managers, white executives, and white managers. For each minority executive, we identified and included a comparable white executive, minority manger, and white manager in the sample. Selection was based on tenure with the organization, educational background, and gender. However, we were not able to create a white female executive match for the one minority female executive in the sample.
4. The records we obtained were created in 1995 and consisted of employment histories for all those holding a division operations

manager or VPGM position at that time. However, the managers who became division operations managers as laterals from outside the Operations function (67 people or 11 percent of the study sample) did not have promotion data for Stage 1 or 2 and thus were eliminated from the analysis. This left a sample of 554 individuals.

5. See Appendix B for an explanation of these procedures and the actual means.

6. See Allison, *Longitudinal Event Data*; Blossfeld and Rohwer, *Techniques of Event History Modeling*; Tuma and Hannan, *Social Dynamics*; and Yamaguchi, *Event History Analysis*, for descriptions of this methodology.

7. Several observers of executive development practices in organizations note that most large organizations identify people with executive potential early in their careers (Kotter, *Leadership Factor*, 90–92; McCall and Lombardo, *Off the Track*, 8). These persons are often given special developmental opportunities and attention in the context of above-average upward mobility.

8. A number of empirical studies of promotion process evince that promotion determinants and criteria for racial minorities and whites differ. See Powell and Butterfield, "Effect of Race on Promotions"; Baldi and McBrier, "Do the Determinants of Promotion Differ"; Paulin and Mellor, "Gender, Race, and Promotions"; Nkomo and Cox, "Gender Differences."

9. "Notes on Affirmative Action," *New York Times*, 24 September 1995, sec. 4, p. 12.

10. In their book *All That We Can Be*, Charles Moskos and John Butler present an extensive discussion of the U.S. Army's efforts to integrate racially and to ensure equal opportunity at all organizational levels. They too cite Powell as an example of how the efforts to create an open environment then allowed talented minorities to compete fairly for top positions.

11. Kram (*Mentoring at Work*, 23–43) discusses the career and psychosocial functions of mentoring relationships in detail. Included in this discussion are the protégé's increased personal development, work satisfaction, and organizational power.

4: The Early Years

1. Useem (*Inner Circle*, 13–14) notes a link between class membership, the social status of parents, and the future success of offspring in his study of business and political activity in large corporations in both the United States and the United Kingdom. In his classic *The Power Elite*, C.

Wright Mills studied the backgrounds and career paths of the leaders of corporations, the executive branch of government, and the military. He found that almost all of the individuals were raised in families from the upper third of the income and occupational pyramids. In fact, a majority came from the 11% of U.S. families headed by businesspeople or highly educated professionals (127–129). Mabel Newcomer studied the highest-ranking businessmen of 1900, 1925, and 1950, and found that 55.7% of the fathers of the 1950 executives had been business executives, and 17.8% were professionals (*Big Business Executive*, 55).

2. All fifteen of Kotter's study participants were white males and shared similarities in their childhood family environment, education, and early career experiences (Kotter, *General Managers*, 44–51)

3. Harrell, *Managers' Performance and Personality*, 99.

4. Johnson, *Blueprint for Success*, 3–4.

5. One comparable sample is the 1985 Korn/Ferry study of senior-level *Fortune 500* executives. In that sample, all nonwhite respondents made up less than 1% of the total. Eighty-five percent of the Korn/Ferry executives graduated from college, and 51% earned a graduate degree. In comparison, 98% of the Executive Leadership Council (ELC) sample of African American executives graduated from college, and 82% earned graduate or professional degrees. Sixty-four percent of the executives in the Korn/Ferry sample had fathers who worked in white-collar jobs, and 24% came from blue-collar homes. Sixty-three percent of their mothers did not work outside the home, 34% worked in clerical jobs, and 17% in blue-collar occupations. The occupations of the ELC sample's fathers varied widely and were distributed as follows: 14.6% in labor, 13% in government, 12.5% in factories, 10.5% professionals, 8% teachers, 8% in construction, and 2% in the ministry. The remaining 31.4% were classified as "various other." Twenty-six percent of the ELC's mothers were homemakers, 20% were teachers, and 14% were domestics. (Johnson, *Blueprint for Success*, 3–4; Korn/Ferry International, *Korn/Ferry International's Executive Profile: A Survey*, 36–41.) In Harrington and Boardman's study of highly successful individuals, the African Americans in the sample reported higher levels of education than their equally successful white counterparts (Harrington and Boardman, *Paths to Success*, 55).

6. The insignificance of education as a predictor of occupational mobility at Acme is evidenced in our event history analysis described in Chapter 3 and Appendix B. Education was not significant in any of the equations. Furthermore, minority executives in the larger Acme sample tended to be better educated. Forty-one percent of minority

executives had college degrees compared with 28% of white executives. The percentages for minority managers and white managers are 26% and 29%, respectively.

7. Michael Useem, for example, uses elite boarding schools, inclusion in the Social Register, and a family income base of over $100,000 in 1967 as indicators of belonging to the "inner circle" of the business world elite (Useem, *Inner Circle*, 66–70). For other discussions of social class, see, for example, Blau and Duncan, *American Occupational Structure*; Featherman and Hauser, *Opportunity and Change*; and Jencks et al., *Who Gets Ahead?*

8. Blau and Duncan, *American Occupational Structure*, 331–337.

9. See Harrington and Boardman for a discussion of sociological variables and upward mobility (Harrington and Boardman, *Paths to Success*, 5–13). Blau and Duncan (*American Occupational Structure*, 405) found that social origin, career origin, ethnic background, region of birth, education, type of community, and other characteristics of family origin are cumulative in their effect on upward mobility of racial minorities, while they are not for whites.

10. Harrington and Boardman found no differences in the positive influence that the Pathmakers' and the Control group's families had on schooling. They did find that the Pathmakers started in and graduated from less selective schools than the Control group. A contributing factor was the lesser financial resources of the Pathmakers' families (*Paths to Success*, 71–72).

11. Hacker, *Two Nations*, 34–38.

12. The ability to cross boundaries is an important contributor to social and professional success, as Zweigenhaft and Domhoff observe in *Blacks in the White Establishment*: "Perhaps there is no more important cultural capital for blacks than to feel comfortable interacting with whites on an equal basis; this is a major contribution of the ABC program to its graduates" (108).

13. Zweigenhaft and Domhoff point out that having white or very light skin seems to benefit Latinos attempting to integrate managerial ranks of corporations or other elite institutions (*Diversity in the Power Elite*, 129–131).

5: Early Career

1. Schein devotes a major portion of his book *Career Dynamics* to the early career period. This period begins with entry into the work

world and is the time when some of the most difficult and critical issues of creating an effective and mutually beneficial fit between the individual and organization occurs. For other discussions of this period, see Levinson et al., *Seasons of a Man's Life*; Hall, *Careers in Organizations*; and Super, *Psychology of Careers*. In addition, most of the empirical research examining organizational socialization is focused on this early career phase. See Chatman, "Matching People"; Caldwell, Chatman, and O'Reilly, "Building Organizational Commitment"; and Louis, "Surprise and Sense Making."

2. In her longitudinal study, *MBAs on the Fast Track*, Wallace did compare the early career mobility of racial minority graduates of the MIT Sloan School of Management with those of white graduates. Her conclusion was that five years after graduation, minority MBA graduates were not as successful as their white counterparts. Minorities received fewer promotions, were more likely to be in staff jobs, described lower aspirations as a result of their experiences, and reported lower salaries. Since race was not the focus of her study, Wallace did not attempt to identify what accounted for these differences. Chapter 6 of *MBAs on the Fast Track* focuses on the experience of minority managers. Dickens and Dickens present a stage theory of development in *The Black Manager*, but the stages are defined by milestones in racial identity development rather than career development.

3. Lawrence, "Organizational Age Norms," 215–219.

4. See Steele and Aronson, "Stereotype Threat"; Steele, "Threat in the Air"; Howard and Hammond, "Rumors of Inferiority"; and Dickens and Dickens, *The Black Manager*.

5. Butler and Waldroop discuss this in Chapters 1 and 2 of *Discovering Your Career in Business*.

6. Kotter, *Power and Influence*, 123–125.

7. Morrison, White, and Velsor at the Center for Creative Leadership found that women are particularly vulnerable when they move too fast (*Breaking the Glass Ceiling*, 38–39). Kotter and Gabarro also note that too-rapid movement can be as detrimental to executive effectiveness as too slow movement (Kotter, *Power and Influence*, 130–133; Gabarro, *Taking Charge*, 138).

8. Morrison, *The New Leaders*, 59–67; Bray, Campbell, and Grant, *Formative Years in Business*, 70–76.

9. McCall, Lombardo, and Morrison, *Lessons of Experience*, 17, 32–41.

10. In coding for these kinds of opportunities we relied on interviewee's descriptions of the nature and benefits drawn from each

assignment as well as our own knowledge of the organizations. See Appendix A for a detailed discussion of the coding categories and procedures.

11. Greenhaus and Parasuraman ("Job Performance Attributions") found evidence of this performance discrepancy between black and white managers in three U.S. companies. Deaux and Emswiller ("Explanations of Successful Performance") and Cash, Gillen, and Burns ("Sexism and 'Beautyism'") found that when women performed tasks traditionally done by men, their success was more likely to be attributed to luck, while when men did the same tasks successfully, it was more likely to be attributed to ability.

12. David Thomas notes that white male superiors and black female subordinates attempting to establish mentoring relations face extra difficulty because of the lack of basis for identification. Those relationships can come under intense scrutiny by whites and blacks who distrust the parties' motives for pairing (D. Thomas, "Mentoring and Irrationality," 279–287).

13. Kanter, *Men and Women of the Corporation*, 164–173.

14. See Wells and Jennings, "Black Career Advances."

15. Roberts and White in *Roberts v. Texaco* devote two chapters to highlighting the importance of Roberts's precollege years and early academic and character-building experiences. She directly attributes her success to Career Stage 1 choices.

16. See Bandura, "Human Agency"; *Social Learning Theory*; "Social Cognitive Theory"; and Bandura et al., "Multifaceted Impact."

17. See Steele and Aronson, "Stereotype Threat"; and Steele, "Threat in the Air."

18. Greenhaus and Parasuraman, "Job Performance Attributions"; Brewer and Kramer, "Psychology of Intergroup Attitudes and Behavior"; Hewstone, "The 'Ultimate Attribution Error'?"; Pettigrew, "The Ultimate Attribution Error"; Weber, "Nature of Ethnocentric Attribution Bias."

6: Breaking Through

1. Higgins and Nohria, "The Side-Kick Effect," in press.

2. Ibarra ("Race, Opportunity and Diversity," 691) found that high-potential minorities had more racially diverse networks than non–high-potential minorities. McCall, Lombardo and Morrison also note that a frequent cause for derailment for managers is overdependence on a single, although powerful mentor. (*Lessons of Experience*, 166–169.)

7: DIVERSITY STRATEGY

1. To cite these written materials here would break the disguise of our companies. When data came directly from the companies, we provide a description of the document.
2. Other scholars have described different models for approaching diversity. For discussions of assimilation, pluralism, and other models, see Cox, *Cultural Diversity*, 165–168; Cox and Finley-Nickelson, "Models of Acculturation"; R. Thomas, *Beyond Race and Gender*, 7–9; and D. Thomas and Ely, "Making Differences Matter," 81–83.
3. Park, *Race and Culture*, 204–220; Will, "The Journey Up From Guilt."
4. "Valuing differences" programs generally have the following five focuses: (1) fostering awareness and acceptance of individual difference; (2) fostering greater understanding of the nature and dynamics of individual differences; (3) helping participants understand their own feelings and attitudes about people who are "different"; (4) exploring how differences might be used as assets in the workplace; and (5) enhancing work relations between people who are different. (R. Thomas, *Beyond Race and Gender*, 24–25.)
5. Our typology is not normative with regard to one approach being more desirable than another. This is because the primary outcome we are concerned with is successful development and advancement of minorities to executive level jobs. Other theorists have identified different approaches that organizations take toward diversity. These typologies tend to be normative, positing that one approach is preferable to another. Cox, for instance, identified three types: monolithic, plural, and multicultural and maintains that the multicultural typology is the most desirable (*Cultural Diversity*, 225–230). Unlike us, he focuses on informal and structural integration of cultural diversity in the organization. D. Thomas and Ely, too, have developed a normative typology ("Making Differences Matter"). Like us they note that multiple approaches can lead an organization to create a diverse management corps. However, all approaches are not equally effective at making racial or gender diversity positive contributors to individual and work group effectiveness. According to that criteria, the learning and effectiveness paradigm is preferable.
6. D. Thomas describes how race blocks the development of deeply personal work-based relationships between whites and African Americans. He maintains that this is related to the painful and threatening history of U.S. race relations and the common assumption of race as a taboo topic. See D. Thomas, "Mentoring and Irrationality."

7. Private communications with Ron Krouk, diversity manager of Lotus Development Corporation, July 1997. Krouk describes affirmative action as a process improvement tool, like total quality management, in which the system is monitored to identify variance in the quality of what is produced.

8. The source of this quote is a company-approved history written by a non-employee in 1990.

9. For a discussion of intergroup theory, see Alderfer, "Intergroup Perspective," 202–204; Brown, *Managing Conflict*; and Alderfer, "Intergroup Relations," 355–371.

8: CREATING AND SUSTAINING CHANGE

1. Ann Morrison's *The New Leaders* is a benchmark study of sixteen companies who have been especially successful in diversifying their leadership, and the most exhaustive study of this type. Morrison identifies over fifty individual practices and tactics that these companies used to achieve racial diversity.

2. Ann Morrison's work in *The New Leaders* is focused on the idea that a company must build a comprehensive diversity strategy. Such an effort must address three areas: education, enforcement, and exposure. The practices and tactics she identifies fall into one or more of these broad categories. This book is a useful guide in assessing an organization's mix of activities. R. Thomas, *Beyond Race and Gender*; Alderfer et al., "Diagnosing Race Relations"; and Alderfer et al., "Race Relations Advisory Group" describe intervention strategies for assessing and improving an organization's current ability to effectively develop and manage a demographically diverse workforce. The best review of this literature can be found in Cox, *Cultural Diversity*, 223–261.

3. See Jones, "The Dream Deferred."

4. D. Thomas, "Racial Dynamics," 180–181; D. Thomas, "Beyond the Simple Demography-Power Hypothesis."

5. D. Thomas illustrates that when parties to cross-racial mentoring relationships are able to discuss race openly, learning about racial differences occurs. This is also viewed as an enhancing feature of the relationship (D. Thomas, "Racial Dynamics," 188–189). D. Thomas also found that openness about race facilitated the mentor's ability to address race-based barriers to the promotion of their protégés (D. Thomas, "Managing Racial Differences").

6. Our insights about the role of these partnerships in managing the anxiety associated with change is informed by psychodynamic stud-

ies of groups and organizations. Bion and his associates at the Tavistock Institute noted the tendency of groups to create pairings that often acted out the conflicts and tensions that arose from members working together (*Experiences in Groups*, 151–152, 162–165). Hirschorn (*Workplace Within*, 60–63) and Gilmore and Krantz ("Projective Identification") also demonstrate this phenomenon in organizations. The basic assumption behind these pairings is the hope that out of them will come answers to the often unexpressed anxieties that block effective system functioning.

7. Cox writes about the importance of support groups in affirming identity and as advisory groups to the organizational leadership (*Cultural Diversity*, 148–149, 246–247). In her study of a diverse group of managers, Morrison found that support groups played a vital role in affirming identity, building confidence, providing information and feedback, and providing a supportive environment where criticism is exchanged and valued (*New Leaders*, 71–73).

8. Raymond Friedman has conducted the most detailed study of minority support groups and networks in corporations. Our conclusions about the benefits of these groups are quite consistent with his findings. See Friedman and Deinard, "Black Caucus Groups," and Friedman, *African American Network Groups*.

9. Jonathan Kaufman and Anita Raghavan, writing for the *Wall Street Journal*, describe the contrasting choices that minority managers make in this regard. Their article focuses on the careers and perspectives of Edward Jones, a former upper-middle manager at AT&T, and his brother, Tom Jones, then vice chairman of Travelers Group. Edward, who plateaued in middle management at AT&T, was outspoken about race and racial issues, which he feels alienated whites and cost him his career. Tom, on the other hand, was not vocal on these issues at work and had a more successful corporate career. (Kaufman and Raghavan, "Two Brothers Divided.")

10. Kanter, *Men and Women of the Corporation*, 48.

11. Zweigenhaft and Domhoff, *Diversity in the Power Elite*, 1–58.

12. See, for example, Beer, Eisenstat, and Biggadike, "Developing an Organization"; Eisenstat and Beer, "Strategic Change"; Miles et al., "Organizational Strategy, Structure, and Process"; Nadler and Tushman, "Designing Organizations."

13. Charles C. Moskos and John S. Butler conducted an in-depth study of the Army's efforts to promote racial equality. Compared to U.S. corporations, the Army appears to have achieved a greater level of success. Moskos and Butler attribute this to an organizational culture

that has zero tolerance for racist behavior and the Army's ability to create a culture that vigilantly works to render racial differences irrelevant (*All That We Can Be*, 133).

14. Beer, Eisenstat, and Spector (*The Critical Path*, 179–208) note the importance of leaders and change partnerships in organizational renewal effort. Nadler and Tushman ("A Model of Diagnosing") also make the point about the criticality for alignment in achieving organizational effectiveness.

15. Our thinking about opportunity is greatly influenced by Kanter's treatment of the subject. (Kanter, *Men and Women of the Corporation*, 164–205.)

9: Corporate Leadership for Minority Advancement

1. There is an extensive literature on the social technologies for bringing about planned change in organizations. Organizational tools for improving an organization's race relations and capacity to manage diversity are presented in Alderfer and Smith, "Studying Intergroup Relations"; Alderfer et al., "Diagnosing Race Relations"; Cox, *Cultural Diversity*; and R. Thomas, *Beyond Race and Gender.*

2. See Morrison's *The New Leaders.*

3. See Alderfer and Tucker, *Measuring Managerial Potential*, and Alderfer et al., "Race Relations Advisory Group."

4. See Kilborn's *New York Times* article on PG&E, "How a Work Force Responds When Equal Rights Is a Goal." D. Thomas also made a visit to PG&E and conducted interviews with managers and executives at the company on April 9 and 10, 1992.

5. A close read of Kanter's exposition on opportunity (*Men and Women of the Corporation*, 129–163) implies that development is a consequence of good opportunity. However, she is never explicit about this or the fact that opportunities can be desirable for their external features (power, prestige, and compensation) but not be developmental.

6. See D. Thomas and Kram, "Promoting Career-Enhancing Relationships."

7. Kram, *Mentoring at Work*, 159–167.

8. See ibid., 167–186.

9. See Kram, *Mentoring at Work*, and Levinson et al., *Season of a Man's Life.* D. Thomas found that younger minorities were more likely to find it acceptable to suppress discussion of issues of race with mentors and to not consider this an important limitation of the relationship ("Racial Dynamics," 178–181).

10. D. Thomas has studied these dynamics extensively. Readers are referred to the following: D. Thomas, "Managing Racial Differences"; "The Impact of Race"; "Racial Dynamics"; D. Thomas and Wetlaufer, "A Question of Color"; D. Thomas and Higgins, "Mentoring and the Boundaryless Career."

11. See, for example, Eden, "Self-Fulfilling Prophecy as a Management Tool."

10: Lessons for the Next Generation of Minority Executives

1. *Soul in Management*, by Richard America and Bernard Anderson, is an excellent source of guidance and perspectives for people of color, though its primary audience is African Americans.

2. Kotter, *General Managers*, 45.

3. New research by Ron Burt at the University of Chicago demonstrates that a negative evaluation by colleagues and superiors results in smaller bonuses for minorities than whites. However, when the information is positive or neutral the allocation process is unaffected by race. Ronald Burt, Organizational Behavior Research Seminar at the Harvard Business School, November 14, 1996.

4. Examples of self-assessment tools and course content can be found in Thomas and Heaphy, "Self-Assessment and Career Development Instructor's Course Overview," a class taught at the Harvard Business School. Other relevant books are Clawson et al., *Self-Assessment and Career Development*; Schein, *Career Anchors*; and Tieger and Barron-Tieger, *Do What You Are*.

5. Ibarra illustrates that high-potential minority managers had greater diversity of social contacts than did minorities who were not viewed as having high potential ("Race, Opportunity and Diversity," 691). D. Thomas found that minorities purposely crossed the boundaries of their department and organization to create diverse networks of career support ("Impact of Race," 486–487). He also found that minorities with relationships that allowed them to be open about race moved further up the hierarchy than those who did not (D. Thomas, "Strategies for Managing Racial Difference").

6. Higgins and D. Thomas, "Constellations and Careers," and D. Thomas and Higgins, "Mentoring and the Boundaryless Career," use the port-folio concept to describe the importance of multiple relationships in the support of an individual's career.

7. Higgins and Nohria, "Side-Kick Effect."
8. Herminia Ibarra has designed an assessment instrument useful for this purpose. See Ibarra, "Network Assessment Exercise."
9. In "Mentoring Alternatives," Kram and Isabella describe the critical role that peers can play in supporting individual professional development. They can act as an alternative to mentoring support from seniors, enabling one to perform effectively and become more attractive as a protégé later based on an excellent record.
10. D. Thomas, "Impact of Race," 487.
11. D. Thomas's work on mentoring documents some of the challenges that confront cross-race relationship formation, including lack of personal identification based on observed similarities. See, for example, D. Thomas, "Mentoring and Irrationality"; "The Impact of Race"; and "Racial Dynamics."
12. Whyte, *Organization Man*.
13. See Cross, *Shades of Black*; Helms, *Black and White Racial Identity*; Jackson and Hardiman, "Racial Identity Development."
14. See Bell, "Bi-Cultural Life Experience."
15. The Efficacy Institute in Lexington, Massachusetts, has pioneered a technology for helping minorities understand these stresses and devise a more authentic, but viable way of presenting themselves in the corporation. See Howard, "Rumors of Inferiority."
16. Amy Chen is a pseudonym for a Harvard Business School graduate who reported this encounter to David Thomas in the fall of 1996.
17. Since we interviewed Ben Richardson, Franklin Raines, an African American, was appointed CEO of Fannie Mae, a *Fortune 100* company.
18. See Carol Hymowitz, "A Promising Career."
19. In *The New Rules*, John Kotter examines how the social and economic changes of the last quarter century have influenced the way in which individuals must now manage their careers. In the 1970s, Douglas Hall anticipated that a new, more flexible career model was needed to reflect a fast-changing corporate reality. He dubbed this model the "protean career" to signify its flexibility and anchoring in the individual's full set of experiences and competencies rather than in the organization (Hall, *Careers in Organizations*, 201). Hall and Mirvis describe the need for new psychological and cognitive orientations about success and learning to cope with the demands of the new career environment (Hall and Mirvis, "Careers as Lifelong Learning," and Mirvis and Hall, "Psychological Success").

Appendix A: Research Design and Methods

1. See Yin ("Case Study," "Case Study Crisis," *Case Study Research*) for a detailed discussion of the technical definitions of various types of case-based research, and of the characteristics that distinguish case research from other strategies (Yin, *Case Study Research*, 22–38); see also Eisenhardt ("Building Theories," 534–544).
2. See Eisenhardt ("Building Theories," 534–544); Yin (*Case Study Research*, 14).
3. See Yin ("Case Study"; *Case Study Research*, 29–40, 49–50); Glaser and Strauss ("Discovery of Grounded Theory," 21–25, 28–34).
4. Yin (*Case Study Research*, 15–25); Eisenhardt ("Building Theories," 547–548).
5. See Glaser and Strauss ("Discovery of Grounded Theory," 45–71).
6. See, for example, Alderfer ("Intergroup Perspective"), D. Thomas and Alderfer ("Influence of Race"), and Berg and Smith ("Exploring Clinical Methods," note especially the introduction). For a more general argument in favor of multiple investigators in field-based research see Pettigrew ("Longitudinal Field Research") quoted in Eisenhardt ("Building Theories").

Appendix B: Event History Analysis

1. Blossfeld and Rohwer, *Techniques of Event History Modeling*, 27–29.
2. Rosenbaum, "Tournament Mobility."
3. Blossfeld and Rohwer, *Techniques of Event History Modeling*, 212–213.
4. SAS Institute, *SAS/STAT Software: Changes and Enhancements through Release 6.11*, 813.
5. Allison, *Regression for Longitudinal Event Data*, 16–18; Yamaguchi, *Event History Analysis*, 18–19.
6. Peterson and Spilerman, "Job Quits From an Internal Labor Market."
7. See chapter 2 in Yamaguchi, *Event History Analysis* (on converting logits to probabilities).

◢ Bibliography

Adelman, Kenneth L., Martin Anderson, Linda Chavez, Mitchell E. Daniels, Jr., Donald J. Devine, Charles Heatherly, Frederick N. Khedouri, Constantine C. Menges, Paul Craig Roberts, Ralph Stanley, John A. Svahn, Norman Ture, James Watt, and Murray L. Weidenbaum. "Where We Succeeded, Where We Failed: Lessons from Reagan Officials for the Next Conservative Presidency." *Policy Review* 43 (1988).

Alderfer, Clayton P. "Intergroup Relations and Organizational Diagnosis." In *Making Organizations Humane and Productive*, edited by H. Meltzer and W. R. Nord, 355–371. New York: Wiley, 1981.

———. "An Intergroup Perspective on Group Dynamics." In *Handbook of Organizational Behavior*, edited by Jay Lorsch, 190–222. Englewood Cliffs, N.J.: Prentice-Hall, 1986.

———. "Changing Race Relations Embedded in Organizations: Report on a Long-Term Project with the XYZ Corporation." In *Diversity in the Workplace: Human Resource Initiatives*, edited by S. Jackson. New York: Guilford, 1992.

Alderfer, Clayton P., Charlene J. Alderfer, Leota M. Tucker, and Robert C. Tucker. "Diagnosing Race Relations in Management." *Journal of Applied Behavioral Science* 16, no. 2 (1980): 135–166.

307

Alderfer, Clayton P., and Kenwyn K. Smith. "Studying Intergroup Relations Embedded in Organizations." *Administrative Science Quarterly* 27, no. 1 (1982): 35–65.

Alderfer, Clayton P., and David A. Thomas. "The Significance of Race and Ethnicity for Understanding Organizational Behavior." In *International Review of Industrial and Organizational Psychology*, edited by C. Cooper. New York: John Wiley & Sons, 1988.

Alderfer, Clayton P., and Robert C. Tucker. *Measuring Managerial Potential and Intervening to Improve the Racial Equity of Upward Mobility Decisions.* Technical Report No. 6. Yale School of Organization and Management.

Alderfer, Clayton P., Robert C. Tucker, Charlene J. Alderfer, and Leota M. Tucker. "The Race Relations Advisory Group: An Intergroup Intervention." In *Research in Organization Development*, edited by William A. Pasmore and Richard W. Woodman. Greenwich, Conn.: JAI Press, 1988.

Allison, Paul David. *Regression for Longitudinal Event Data.* Newbury Park, Calif.: Sage Publications, 1984.

Amaker, Norman C. *Civil Rights and the Reagan Administration.* Washington, D.C.: The Urban Institute Press, 1988.

America, Richard F., and Bernard E. Anderson. *Soul in Management: How African-American Managers Thrive in the Competitive Corporate Environment.* Secaucus, N.J.: Birch Lane Press, 1996.

Amott, Teresa, and Julie Matthaei. *Race, Gender and Work: A Multi-Cultural Economic History of the United States.* Boston: South End Press, 1996.

Ashenfelter, Orley, and James Heckman. "Measuring the Effect of an Anti-discrimination Program." In *Evaluating the Labor Effects of Social Programs*, edited by Orley Ashenfelter and James Blu. Princeton, N.J.: Princeton University Press, 1976.

Bailyn, Lotte. *Breaking the Mold: Women, Men, and Time in the New Corporate World.* New York: The Free Press, 1993.

Baldi, Stephane, and Debra Branch McBrier. "Do the Determinants of Promotion Differ for Blacks and Whites?" *Work and Occupations* 24, no. 4 (1997): 478–497.

Bandura, Albert. *Social Learning Theory.* Englewood Cliffs, N.J.: Prentice-Hall, 1977.

———. "Human Agency in Social Cognitive Theory." *The American Psychologist* 44, no. 9 (1989): 1175–1184.

———. "Social Cognitive Theory of Self-Regulation." *Organizational Behavior & Human Decision Processes* 50, no. 2 (1991): 248–287.

Bandura, Albert, Claudio Barbarnelli, Gian Vittorio Caprara, and Concetta Pastorelli. "Multifaceted Impact of Self-Efficacy Beliefs on Academic Functioning." *Child Development* 67, no. 3 (1996): 1206–1223.

Bastian, Lisa D., and Bruce M. Taylor. *Young Black Male Victims: National Crime Victimization Survey.* Washington, D.C.: Department of Justice, Office of Justice Programs, Bureau of Justice Statistics, 1994.

Becker, Gary. *Human Capital.* New York: Columbia University Press, 1975.

Beer, Michael, Russell Eisenstat, and Bert Spector. *The Critical Path to Corporate Renewal.* Boston: Harvard Business School Press, 1990.

———. "Why Change Programs Don't Produce Change." *Harvard Business Review* 68, no. 6 (1990): 158–166.

Beer, Michael, Russell Eisenstat, and E. Ralph Biggadike. "Developing an Organization Capable of Strategy Implementation and Reformulation: A Preliminary Test." Working Paper 92-064, Harvard Business School.

Beer, William A. "Resolute Ignorance: Social Science and Affirmative Action." *Society* 24 (1987): 63–69.

———. "Whose Straw Man? " *Society* 25, no. 2 (1988): 70–71.

Bell, Ella E., and Stella M. Nkomo. *Our Separate Ways.* New York: Doubleday, 1998.

Bell, Ella L. "The Bicultural Life Experience of Career-Oriented Black Women." *Journal of Organizational Behavior* 11, no. 6 (1990): 459–477.

Bell, Ella L. J. Edmondson, and Stella M. Nkomo. "Barriers to Workplace Advancement Experienced by African-Americans." Monograph prepared for The Glass Ceiling Commission, Washington, D.C.: United States Department of Labor, 1994.

Belz, Herman. *Equality Transformed: A Quarter-Century of Affirmative Action.* Bowling Green, Ohio: Social Philosophy and Policy Center, 1991.

Berg, David N., and Kenwyn K. Smith. *Exploring Clinical Methods for Social Research.* Beverly Hills, Calif.: Sage Publications, 1985.

Bergmann, Barbara. *In Defense of Affirmative Action.* New York: Basic Books, 1996.

Bion, Wilfred R. *Experiences in Groups, and Other Papers.* New York: Basic Books, 1961.

Blau, Peter, and Otis Dudley Duncan. *The American Occupational Structure.* New York: Wiley, 1967.

Blossfeld, Hans-Peter, and Gotz Rohwer. *Techniques of Event History Modeling: New Approaches to Casual Analysis.* Mahwaw, N.J.: L. Erlbaum, 1995.

Bobo, Lawrence, and Vincent L. Hutchings. "Perceptions of Racial Group Competition: Extending Blumer's Theory of Group Position to a Multiracial Social Context." *American Sociological Review* 61, no. 6 (1996): 951–972.

Bobo, Lawrence, and James R. Kluegel. "Opposition to Race-Targeting: Self-Interest, Stratification Ideology, or Racial Attitudes?" *American Sociological Review* 58, no. 4 (1993): 443–464.

Bourdieu, Pierre. "Cultural Reproduction and Social Reproduction." In *Power and Ideology in Education*, edited by J. Karabel and A. H. Halsey. New York: Oxford University Press, 1977.

Braddock, Jomills Henry, and James M. McPartland. "How Minorities Continue to Be Excluded from Equal Employment Opportunities: Research on Labor Market and Institutional Barriers." *Journal of Social Issues* 43, no. 1 (1987): 5–39.

Bray, Douglas, Richard Campbell, and Donald Grant. *Formative Years in Business.* Malabar, Fla.: Robert E. Krieger, 1979.

Brewer, M. B., and R. M. Kramer. "The Psychology of Intergroup Attitudes and Behavior." *Annual Review of Psychology* 36 (1985): 219–243.

Brief, Arthur P., and Hayes, Erika L. "The Continuing American Dilemma: Studying Racism in Organizations." *Journal of Organizational Behavior* 4 (1997): 89–105.

Brown, L. David. *Managing Conflict at Organizational Interfaces.* Reading, Mass.: Addison-Wesley, 1983.

Bruderl, Josef, Andreas Diekmann, and Peter Preisendorfer. "Patterns of Intraorganizational Mobility: Tournament Models, Path Dependency, and Early Promotion Effects." *Social Science Research* 20, no. 3 (1991): 197–216.

Burrough, Bryan. *Barbarians at the Gate.* New York: Harper & Row, 1990.

Butler, Timothy, and James Waldroop. *Discovering Your Career in Business.* Reading, Mass.: Addison-Wesley, 1997.

Caldwell, David F., Jennifer A. Chatman, and Charles A. O'Reilly. "Building Organizational Commitment: A Multifirm Study." *Journal of Occupational Psychology* 63, no. 3 (1990): 245–261.

Calvert, Robert, Jr. *Equal Employment Opportunity for Minority Group College Graduates: Locating, Recruiting, Employing.* Garrett Park, Md.: Garrett Park Press, 1972.

Cash, Thomas F., Barry Gillen, and D. S. Burns. "Sexism and 'Beautyism' in Personnel Consultant Decision Making." *Journal of Applied Psychology* 62, (1977): 301–310.

Catalyst. *Women of Color in Corporate Management: A Statistical Picture.* New York: Catalyst, 1997.

———. *Women of Color in Corporate Management: Dynamics of Career Advancement.* New York: Catalyst, 1998.

Chatman, Jennifer A. "Matching People and Organizations: Selection and Socialization in Public Accounting Firms." *Administrative Science Quarterly* 36, no. 3 (1991): 459–484.

Clawson, James C., John P. Kotter, Victor A. Faux, and Charles C. McArthur. *Self-Assessment and Career Development*, 3rd ed. Englewood Cliffs, N.J.: Prentice-Hall, 1992.

Collins, James C., and Jerry I. Porras. *Built to Last.* New York: Harper Business, 1994.

Collins, Sharon. "The Marginalization of Black Executives." *Social Problems* 36, no. 4 (1989): 317–331.

———. *Black Corporate Executives: The Making and Breaking of a Black Middle Class.* Philadelphia: Temple University Press, 1997.

Cose, Ellis. *The Rage of a Privileged Class: Why Are Middle-Class Blacks Angry? Why Should America Care?* New York: Harper Collins, 1993.

Cox, Taylor, Jr. *Cultural Diversity in Organizations: Theory, Research, and Practice.* San Francisco: Berret-Koehler Publishers, 1993.

Cox, Taylor, Jr., and S. Blake. "Managing Cultural Diversity: Implications for Organizational Competitiveness." *Academy of Management Executive* 5, no. 3 (1991): 45–56.

Cox, Taylor, Jr., and J. Finley-Nickelson. "Models of Acculturation for Intraorganizational Cultural Diversity." *Canadian Journal of Administrative Sciences* 8, no. 2 (1991): 90–100.

Cox, Taylor, Jr., and Stella M. Nkomo. "Invisible Men and Women: A Status Report on Race as a Variable in Organization Behavior Research." *Journal of Organizational Behavior* 11, no. 6 (1990): 419–431.

Crocker, Jennifer, and Brenda Major. "Social Stigma and Self-Esteem: The Self-Protective Properties of Stigma." *Psychological Review* 96, no. 4 (1989): 608–630.

Cross, William. *Shades of Black: Diversity in African-American Identity.* Philadelphia: Temple University Press, 1991.

Dalton, Gene W., et. al. "The Four Stages of Professional Careers: A New Look at Performance Appraisal." *Organizational Dynamics* 6, no. 1 (1977): 19–42.

Davis, George, and Glegg Watson. *Black Life in Corporate America: Swimming in the Mainstream.* New York: Doubleday, 1982.

Deaux, K., and T. Emswiller. "Explanations of Successful Performance in Sex-Linked Tasks: What Is Skill for the Male is Luck for the Female." *Journal of Personality and Social Psychology* 29, (1974): 80–85.

Denton, Toni C. "Bonding and Supportive Relationships Among Black Professional Women: Rituals of Restoration." *Journal of Organizational Behavior* 11, no. 6 (1990): 447–457.

Dickens, Floyd Jr., and Jacqueline B. Dickens. *The Black Manager: Making It in the Corporate World.* 2d ed. New York: AMACOM, 1991.

DiTomaso, Nancy, and Donna E. Thompson. "The Advancement of Minorities into Corporate Management: An Overview." *Research in the Sociology of Organizations* 6 (1988): 281–312.

DiTomaso, Nancy, Donna E. Thompson, and D. H. Blake. "Corporate Perspectives on the Advancement of Minority Managers." In *Ensuring Minority Success in Corporate Management*, edited by D. E. Thompson and N. DiTomaso. New York: Plenum, 1988.

Dreyfuss, Joel, and Charles Lawrence III. *The Bakke Case: The Politics of Inequality.* New York: Harcourt, Brace, Jovanovich, 1979.

Durr, Marlese, and John R. Logan. "Racial Submarkets in Government Employment: African American Managers in New York State." *Sociological Forum* 12, no. 3 (1997): 353–370.

Eccles, Mary. "Race, Sex, and Governmental Jobs: A Study of Affirmative Action Programs in Federal Agencies." Ph.D. diss., Harvard University, 1975.

Eccles, Robert, and Nitin Nohria, with James Berkley. *Beyond the Hype: Rediscovering the Essence of Management.* Boston: Harvard Business School Press, 1992.

Eden, Dov. "Self-Fulfilling Prophecy as a Management Tool: Harnessing Pygmalion." *Academy of Management Review* 9, no. 1 (1984): 64–74.

———. "Industrialization as a Self-Fulfilling Prophecy: The Role of Expectations in Development." *International Journal of Psychology* 25 (1990): 871–886.

Eisenhardt, Kathleen M. "Building Theories from Case Study Research." *Academy of Management Review* 14, no. 4 (1989): 532–550.

Eisenstat, Russell A., and Michael Beer. "Strategic Change: How to Realign the Organization to Implement Strategy." In *The Portable MBA*, edited by L. Fahey and J. Mahaney. New York: Wiley, 1994.

Ely, Robin. "The Effects of Organizational Demographics and Social Identity on Relationships Among Professional Women." *Administrative Science Quarterly* 39 (1994): 203–238.

———. "The Power of Demography: Women's Social Constructions of Gender Identity at Work." *Academy of Management Journal* 38 (1995): 589–634.

Farley, Reynolds. "Trends in Racial Inequalities: Have the Gains of the 1960's Disappeared in the 1970's?" *American Sociological Review* 42, no. 2 (1977): 189–208.

———. *The Color Line and the Quality of Life in America.* New York: Russell Sage, 1987.

Feagin, Joe R., and Melvin P. Sikes. *Living with Racism: The Black Middle-Class Experience.* Boston: Beacon, 1994.

Featherman, David L., and Robert M. Hauser. *Opportunity and Change.* New York: Academic Press, 1978.

Fernandez, John P. *Racism and Sexism in Corporate Life: Changing Values in American Business.* New York: Lexington Books, 1981.

———. *Survival in the Corporate Fishbowl: Making It into Upper and Middle Management.* New York: Lexington Books, 1987.

———. *Managing a Diverse Work Force: Regaining the Competitive Edge.* New York: Lexington Books, 1991.

Friedman, Judith, and Nancy DiTomaso. "Myths about Diversity: What Managers Need to Know About Changes in the U.S. Labor Force." *California Management Review* 38, no.4 (1996): 54–77.

Friedman, Raymond A. *African American Network Groups: Their Impact and Effectiveness.* Washington, D.C.: Executive Leadership Council, 1992.

Friedman, Raymond A., and Caitlin Deinard. "Black Caucus Groups at Xerox Corp. (A)." Case 9-491-047. Boston: Harvard Business School, 1991.

Fryxell, Gerald E., and Linda D. Lerner. "Contrasting Corporate Profiles: Women and Minority Representation in Top Management Positions." *Journal of Business Ethics* 8, no. 5 (1989): 341–352.

Gabarro, John J. *The Dynamics of Taking Charge.* Boston: Harvard Business School Press, 1987.

Gallup Organization. *Votes by Groups in Presidential Elections.* Princeton, N.J.: Gallup Organization.

Gilmore, Thomas N., and James Krantz. "Projective Identification in the Consulting Relationship: Exploring the Unconscious Dimensions of a Client System." *Human Relations* 38, no. 12 (1985): 1159–1177.

Glaser, Barney, and Auselm L. Strauss. *The Discovery of Grounded Theory: Strategies for Qualitative Research.* Chicago: Aldine, 1967.

Glazer, Nathan. *Affirmative Discrimination: Ethnic Inequality and Public Policy.* New York: Basic Books, 1975

Goldstein, Morris, and Robert Smith. "The Estimated Impact of the Anti-discrimination Program Aimed at Federal Contractors." *Industrial and Labor Relations Review* 29, no. 4 (1976): 523–543.

Greene, Jay. "Black Execs Believe Discrimination Hinders Their Careers—Survey." *Modern Healthcare* 23, no. 10 (1993): 4.

Greenhaus, Jeffrey H., and Saroj Parasuraman. "Job Performance Attributions and Career Advancement Prospects: An Examination of Gender and Race Effects." *Organizational Behavior and Human Decision Processes* 55, no. 2 (1993): 273–297.

Greenhaus, Jeffrey H., Saroj Parasuraman, and Wayne M. Wormley. "Effects of Race on Organizational Experiences, Job Performance Evaluations, and Career Outcomes." *Academy of Management Journal* 33, no. 1 (1990): 64–86.

Griswold de Castillo, Richard. "The Chicano Movement and the Treaty of Guadalupe Hidalgo." In *Times of Challenge: Chicanos and Chicanas in American Society,* edited by Juan R. Garcia et al. Houston: University of Houston, 1988.

Griswold de Castillo, Richard, and Arnoldo de León. *North to Aztlán: A History of Mexican Americans in the United States.* New York: Twayne Publishers, 1996.

Hacker, Andrew. *Two Nations: Black and White, Separate, Hostile, Unequal.* New York: Scribner's, 1992.

Hall, Douglas T. *Careers in Organizations.* Pacific Palisades, Calif.: Goodyear, 1976.

Hall, Douglas T., and P. H. Mirvis. "Careers as Lifelong Learning." In *The Changing Nature of Work,* edited by A. Howard. San Francisco: Jossey-Bass, 1995.

Hammersback, John C., Richard C. Jensen, and José Angel Gutierrez. *War of Words: Chicano Protest in the 1960s and 1970s.* Westport, Conn.: Greenwood Press, 1985.

Harrell, Thomas W. *Managers' Performance and Personality.* Dallas: Southwest Publishing Co., 1961.

Harrington, Charles C., and Susan K. Boardman. *Paths to Success: Beating the Odds in American Society.* Cambridge, Mass.: Harvard University Press, 1997.

Hayes, Erika L. "It's Not What You Know, It's Who You Know: The Effects of Human and Social Capital on Race Differences in Promotion and Support." Ph.D. diss., University of Michigan, 1995.

Heckman, James, and Kenneth Wolpin. "Does the Contract Compliance Program Work? An Analysis of Chicago Data." *Industrial and Labor Relations Review* (1976): 544–564.

Helms, Janet E. *Black and White Racial Identity.* New York: Greenwood, 1990.

Herriot, Peter, Gwendy Gibson, Carole Pemberton, and Robert Pinder. "Dashed Hopes: Organizational Determinants and Personal Perceptions of Managerial Careers." *Journal of Occupational & Organizational Psychology* 66, no. 2 (1993): 115–123.

Herrnstein, Richard S., and Charles Murray. *The Bell Curve.* New York: Free Press, 1994.

Hewstone, M. "The 'Ultimate Attribution Error'? A Review of the Literature on Intergroup Causal Attribution." *European Journal of Social Psychology* 20 (1992): 311–335.

Higgins, Monica C., and Nitin Nohria. "The Side-Kick Effect: Mentoring Relationships and the Development of Social Capital." In *Corporate Social Capital,* edited by R. Leenders and S. Gabbay. Reading, Mass.: Addison-Wesley, in press.

Higgins, Monica C., and David A. Thomas. "Constellations and Careers: Toward Understanding the Effects of Multiple Developmental Relationships." Working paper 97-080, Harvard Business School, 1997.

Hill, Linda A. *Becoming a Manager: Mastery of a New Identity.* Boston: Harvard Business School Press, 1992.

Hirschorn, Larry. *The Workplace Within: The Psychodynamics of Organizational Life.* Cambridge, Mass.: MIT Press, 1988.

Holloway, Charles M. *The Bakke Decision, Retrospect and Prospect.* Summary Report on Six Seminars Held by the College Board in July and August 1978. Washington, D.C.: United States Commission on Civil Rights, May 1979.

Howard, Ann, and Douglas Bray. *Managerial Lives in Transition: Advancing Age and Changing Times.* New York: Guilford Press, 1988.

Howard, Jeff, and Ray Hammond. "Rumors of Inferiority: The Hidden Obstacles to Black Success." *The New Republic,* 193, no. 5 (1985): 17.

Hudson Institute. *Workforce 2000: Work and Workers for the Twenty-first Century.* Indianapolis, Ind.: Hudson Institute, 1987.

Hymowitz, Carol. "A Promising Career Comes to a Tragic End, and a City Asks Why." *Wall Street Journal*, 9 May 1997.

Ibarra, Herminia. "Race, Opportunity, and Diversity of Social Circles in Managerial Networks." *Academy of Management Journal* 38 (1995): 673–703.

———. "Network Assessment Exercise: Executive Version." HBS Exercise 9-497-003, Harvard Business School, 1997.

Jackson, Bailey, and Rita Hardiman. "Racial Identity Development: Implications for Managing the Multiracial Work Force." In *The National Training Laboratories Managers Handbook*, edited by R. Rityo and A. Sargent, 67–78. Arlington, Va.: NTL Press, 1983.

Jencks, Christopher. *Who Gets Ahead? The Determinants of Economic Success in America*. New York: Basic Books, 1979.

Johnson, Jeffalyn. *A Blueprint for Success: An Executive Leadership Council Study*. Washington, D.C.: Executive Leadership Council, 1991.

Jones, Edward W., Jr. "What It's Like to Be a Black Manager." *Harvard Business Review* 51, no. 4 (1973): 108–116.

———. "Black Managers: The Dream Deferred." *Harvard Business Review* 64, no. 3 (1986): 84–93.

Journal Graphic Transcripts. "Thomas W. Jones Talks about Race in America." 18 May 1995. Transcript #1380-3.

Kanter, Rosabeth Moss. *Men and Women of the Corporation*. New York: Basic Books, 1977.

———. "Some Effects of Proportions on Group Life: Skewed Sex Ratios and Responses to Token Women." *American Journal of Sociology* 82, no. 5 (1977): 965–990.

———. "Differential Access to Opportunity and Power." In *Discrimination in Organizations*, edited by Adolfer Alvarez. San Francisco: Jossey-Bass, 1978.

Kaufman, Jonathan, and Anita Raghavan. "Two Brothers Divided: Can Blacks in Corporations Hold Selves True?" *Wall Street Journal*, 21 November 1997.

Kilborn, Peter T. "How a Work Force Responds When Equal Rights Is a Goal." *New York Times*, 12 May 1991.

Korn/Ferry International. *Korn/Ferry International's Executive Profile: A Survey of Corporate Leaders in the 80's*. New York: Korn/Ferry International, 1986.

———. *Korn/Ferry International's Executive Profile: A Decade of Changes in Corporate Leadership*. New York: Korn/Ferry, 1990. Pamphlet.

Korrol, Virginia E. Sanchez. *From Colonia to Community: The History of Puerto Ricans in New York City.* Berkeley: University of California Press, 1994.

Kossek, Ellen Ernst, and Susan C. Zonia. "Assessing Diversity Climate: A Field Study of Reactions to Employer Efforts to Promote Diversity." *Journal of Organizational Behavior* 14, no. 1 (1993): 61–81.

Kotter, John P. *The General Managers.* New York: Free Press, 1982.

———. *Power and Influence.* New York: Free Press, 1985.

———. *The Leadership Factor.* New York: Free Press, 1988.

———. *A Force For Change.* New York: Free Press, 1990.

———. "What Leaders Really Do: Good Management Controls Complexity; Effective Leadership Produces Useful Change." *Harvard Business Review* 68, no. 3 (1990): 103–111.

———. *The New Rules: How to Succeed in Today's Post-Corporate World.* New York: Free Press, 1995.

Kram, Kathy E. *Mentoring at Work: Developmental Relationships in Organizational Life.* Glenview, Ill.: Scott, Foresman, 1985.

Kram, Kathy E., and Lynne Isabella. "Mentoring Alternatives: The Role of Peer Relationships in Career Development." *Academy of Management Journal* 28, no. 1 (1985): 110–132.

Landau, Jacqueline. "The Relationship of Race and Gender to Managers' Ratings of Promotion Potential." *Journal of Organizational Behavior* 16, no. 4 (1995): 391–400.

Lawrence, Barbara S. "Age Grading: The Implicit Organizational Timetable." *Journal of Occupational Behaviour,* 5 (1984): 23–25.

———. "Historical Perspective: Using the Past to Study the Present." *Academy of Management Review* 9, no. 2 (1984): 307–312.

———. "New Wrinkles in the Theory of Age: Demography, Norms, and Performance Ratings." *Academy of Management Journal* 31, no. 2 (1988): 309–337.

———. "Organizational Age Norms: Why Is It So Hard to Know When You See One?" *The Gerontologist* 36, no. 2 (1996): 209–220.

Leonard, Jonathan. "Employment and Occupational Advance Under Affirmative Action." *Review of Economics and Statistics* 66, no. 3 (1984): 377–385.

Levinson, Daniel S., Charlotte N. Darrow, Edward B. Klein, Maria M. Levinson, and Braxton McKee. *Seasons of a Man's Life.* New York: Knopf, 1978.

Lewis, Reginald, and Blair S. Walker. *Why Should White Guys Have All the Fun? How Reginald Lewis Created a Billion-Dollar Business Empire.* New York: Wiley, 1995.

Lichtblau, Eric. "Attacks, Bias Against Gays on Upswing, Survey Finds." *Los Angeles Times*, 8 June 1988.

Lifshey, Adam. "The Yellow Power Genesis: Asian American Radicalism in the Sixties." Thesis submitted for undergraduate honors, Harvard College, 1991.

Louis, Meryl R. "Surprise and Sense Making: What Newcomers Experience in Entering Unfamiliar Organizational Settings." *Administrative Science Quarterly* 25, no. 2 (1980): 226–251.

Loury, Glenn. "Beyond Civil Rights: The Better Path to Black Progress." *The New Republic* 193 (1985): 22.

Lynch, Frederick. *The Diversity Machine: The Drive to Change the 'White Male' Workplace.* New York: Free Press, 1997.

Luthans, Fred, Richard Hodgetts, and Stuart Rosenkrantz. *Real Managers.* Cambridge, Mass.: Ballinger, 1988.

March, James C., and James G. March. "Performance Sampling in Social Matches." *Administrative Science Quarterly* 23, no. 3 (1978): 434–453.

March, James G., and Robert I. Sutton. "Organizational Performance as a Dependent Variable." *Organization Science* 8, no. 6 (1997): 698–706.

McCall, Morgan, Jr. *High Flyers: Developing the Next Generation of Leaders.* Boston: Harvard Business School Press, 1998.

McCall, Morgan W., Jr., and Michael M. Lombardo. *Off the Track: Why and How Successful Executives Get Derailed.* Greensboro, N.C.: Center for Creative Leadership, 1983.

McCall, Morgan W., Jr., Michael M. Lombardo, and Ann M. Morrison. *The Lessons of Experience: How Successful Executives Develop on the Job.* New York: Lexington Books, 1988.

Mertzer, H., and W. R. Nord, "Intergroup Relations and Organizational Diagnosis." In *Making Organizations Humane and Productive*, 355–371. New York: Wiley, 1981.

Miles, Raymond E., Charles C. Snow, Alan D. Meyer, and Henry J. Coleman, Jr. "Organizational Strategy, Structure, and Process." *Academy of Management Review* 3, no. 3 (1978): 546–562.

Mills, C. Wright. *The Power Elite.* New York: Oxford University Press, 1956.

Mirvis, Philip, and David Berg. *Failures in Organization Development and Change: Cases and Essays for Learning.* New York: John Wiley & Sons, 1977.

Mirvis, Philip H., and Douglas T. Hall. "Psychological Success and the Boundaryless Career." In *The Boundaryless Career: A New Employment Princi-*

ple for a New Organizational Era, edited by Michael B. Arthur and Denise M. Rousseau, 237–255. New York: Oxford University Press, 1996.

Moody, Charles D. "On Becoming a Superintendent: Contest or Sponsored Mobility?" *The Journal of Negro Education* 52, no. 4 (1983): 382–397.

Mooney, Patrick H., and Theo H. Majka. *Farmers' and Farm Workers' Movements*. New York: Twayne Publishers, 1995.

Morrison, Ann. *The New Leaders*. San Francisco: Jossey-Bass, 1992.

Morrison, Ann, and Kristen M. Crabtree. *Developing Diversity in Organizations: A Digest of Selected Literature*. Greensboro, N.C.: Center for Creative Leadership, 1993.

Morrison, Ann M., Randall P. White, and Ellen Van Velsor. *Breaking the Glass Ceiling: Can Women Reach the Top of America's Largest Corporations?* Reading, Mass.: Addison-Wesley, 1987.

Moskos, Charles C., and John S. Butler. *All That We Can Be: Black Leadership and Racial Integration the Army Way*. New York: Harper Collins, 1996.

Murray, Charles. *Losing Ground: American Social Policy, 1950–1980*. New York: Basic Books, 1984.

Murray, M. M. "The Middle Years of Life of Middle Class Black Men: An Exploratory Study." Ph.D. dissertation, University of Cincinnati, 1982.

Nadler, David A., Marc S. Gerstein, and Robert B. Shaw & Associates. *Organizational Architecture*. San Francisco: Jossey-Bass, 1992.

Nadler, David, and Michael Tushman. "A Model for Diagnosing Organization Behavior." *Organization Dynamics* 9, no. 2 (1980): 148–163.

Nadler, David A., and Michael L. Tushman. "Designing Organizations That Have Good Fit: A Framework for Understanding New Architectures." In *Organizational Architecture*, edited by David Nadler et al. San Francisco: Jossey-Bass, 1992.

"National City Crime Growth Down." *San Diego Union-Tribune*, 9 March 1988.

Newcomer, Mabel. *The Big Business Executive: The Factors That Made Him, 1900–1950*. New York: Columbia University Press, 1955.

Nilson, L. B. "The Occupational and Sex-Related Components of Social Standing." *Social Research* 60 (1976): 328–336.

Nkomo, Stella M., and Taylor Cox, Jr. "Gender Differences in the Upward Mobility of Black Managers: Double Whammy or Double Advantage? *Sex Roles* 21 (1989): 825–839.

"Notes on Affirmative Action." *New York Times*, 24 September 1995.

Parikh, Sunita. *The Politics of Preference: Democratic Institutions and Affirmative Action in the United States and India.* Ann Arbor: The University of Michigan Press, 1997.

Park, Robert E. *Race and Culture.* Glencoe, Ill.: Free Press, 1950.

———. "The Race Relations Cycle in Hawaii." In *Race and Culture*, edited by Robert E. Park. Glencoe, Ill.: Free Press, 1950.

Paulin, Elizabeth A., and Jennifer M. Mellor. "Gender, Race, and Promotions within a Private-Sector Firm." *Industrial Relations* 35, no. 2 (1996): 276–295.

Peterson, Trond, and Seymour Spilerman. "Job Quits from an Internal Labor Market." In *Event History Analysis in Life Course Research*, edited by K. Mayer and N. Tuma, 69–95. Madison: University of Wisconsin Press, 1990.

Pettigrew, A. "Longitudinal Field Research on Change: Theory and Practice." Paper presented at the National Science Foundation Conference on Longitudinal Research Methods in Organizations, Austin, 1988.

Pettigrew, T. F. "The Ultimate Attribution Error: Extending Gordon Allport's Cognitive Analysis of Prejudice." *Personality and Social Psychology* 5 (1979): 461–477.

Pettigrew, T. F., and Joanne Martin. "Shaping the Organizational Context for Black American Inclusion." *Journal of Social Issues* 43, no. 1 (1987): 41–78.

Powell, Gary N., and D. Anthony Butterfield. "Effect of Race on Promotions to Top Management in a Federal Department." *Academy of Management Journal* 40, no. 1 (1997): 112–128.

Powell, R. M. "Race, Religion and the Promotion of the American Executive." College of Administrative Science monograph no. AA-3, Ohio State University, 1969.

Ragins, Belle Rose. "Diversified Mentoring Relationships in Organizations: A Power Perspective." *Academy of Management Review* 22, no. 2 (1997): 482–521.

Richie, Beth Sperber, Ruth E. Fassinger, Sonja Geschmay Linn, Judith Johnson, Sandra Robinson, and Joann Prosser. "Persistence, Connection, and Passion: A Qualitative Study of the Career Development of Highly Achieving African American-Black and White Women." *Journal of Counseling Psychology* 44, no. 2 (1997): 133–148.

Roberts, Bari-Ellen, and Jack E. White. *Roberts vs. Texaco: A True Story of Race and Corporate America.* New York: Avon Books, 1998.

Rosales, Artur F. *Chicano! A History of the Mexican American Civil Rights Movement.* Houston: University of Houston, 1996.

Rosenbaum, James. "Tournament Mobility: Career Paths in a Corporation." *Administrative Science Quarterly* 24, no. 2 (1979): 220–241.

———. *Career Mobility in a Corporate Hierarchy.* New York: Academic Press, 1984.

Sanchez, Jay Anthony. "The Young Lords: Past, Present and Promise." Thesis submitted for undergraduate honors, Harvard College, 1989.

SAS Institute, Inc. *SAS/STAT Software: Changes and Enhancements through Release 6.11.* Cary, N.C.: SAS Institute, 1996.

Schein, Edgar. *Career Dynamics: Matching Individual and Organizational Needs,* Reading, Mass · Addison Wesley, 1978.

———. *Career Anchors: Discovering Your Real Values.* Pfeffer and Co.: San Diego, 1990.

Schuman, Howard, Charlotte Steeh, and Lawrence Bobo. *Racial Attitudes in America: Trends and Interpretations.* Cambridge, Mass.: Harvard University Press, 1985.

Scott, Bill. *Kent State/May 4: Echoes Through a Decade.* Kent, Ohio: Kent State University Press, 1982.

Sheridan, John E., John W. Slocum, Jr., Richard Buda, and Richard C. Thompson. "Effects of Corporate Sponsorship and Departmental Power on Career Tournaments." *Academy of Management Journal* 33, no. 3 (1990): 578–602.

Shipler, David K. *A Country of Strangers: Blacks and Whites in America.* New York: Knopf, 1997.

Sowell, Thomas. *Civil Rights, Rhetoric or Reality?* New York: W. Morrow, 1984.

Steele, Claude M. "A Threat in the Air: How Stereotypes Shape the Intellectual Identities and Performance of Women and African Americans." *American Psychologist* 52, no. 6 (1997): 613–629.

Steele, Claude M., and James Aronson. "Stereotype Threat and the Intellectual Test Performance of African Americans." *Journal of Personality and Social Psychology* 69, no. 5 (1995): 797–811.

Steele, Shelby. *The Content of Our Character: A New Vision of Race in America.* New York: St. Martin's, 1990.

Stith, Anthony. *Breaking the Glass Ceiling: Racism and Sexism in Corporate America: The Myths, the Realities and the Solutions.* Orange, N.J.: Bryant & Dillon, 1996.

Super, Donald. *The Psychology of Careers: An Introduction to Vocational Development*. New York: Harper and Row, 1957.

Szafran, Robert F. "Female and Minority Employment Patterns in Banks: A Research Note." *Work and Occupations* 11, no. 1 (1984): 55–76.

Tang, Joyce. "The Model Minority Thesis Revisited: (Counter) Evidence from the Science and Engineering Fields." *Journal of Applied Behavioral Science* 33, no. 3 (1997): 291–315.

Thomas, Clarence. "Why Black Americans Should Look to Conservative Policies." *Heritage Foundation Reports* 119, 1968.

Thomas, David A. "An Intra-Organizational Analysis of Black and White Patterns of Sponsorship and Dynamics of Cross-Racial Mentoring." Ph.D dissertation, Yale University, 1986.

———. "Mentoring and Irrationality: The Role of Racial Taboos." *Human Resource Management* 28, no. 2 (1989): 279–290.

———. "Strategies for Managing Racial Differences in Work Centered Developmental Relationships." Unpublished Working Paper, Wharton School of the University of Pennsylvania, 1989.

———. "The Impact of Race on Managers' Experiences of Developmental Relationships." *Journal of Organizational Behavior* 2, no. 4 (1990): 479–492.

———. "Racial Dynamics in Cross-Race Developmental Relationships." *Administrative Science Quarterly* 38, no. 2 (1993): 169–194.

———. "Beyond the Simple Demography-Power Hypothesis: How Blacks in Power Influence Whites to Mentor Blacks." In *Mentoring Dilemmas: Developmental Relationships in Multicultural Organizations*, edited by F. Crosby, A. Murell, and R. Ely. New York: Lawrence Earlbaum Publisher, 1999.

Thomas, David A., and Clayton P. Alderfer. "The Influence of Race on Career Dynamics." In *Handbook of Career Theory*, edited by M. Arthur, D. T. Hall, and B. Lawrence. Cambridge, England: Cambridge University Press, 1989.

Thomas, David A., and Robin Ely. "Making Differences Matter: A New Paradigm for Managing Diversity." *Harvard Business Review* 74, no. 5 (1996): 79–90.

Thomas, David A., John B. Hammond, and Elise D. Phillips. "Perceptions of Minority and White Executives and Managers: A Comparative Study of the Relationships Between Race, Status and Managerial Behavior." Unpublished Working Paper, Harvard Business School, 1997.

Thomas, David A., and Emily D. Heaphy. "Developmental Relationships." Teaching Note 498-071. Boston: Harvard Business School, 1998.

———. "Self-Assessment and Career Development Instructor's Course Overview." Teaching Note 498-072. Boston: Harvard Business School, 1998.

Thomas, David A., and Monica Higgins. "Mentoring and the Boundaryless Career: Lessons from the Minority Experience." In *Boundaryless Careers: A New Employment Principle for a New Organizational Era*, edited by M. Arthur and D. Rousseau. New York: Oxford University Press, 1996.

Thomas, David A., and Kathy E. Kram. "Promoting Career-Enhancing Relationships in Organizations: The Role of the Human Resource Professional." In *Career Growth and Human Resource Strategies*, edited by M. London and E. Mone. New York: Quorum Books, 1988.

Thomas, David A., and Karen Proudford. "Theory for Practice: Making Sense of Race Relations in Organizations." In *Cultural Diversity in Organizations*, edited by R. Carter. New York: Sage Publications, 1999.

Thomas, David A., and Suzy Wetlaufer. "A Question of Color: A Debate on Race in the U.S. Workplace." *Harvard Business Review* 75, no. 5 (1997): 118–132.

Thomas, R. Roosevelt, Jr. "From Affirmative Action to Affirming Diversity." *Harvard Business Review* 68, no. 2 (1990): 107–117.

———. *Beyond Race and Gender: Unleashing the Power of Your Total Work Force by Managing Diversity.* New York: AMACOM, 1991.

Tieger, Paul D., and Barbara Barron-Tieger. *Do What You Are: Discover the Perfect Career for You Through the Secrets of Personality Type.* 2d ed. Boston: Little, Brown, 1995.

Tokunaga, Howard, and Tracy Graham. "Career Progression in a Fortune 500 Company: Examination of the 'Glass Ceiling'." *IEEE Transactions on Engineering Management* 43, no. 3 (1996): 262–272.

Traub, James, "Nathan Glazer Changes His Mind, Again." *New York Times*, 28 June 1998.

Tsui, Anne, Terry Egan, and Charles A. O'Reilly. "Being Different: Relational Demography and Organizational Attachment." *Administrative Science Quarterly* 37, no. 4 (1992): 549–579.

Tsui, Anne, and Charles O'Reilly. "Beyond Simple Demographic Effects: The Importance of Relational Demography in Superior-Subordinate Dyads." *Academy of Management Journal* 32, no. 2 (1989): 402–423.

Tuma, Nancy Brandon, and Michael T. Hannan. *Social Dynamics: Models and Methods.* Orlando, Fla.: Academic Press, 1984.

Turner, Ralph H. "Modes of Social Ascent through Education: Sponsored and Contest Mobility and the School System." *American Sociological Review* 25, no. 6 (1960): 855–867.

U.S. Bureau of the Census. "Average Annual Growth Rates of Gross National Product (Percent): 1909–1970." In *Historical Statistics of the United States: Colonial Times to 1970.* Washington, D.C.: U.S. Department of Commerce, Bureau of the Census, 1997 (CD-ROM).

———. *Statistical Abstract of the United States.* Austin, Tex.: The Reference Press, 1996.

———. "Percent of Persons 25 Years Old and Over Who Have Completed High School or College, by Race, Hispanic Origin and Sex: Selected Years 1940–1995." In *Education and Social Stratification.* Available from www.census.gov.

U.S. Commission on Civil Rights. *Toward an Understanding of Bakke.* Washington, D.C.: U.S. Commission on Civil Rights, 1979.

U.S. Department of Labor. *A Report on the Glass Ceiling Initiative.* Washington, D.C.: U.S. Department of Labor, 1991.

U.S. Kerner Commission. *Report of the National Advisory Commission on Civil Disorders.* New York: Bantam Books, 1968.

U.S. National Advisory Commission. *Report of National Advisory Commission on Civil Disorders.* New York: Bantam Books, 1968.

Useem, Michael. *The Inner Circle: Large Corporations and the Rise of Business Political Activity in the US and UK.* New York: Oxford University Press, 1984.

Wallace, Phyllis. *MBAs on the Fast Track: The Career Mobility of Young Managers.* New York: Ballinger, 1989.

Webber, Ross A. "Majority and Minority Perceptions and Behavior in Cross-cultural Teams." *Human Relations* 27 (1974): 873–890.

Weber, J. "The Nature of Ethnocentric Attribution Bias: In-Group Protection or Enhancement?" *Journal of Experimental Social Psychology* 30 (1994): 482–504.

Wei, William. *The Asian America Movement.* Philadelphia: Temple University Press, 1994.

Wells, Leroy, Jr., and Carl L. Jennings. "Black Career Advances and White Reactions: Remnants of Herrenvolk Democracy and the Scandalous Paradox." In *Sunrise Seminars*, edited by D. Vails-Webber and W. N. Potts, 41–47. Arlington, Va.: NTL Institute, 1983.

Whitely, William T., and Pol Coetsier. "The Relationship of Career Mentoring to Early Career Outcomes." *Organization Studies* 14, no. 3 (1993): 419–441.

Whyte, William H., Jr. *The Organization Man.* New York: Simon and Schuster, 1956.

Wiley, Mary Glenn, and Arlene Eskilson. "Interaction of Sex and Power Base on Perceptions of Managerial Effectiveness." *Academy of Management Journal* 25, no. 3 (1982): 671–677.

Wilkins, David B., and G. Mitu Gulati. "Why Are There So Few Black Lawyers in Corporate Law Firms? An Institutional Analysis." *California Law Review* 84, no. 3 (1996): 493–625.

Will, George F. "The Journey Up From Guilt." *Newsweek*, 18 June 1968.

Wolfe, Tom. *The Bonfire of the Vanities.* New York: Bantam Books, 1987.

Work, John. "Management Blacks and the Internal Labor Market: Responses to a Questionnaire." *Human Resource Management* 19, no. 3 (1980): 27–31.

———. *Race, Economics, and Corporate America.* Wilmington, Del.: Scholarly Resources, 1984.

Yamaguchi, Kazuo. *Event History Analysis.* Newbury Park, Calif.: Sage Publications, 1991.

Yin, Robert K. "The Case Study as Serious Research Strategy." *Knowledge: Creation, Diffusion, Utilization* 3 (1981): 97–114.

———. "The Case Study Crisis: Some Answers." *Administrative Science Quarterly* 26, no. 1 (1981): 58–65.

———. *Case Study Research: Design and Methods.* Newbury Park, Calif.: Sage Publications, 1984/1989.

Zweigenhaft, Richard L., and G. William Domhoff. *Blacks in the White Establishment: A Study of Race and Class in America.* New Haven, Conn.: Yale University Press, 1991.

———. *Diversity in the Power Elite: Have Women and Minorities Reached the Top?* New Haven, Conn.: Yale University Press, 1998.

◢ Index

327

◢ About the Authors

DAVID A. THOMAS is a professor of business administration at the Harvard Business School. For fifteen years his research, writing, and consulting have focused on the role of race in the career development of executives and managers of color, and the challenges of managing a culturally diverse workforce. His articles and case studies appear in numerous journals, edited volumes, and magazines. He is the 1998 recipient of the Executive Development Roundtable's Annual Award for scholarly contributions in the field of executive development.

JOHN J. GABARRO is the UPS Professor of Human Resource Management at the Harvard Business School. He has served as the faculty chair of Harvard's Senior Management Program and of Harvard's organizational behavior faculty. Gabarro's research has focused on the development of working relationships, managerial effectiveness, and executive succession. He is the author of six books, including *The Dynamics of Taking Charge*, which won the New Directions in Leadership Award and was named one of the ten best business books of the year by the *Wall Street Journal*.